MW00576074

# PRAISE FOR
# *BORN TO CREATE*

"*Born to Create* not only highlights the importance of creativity but also offers insights into fostering it in various work environments, including in-office and remote settings. Creative leadership is presented as the way forward, replacing outdated command-and-control models with environments that encourage aha moments and out-of-the-box thinking. As technology continues to dominate our lives and attention spans, creativity is posited as the human differentiator that sets us apart from robots and algorithms. The narrative emphasizes that creativity isn't a random act but a skill that can be honed and utilized to navigate the uncertainties and complexities of the modern workplace.

There's no doubt creativity will play a key role in designing the new world of work. Anne masterfully provides a path in this book that unlocks creativity for everyone."

—Lars Schmidt, founder and CEO, Amplify Talent

"As a creator, I've lived what it feels like to get bogged down in the creative process. Anne's remarkable book cuts through the jargon and the noise and brings the learnable practice of creativity into modern-day workplaces. If you're looking for practical tools to live and lead creatively, this is a must-read."

—Ian Brennan, writer, director, and co-creator, *Glee*

"With the increased speed of business and changes in external environments, the problems that leaders are asked to solve today are unprecedented, and only those who lean in with individual creativity will be effective. Anne provides a clear road map that anyone can follow to be a more effective, inspiring creative force in work and life."

—Cara Brennan Allamano, chief people officer,
Lattice, and founding partner, PeopleTech Partners

*"Born to Create* delivers helpful exercises and insights for those looking to innovate in a changing workplace. It's the perfect handbook for today's creative leader."

—Melissa Daimler, chief learning officer, Udemy, and author of *ReCulturing*

*"Born to Create* is full of ideas, exercises, and dialogues inspiring for anyone in business—and in life. Creative leadership in today's environment is challenging and extends beyond the workplace. Anne Jacoby's tools are fun, logical, succinct, and high impact. I recommend *Born to Create* to anyone looking for ways to innovate. An excellent and enjoyable read!"

—Katherine Beyda, executive vice president of physical production, New Line Cinema

"Be prepared to be surprised and delighted! *Born to Create* is a collection of the practical and the inspirational—stories and tools, drills, and insights—everything you need to find and cultivate the creative leader you are. Whatever stage of your career, *Born to Create* provides a fulsome framework for reflecting on creative leadership and taking steps to improve. I will keep a copy on my bookshelf as a handy reference for approaching those special challenges I face."

—Arnold A. Pinkston, corporate vice president and general counsel, Edwards Lifesciences

# BORN TO CREATE

How Creativity Sparks Connection,
Innovation, and Belonging in
Our New World of Work

# BORN

# TO

# CREATE

## Anne Jacoby

**FC**

**FAST
COMPANY**
*Press*

Fast Company Press
New York, New York
www.fastcompanypress.com

This work is being published under the Fast Company Press imprint by an exclusive arrangement with Fast Company. Fast Company and the Fast Company logo are registered trademarks of Mansueto Ventures, LLC. The Fast Company Press logo is a wholly owned trademark of Mansueto Ventures, LLC.

Distributed by Greenleaf Book Group

For ordering information or special discounts for bulk purchases, please contact Greenleaf Book Group at PO Box 91869, Austin, TX 78709, 512.891.6100.

Design and composition by Greenleaf Book Group
Cover design by Kelvin Zlochevsky

Publisher's Cataloging-in-Publication data is available.

Print ISBN: 978-1-63908-071-7

eBook ISBN: 978-1-63908-072-4

To offset the number of trees consumed in the printing of our books, Greenleaf donates a portion of the proceeds from each printing to the Arbor Day Foundation. Greenleaf Book Group has replaced over 50,000 trees since 2007.

Printed in the United States of America on acid-free paper

24 25 26 27 28 29 30 31   10 9 8 7 6 5 4 3 2 1

First Edition

*For Mom and Dad, who always believed*
*I was born to create,*
*&*
*For all the teachers who spark creativity*

*"Creativity is a wild mind and a disciplined eye."*

—Dorothy Parker

# CONTENTS

# CREATIVITY IS NOT ROCKET SCIENCE

In the thick of the pandemic, I got ready to launch a workshop for a leadership team of a high-growth organization. It was the typical setup: me at my desk in my home office, and my client's leadership group, individually filling little Zoom boxes on my screen.

Now, I'm far from a rocket scientist myself—the closest I've been to a launch pad is climbing into the hot-air-balloon basket at the end of a production of *The Wizard of Oz*—but I leapt at the chance to work with this team. This was an almost immeasurably brilliant group of people—I mean, they were *literal rocket scientists*—and I love consulting sessions with leaders open to those deep, probing discussions of theory and possibility. These people dealt with complex equations and abstract concepts all day long. Surely my open-ended questions about work culture would be child's play for them.

It was a little difficult to get a read on the energy in the room, what with the inevitable arm's-length feeling of a Zoom session, as well as some masked-up team members covering most of their facial expressions. But, as every actor knows, you can't rely on your audience to give you *all* the energy, so I took to the stage (of my webcam) with enthusiasm regardless.

"How does creativity show up in your work?" I asked.

Nothing. Just silence and blank expressions (at least, as far as I could tell through the masks). It wasn't intended to be a hardball question. In fact, this was my *opener,* my intro to get the group talking before transitioning into a bigger discussion of culture building and shared values.

But no one knew quite how to answer. No one felt ready to even *attempt* an answer.

Clearly, creativity is not rocket science. So why does it feel so hard?

Maybe you're wondering why I was even *asking* this team about creativity in the first place. My work is in helping companies and executives develop their business culture strategy and learning programs, which includes cultivating core leadership skills. Here I was, inviting them to home in on and consider a particular skill they used at work: creativity. As it turns out, it's hard for a lot of us to see creativity as a skill. Yet defining creativity and making it a disciplined part of our work is precisely what's needed.

First, creativity *can* be defined. "There is a surprising level of unanimity in the field when it comes to a boilerplate definition (of creativity)," neurologist Anna Abraham told *Scientific American*. Creative thinking is the process of generating ideas that are "original, unusual or novel in some way" but also "satisfying, appropriate, or suited to the context in question."[1]

By that definition, everyone is creative, or can learn to be. Anyone who's ever solved an abstract problem has exercised creativity. Really, anyone who's ever learned a skill has flexed their creative muscles: because—quoting Anna Abraham again—"creative thinking involves the discovery of novel connections and is therefore intimately connected to learning."[2]

Second, as Anna Abraham and other researchers have shown, creativity is in fact a *skill,* not some kind of miracle bestowed by the gods. Certainly there are "artsy types"—the singers and actors, the painters and poets—more inclined to overtly creative pursuits, careers, and industries. But accepting creativity as a skill doesn't *negate* the existence of talent, nor does it require all of us to identify as "artsy."

Finally, shifting our conception of creativity from "inborn gift" to "developable skill" reveals a hidden truth about those so-called creative types: even *they* don't rely on the whims of the muse. I've seen this through my long career in the arts, but if you haven't been privy to the up-close-and-personal workings of a live theatre production, a massive art installation, or a TV writers' room, you might be surprised to learn that these artsy types aren't doing their work devoid of structure.

In fact, they thoughtfully construct their environments—and lead their teams—to foster *aha* moments, brilliant solutions, and one-of-a-kind, out-of-the-box insights. They instill a bespoke sense of discipline to the work at hand and the team on board to undertake it.

Yet, at the same time, they don't shy away from the black box. They recognize and welcome the unpredictable part of the process, because they know predictable processes can only create, at best, predictable results.

Predictable isn't *bad*. But it simply isn't—by definition—innovative. It isn't personal—it can't be, not if it's always the same. And it can't adapt when inputs and contexts change. Like when a pandemic stops everyday life in its tracks. Or when the global supply chain chokes up. Or when one generation ages out and a new one ages in.

Predictable isn't going to cut it. It never really has.

We *need* creativity to adapt. To grow. To thrive. And yet . . . we resist it.

I've encountered this resistance time and again. I saw it on that Zoom window of clammed-up rocket scientists. Even managers who embrace the concept of a growth mindset and eagerly pursue personal development seem to balk at the idea of "being creative" when we sit one-on-one.

I don't fault anyone for this. Like I said, our cultural picture of creativity is pretty flawed. Plus, plenty of people associate creative pursuits with shame or falling short—a few early dabbles with art or music that fizzled out, or a one-time passion extinguished by a don't-quit-your-day-job attitude. These can leave us feeling lacking and closed off.

But by the same token, this misconception about creativity is part of why I'm so passionate about teaching creativity as a personal mindset and leadership practice. There's so much room to grow once we shift from "I'm uncreative" to "I'm a beginner." To do that, we must be willing to see creativity as a skill.

All of the high-achieving leaders I've worked with are skilled. They have learned countless complex concepts, procedures, theories, and practices. No

matter how good with numbers you are, no one's born with an inherent understanding of corporate tax strategies! So I know they can acquire skills. And I
know they can learn creativity.

*You* can learn creativity. And you very much should.

Even without knowing specifics—your industry, your role, your team—I
can say with confidence that creativity is what you and your organization need.
One way or another, no matter the challenges you face, creativity will be a part
of the solution.

So that's why I was asking those rocket scientists how they're creative in their
work. Not for any woo-woo notions of the inner self. Not to get them to loosen
up and break the ice before the *real* work started. But rather, because finding
creativity *is* the real work.

I believe creativity at work is essential to doing whatever your organization does, but doing it better—more effectively, more joyfully, and more
authentically.

And while the upshot of creativity at work might not be predictable, it is
*provable*. Forrester Research found that companies that cultivate more creative
workplace cultures significantly outperformed their peers.[3] BetterUp Labs quan-
tified the benefits of creativity at work as including a 25 percent gain in not
just productivity, but also well-being—and a stunning 32 percent increase in
*happiness*.[4] The *New York Times* reported that mandatory in-office work hours
can "drive out innovation," but flexible online collaboration can allow ideas to
easily "bubble up," as well as enable a more diverse workforce.[5]

Nevertheless, creativity still feels risky. It can easily come off as naive to
suggest—let alone insist—that work can be a place of shared joy. But I promise
you, it can.

The risk is worth it.

We need creativity at work not because our teams need to express their
inner Picasso, but because creativity is, at its core, innovation. It's novel solutions to pressing problems made with unexpected connections. And in these
volatile, uncertain, complex, and ambiguous times, it's hard to overstate the
need for novel solutions at work. But sometimes we need a little help to fan
the flames.

## OUR PROBLEM WITH CREATIVITY

As I discovered with the rocket scientists, we have a problem with creativity. And let's face it: even the word *creativity* can feel elusive. We may make that leap to *artsy*. An Impressionist masterpiece, a Beethoven symphony, a Shakespearean actor monologuing to a skull. We think of prodigies, special people with special talents, and we *don't* usually think about our work. Maybe we think it belongs to the twenty-year-old entrepreneur building a business from the garage. Or the temperamental artist splattering paint on the walls. Or lightning striking an ego-driven genius.

When *we're* asked to be more creative at work, we might dread a haphazard lack of structure or feel the pressure to perform. Part of the challenge is that by its very nature, creativity at work takes many forms. You might hope it shows up as you rethink your recruitment process to attract a more diverse talent pool. Perhaps it pokes you in the eye in your sales role as you reconsider your target customer. You may long for creativity to emerge as you tweak your cutting-edge product to be a better market fit. Each of these cases relies on your brain's ability to imagine, think differently, and push beyond the status quo. This requires the application of (you guessed it) creativity in your work.

The concept of creativity can generate other common discomforts. Maybe the thought of being creative drums up our own personal excuses: *I can't draw a straight line, I can't sing a note, I have two left feet*. Perhaps we've shaped our professional self-image in opposition to work that's deemed creative, proclaiming we're left-brained—as if our rational, non-creative side is as defined in our body as in our dominant hand.

Whatever the reason, creativity feels out of reach. It's not that we don't have it but, for whatever reason, we *think* we don't.

A huge part of this problem lies in that cultural conception we have of creativity—that idea that it's a *gift from the gods*. We see creative ability as squishy and undefinable in the abstract, but obvious (or obviously lacking) in the individual. In other words, it's a hard binary: you're creative or you're not.

The big missing realization is that creativity is accessible to each of us. As we'll discover, the value in expressing our creativity shows just why it's so crucial for us to learn—even if we *are* rocket scientists.

Creativity is what moves us from the stale, worn-out status quo to novel, useful, and unexpected solutions. Creative energy prompts us to text our colleague first thing in the morning to collaborate on a new idea or explore a problem in a new light. It invites us to connect through stories, imprinting the moment we heard about our colleague's epic fail with a client that led to changing our offering and doubling our business. Today, more than ever, creativity is essential. Creativity can be cultivated. But it must be practiced.

## THE AUDIENCE FOR THIS BOOK

You may have picked up this book early in your career, curious about how to bring more creativity into your life. Maybe you're a rising leader, ready for your next challenge and hoping to steer your career in a direction that feels more fulfilling. You could be a team or project leader whose work depends on drawing out creativity in others. Or you may be an executive who knows deep down that your team isn't functioning at its creative best, but you're not quite sure how to address it. This book is for each one of you.

Across the twenty-plus years I've partnered with people in organizations of various sizes, industries, functions, and locations around the globe, I've found that most people claim a desire to innovate. They want to develop new ideas that have practical value for their customers. They want to use creativity to inspire others and lead effectively in our new world of work. They need creativity more than ever.

But they're not quite sure how to get it. This isn't a book for work as we know it. This is a book for what work is *becoming*.

## THE SOUND OF CREATIVITY

In early March of 2020, right before the world came to a screeching halt, I attended BetterUp's *Uplift* Conference in Berkeley, California. (BetterUp is a scalable coaching platform perhaps now best known for adding Prince Harry, the Duke of Sussex, to its leadership team.) It was during that early, awkward, elbow-bumping phase of the pandemic when no one yet wore masks. I had launched my consulting practice only a couple of weeks prior, still wobbly from getting my sea legs after leaving my in-house role. Here I was, a newly sprung business owner, primed to advise executive leaders on how to build a thriving workforce for the future yet still naively thinking that COVID-19 would be a few-week blip in our professional lives.

What we know now is that March of 2020 marked the jolt of a seismic shift in how knowledge work gets done. Forever.

Time to rethink *where* and *when* work is performed.

Time to rethink *how* teams collaborate.

Time to rethink our relationship to work itself.

I sat in the third row of this hotel conference room full of fellow business leaders and HR consultants. We were waiting for Leslie Odom Jr., beloved star of *Hamilton*, for his closing keynote. As you'll learn later in this book, my roots to the world of theatre run deep, so I was eager to watch how Odom would connect with this corporate audience.

Perhaps of no surprise, Odom's presence captivated all of us. It was easy to feel an instant kinship with him and his creative journey: the struggle and sacrifice of practicing his craft in his youth, the financial tradeoffs of pursuing a career in the theatre, and the familiar experience of fumbling as you learn how to trust your instincts.

What did surprise me was his powerful and provocative challenge to the audience: *The role of an artist is to work to return to the moment when our heart first opened.*

That was it. The creative spark. And to me, the sound of that moment is still clear.

I was about eight years old, performing in a musical at the Pacific Conservatory of the Performing Arts (PCPA) in Santa Maria, California. Not yet called to "places," I snuck backstage and stood in the wings. The old stage had a musty heaviness you could feel in the air, carrying countless performances from generations past.

Right before the curtain went up, the orchestra tuned its instruments. (For theatre- or symphony-goers, this is a common performance precursor.) That cacophony: the muted chatter of the audience in the house seats, the flurry of the flutes and fellow woodwinds' scales, the resonant hum of the cello and bass bending their notes against the violins' perfect fourths, the horns practicing perfect fifths, all pattering, searching, and creatively fine-tuning; until finally, the oboe's piercing "A" note calms the restless storm, synthesizes the group into one steady note, diverse tones coalescing into one. Suddenly, it all falls silent. Everyone takes a breath. There's a collective, sacred hush.

That was it. The moment my heart first cracked open.

In that instant, I was pulled to a lifelong pursuit of the creative spark: in the arts, in business, and in life.

Your moment might be when you first felt your bare feet sink into the wet sand at the edge of the ocean or saw a spectacular golden sunset. Maybe it's when you first lost yourself in drawing a picture, won someone over in a difficult conversation, or discovered a genuine connection with a customer as you solved their problem. Chances are you still carry that moment with you, even if it's tucked deep down and hidden out of sight.

But tapping into that creative spirit, the moment your heart first opened, may just bring you closer to what you were put on this earth to be. That moment can signal the very essence of who we are and what we value. (And if no clear moment is coming to mind, that's okay, too. You may stumble upon it as you read this book.) That's the spark that lights us up in our work.

## CREATIVITY IN THE *NOW* OF WORK

Creativity at work has never been more important. With the accelerating pace of change in business, creativity is what keeps companies relevant. Creativity is why Pixar, Zappos, and Squarespace lead the pack among the competition. (Creativity is also what may have saved Kodak, BlackBerry, and Blockbuster Video from going under.) It's how some people in our life seem to effortlessly reinvent themselves, constantly learning, seeking out new challenges, and building the life and career they envision, even amid setbacks.

As humans, creativity is what fuels us. When our creativity is expressed and understood by others at work, it nourishes our souls. It binds us to each other, something our business world desperately needs. As we all wrestle with the *why* and *how* of work, creativity helps us reimagine our unique path or feel more connected to the one we're already on. It helps us stay agile in a jungle gym career or finally get the courage to launch our own company.

Our workforce is experiencing a profound revolution. Unemployment is at historic lows. Amid the Great Reinvention, the era following the heavy loss of the pandemic years, it's impossible to ignore our war for talent. Workers want choice. They demand greater flexibility in when, where, and how they work. They clamor for autonomy and control over navigating their careers. And now with five generations in the workforce, many of us no longer gain satisfaction from the outdated models of what *making it* at work is really supposed to mean.

Instead, we value greater purpose in our work. We want alignment with our values and belonging within a community that supports us. We aspire to feel safe to show up authentically at work, tapping into that moment our heart first opened. We long to learn from diverse colleagues who inspire us. As the command-and-control leadership style sunsets, even the way we motivate others is experiencing reinvention. Creativity—bringing your fresh ideas to innovate and deliver customer value while being uniquely you—is what our workplace needs.

## IT'S TIME TO BE A ZEBRICORN

The seismic shift across our work experience may have been brought on by the pandemic, but change had been mounting from the increased use of artificial intelligence and disruptive technology in our workplaces; consequently, the rallying cry to activate our creativity has never been louder. Throughout this book, I'll introduce how we can all show up more creatively—for ourselves, and for others. I like to think of it as embracing our inner zebricorn: part zebra, part unicorn, we are each perfectly imperfect. With creativity, we can each bring different, unique strengths to our teams and show up unabashedly as ourselves. *That's not to say it's always easy.* But embracing our creative thinking to build the work and life we desire often means choosing the less-traveled path. It takes guts. Sometimes it's messy. It demands we show up as ourselves, rather than always trying to fit in. It calls us to activate our creativity.

Although I've made a career out of activating creativity, I'm intimately familiar with struggling to tap into it, too. I'll share the struggle of trying to find a mere five minutes of creative energy amid significant constraints (ever try starting a business while home-schooling a kindergartner and entertaining a three-year-old?). But ah, you'll be amazed by what those five minutes can yield. I'll share some practical ways you can do this, too, regardless of where you are on your creative path.

Today I blend my roots in the performing arts, my MBA, and twenty years of business know-how to help my clients tap into their creative thinking and build the workplace cultures they crave. Before launching my culture consultancy, Spring Street Solutions, I helped scale a company from seven people to thousands around the globe, led large culture change initiatives, launched new offices, and built new functions. I've co-developed culture programs for F500 organizations, coached and advised start-up CEOs, led countless leadership off-sites, and spoken to hundreds of undergraduates just beginning their creative work journeys.

I've also failed. A lot. I've tried things that didn't work and learned from each experience. I've watched my own kids play creatively, inventing newfangled customer reward programs and transforming kitchen stools to airplane seats as the pandemic kept us all grounded.

Throughout these experiences, there's been one constant. It's the pure joy and wisdom that creativity can gift us. Amid the headwinds of challenges and discomfort of uncertainty, creativity can transport us to an energizing future possibility. Creativity has saved me from dark and lonely *what-the-heck-am-I-supposed-to-be-doing-with-my-life* moments and offered a bit of pixie dust when I needed it the most. It can do that for you, too.

## BEING FUTURE-FOCUSED

The Future of Work landed in our laps in mid-March 2020. Suddenly a focus on workplace culture (and how to achieve a thriving one) was on every HR and business leader's mind. I'll explore what it means to be a creative leader in today's ever-changing work world, and dive into how creative leadership applies to in-office and remote-first team structures. While creativity cultures can exist anywhere, we'll explore some best practices to optimize for your workplace environment.

Being prepared for the future will require a deep understanding of how creativity will help us navigate these great unknowns. Throughout the book we'll break down how to strengthen creativity in ourselves, in others, and across our organizations to be the fuel that propels us forward. The universal skill of creativity transcends industries, global cultures, and business sizes. As technology dominates more of our lives—buzzing and dinging with notifications that steal our attention and focus—creativity can be the antidote. It's the shared human experience that differentiates us from the robots. This book will help you access your creative superpower to use for years to come.

## YOUR CREATIVE JOURNEY WITH THIS BOOK

You're now officially invited to the party to get all fired up about work. And if your work doesn't currently light you up, it could be time to focus on something else that does. Life is short. With an estimated one-third of our lives spent at work, I believe more creativity can help it become something that fuels you.

I've structured this book as nine scenes within three acts as a nod to my roots in the theatre, but also as recognition that creativity leads to *performance*, "the action or process of carrying out or accomplishing an action, task, or function." I won't just talk abstractly about creativity; I'll help you apply the skills to get things done.

Act I is The Spark, where we'll focus on your individual creativity. There, we'll dive into the power of creative confidence, how to strengthen your imagination and put things on their feet, and the importance of continuously gathering and integrating feedback.

Act II is The Blaze. That's the section to learn how to lead more creatively and develop creativity in others to innovate. I'll share insights from famous directors, CEOs, musicians, and project leaders who reveal their creative process of building trust. We'll examine how our workspaces influence creativity and ways in which the workplace is changing, including the rise in remote-first cultures. We'll also take a closer look at how creativity can build collaborative team dynamics.

And finally, Act III is The Bonfire, where we'll discover how to build the creativity culture that we all crave. Filled with practical exercises to create an organizational North Star, this section will include the building blocks of creativity culture and the rituals that enable us to authentically foster this connection at work.

Throughout this journey, you'll meet creative artists, business leaders, and entrepreneurs who have embraced—and sometimes tangled with—creativity in their lives and work. You'll hear stories of my creative journey: some struggles and some triumphs. I'll share examples of how I've partnered with clients and learned from countless teachers along the way, including my own kids. And you'll have a chance to reflect on your early memories with creativity, and when, where, and how you feel most creative today.

At the end of each scene, you'll get practical exercises, key questions to ask, and assessment tools to carry with you. Woven throughout, I'll point you to the Recommended Resources section at the end of the book, where you can learn and do even more. Creativity is about action. Even if you don't use these tools right away, I hope you'll find time to revisit them to try them out. I'll wrap up each scene with the Show Notes, which will include some takeaway nuggets to consider. The end of Act I and II will include a brief intermission, a chance to take a breather and reflect.

My great hope is that this book will help you discover how to access more of your creativity at work, unlock ways to elevate creativity as a leadership power skill, and learn how to influence the culture around you to inspire more connection, innovation, and inclusion in your work. Creativity doesn't have to feel elusive. You've already got it inside you.

Let's get the fire started.

**Act I.**

# The Spark:
# Igniting Your
# Creative Mindset

O ne day, in the summer of 2003, my dad flew out to New York from California to help me move from an apartment in Brooklyn to a place on Mulberry Street in Manhattan. As fate would have it, this was also the day of the 29-hour New York City blackout. The whole city shut down. Along with thousands of others, I trudged home across the Brooklyn Bridge in the sweltering heat, passing opportunists selling small bottles of water for five bucks a pop. By the time I had crossed the bridge to Windsor Terrace off Prospect Park, I was exhausted, dehydrated, and consequently sick all night.

Shortly after my dad landed to find the city's electric grid shut down, he quickly pivoted from his original plan to meet me in Manhattan, as the subway wasn't operating, and no cabs were running in that direction. With no form of communication between us, he arrived in Brooklyn to an incapacitated daughter recovering from heat exhaustion. Ever the lifesaver, my dad spent the weekend single-handedly packing up my old tap shoes, candles, baking pans, and half-finished books on *How to Learn Guitar in Three Easy Steps* (or not-so-easy in my case). Turns out, even as a young twenty-something, I had accumulated a lot of stuff.

Now that time in my life was a period of creativity by necessity. Recovering from a bad break-up, I juggled multiple jobs to make ends meet: waiting tables, babysitting, and office work at a start-up on Spring Street in Soho. Creativity meant figuring out how to save money to slowly pay off my student loans (without a degree yet to show for it) and still flirt with the idea of pursuing my career in the performing arts. It meant making cold calls all day and doing a restaurant shift from 5 p.m. until 3 a.m., often followed by an impromptu jam session in the Lower East Side. (The mere thought of this schedule now triggers the need for a nap.)

The next morning, when my dad and I got the moving van to Little Italy, he helped me carry countless loads of books and clothes up six flights of stairs to my new postage-stamp-sized apartment. Finally feeling hydrated enough to stay on my feet for eight hours, I scooted off to my restaurant job, leaving my dad with more boxes left to unpack.

Here's where things get interesting.

He locked himself out of my new apartment. Six floors down. In an unfamiliar neighborhood nestled at the intersection of Little Italy and Chinatown. To hear him tell the story is true creative thinking at work. *Do I wait for her until she gets back? Maybe one of her new neighbors has a spare key . . . but even if they did, it would be weird for them to let me into her apartment . . . Perhaps I can break in . . . That's it. I'll just climb up on the outside of the building.*

My dad spent the next hour scaling the stone wall bordering the old brick building like a middle-aged Spider-Man, flinging his body up to the fire escape, gingerly climbing up the rickety stairs that likely never intended to hold his weight. Curious neighbors, mid-bite of lo mein, peered out their windows to watch this man risking life and limb to ascend the side of the building; my dad responded by flashing a friendly thumbs-up, as if to signal: *I'm okay! I belong here!* until successfully making it up to the miniaturized bedroom window of my sixth-floor walk-up. With a little risk-taking, confidence, and a positive mindset, he found a solution.

What we'll discover in Act I is how this kind of individual creative thinking is exactly what's needed in our workplaces. We all encounter situations where the door we thought was open is unexpectedly locked. It's up to us to find a new way in. The next three scenes will reveal how creativity can help you conquer the inevitable obstacles at work—and find joy while doing it. Like my dad, we can all activate our individual creative mindset. We just need a little practice.

# BUILDING YOUR CREATIVE CONFIDENCE

*"It takes confidence as a leader to come up with a ton of bad ideas.*
*But that's what's necessary to come up with something useful."*

—Alec Guettel, co-founder of Axiom, Sungevity, and Knowable

W hen we cultivate the confidence to welcome our own bad ideas, to not hold back, we can foster creativity. Alec does this seemingly without effort. Not because he's a born creative, but because he's worked to build that confidence.

When I interviewed for an executive assistant role at Axiom back in 2002, I was surprised (and delighted) to learn that Alec Guettel was not only an entrepreneur and Stanford Business School graduate, but *also* the scion of a legendary musical theatre family. His brother Adam Guettel's *Floyd Collins* was a favorite of mine to belt out while brewing hazelnut coffee and baking cookies at my off-campus Sweet Shoppe job, his mother Mary Rodgers Guettel wrote classics like *Once Upon a Mattress*, and his grandfather Richard Rodgers was *the* Richard Rodgers, of Rodgers & Hammerstein fame.

So perhaps it's no surprise that Alec—now a friend and mentor—is one of the most dynamically creative leaders I've ever met. He's co-founder of multiple companies, holder of several patents, and filled with positive energy that leaves people more good-natured, thoughtful, and funnier than when he found them.

But he also admitted that, for a long time, he resisted the term *creativity*.

"If you're worried about being mocked, or concerned about the consequence of sharing bad ideas, you hold back," he elaborated. "It takes someone confident in the process to create the right kind of environment that enables creativity."

Creative confidence is a core skill, yet for many of us—even those with an impressively artistic family tree—trusting in our own creativity isn't something we're used to doing.

Katty Kay and Claire Shipman's book *The Confidence Code* reveals a tipping point when people (particularly women) begin to lose confidence in their capabilities. Self-doubt starts to creep in. It turns out our baseline confidence is a mix of things within and outside of our control. Things like our genetic wiring, lived experiences, and the early encouragement of those who raised us combine to make our unique confidence cocktail.[1] To reclaim more control over this confidence factor, it helps to reflect on instances when we've applied our grit to cope with setbacks. We recognize that even in the lowest points of learning a new skill, there are insights to discover that might shift the tide. That's how we ride the wave of uncertainty—by holding the inner belief that we have what it takes to get through it. That core belief is also critical for creativity; otherwise, it's unlikely any of us would risk putting ourselves out there.

## BORN TO CREATE

Much of my creative confidence was nurtured during my experience at the Los Angeles County High School for the Arts (LACHSA). I practically begged my parents to let me go there. After performing in countless community theatre and Equity shows growing up, attending LACHSA felt like moving to the big leagues. And it required a big (real) move, too. LACHSA is an audition-based, conservatory-style public high school on the campus of Cal State Los Angeles. By the time I approached my sophomore year, we still lived in Santa Maria, a good three hours north of Los Angeles.

Visiting the school was like a trip to a magical place: a utopia of creative thinkers and artists. These teenagers were unabashedly *themselves*. It was the height of the '90s grunge era, and among the pink hair, piercings, and baggy jeans were also preppy kids, crunchy hippies, and everything in between. Rather than the typical high school pressure to conform, there was a *come-as-you-are* energy, where everyone effortlessly worked well together. A jewel in the crown of the music department, we watched the gospel choir rehearse with students of all colors, shapes, sizes, and a unified sound that could blow off a rooftop. After I got accepted to the school, my family willingly uprooted and moved south.

I started at LACHSA with a well-worn passion for singing, acting, and dancing. I left with discipline that would carry me through my arts and business career. With a grueling 6:45 a.m. departure from home, school lasted until 4 p.m., often followed by rehearsals and performances well into the evening. Purpose-built to help emerging artists practice their craft, LACHSA also helped me discover keys to collaborating with diverse colleagues and gain a deep understanding of how creative thinking enables us to interconnect with the world around us.

What's special about this school—as is the case with many creative communities and organizations—is its unyielding commitment to inviting in personal creativity. By design, creativity isn't a *nice to have*. Creativity *is the solution.* Learning about Black history? Put on a show filled with African dance and staged scenes from the Underground Railroad. Prepping for a chemistry test on ionic bonding? Interpret them on canvas. Studying the US founding fathers? Reenact it as a musical. (Lin-Manuel Miranda got that message loud and clear—more on that later.)

We were constantly challenged to learn, synthesize our learning, and then create a new interpretation of what we had just learned. The output of this disciplined approach, combined with a racially and socioeconomically diverse group of students from across Los Angeles County, led to unexpected creative expressions in many forms. It bred creative confidence.

In many ways, my LACHSA experience was an introduction to an optimal organizational culture. Much like a diverse company workforce, we all came with different backgrounds to unite around a shared purpose. At work, we hope to be celebrated as individuals. You might be the one person on the team with an understanding about how to monetize your product. Or maybe you've got a designer's eye and can instantly beautify a PowerPoint slide. We want to be recognized for our unique strengths and talents yet committed to operating cooperatively as part of a bigger organism. As we improve our ability to tap into our individual creative energy, we elevate the creativity of all of those around us.

In the years before I launched my own business, I served on LACHSA's foundation board. At one of our board retreats, we sat in the offices of fellow board member David Angelo's creative brand firm, David & Goliath (D&G). His firm was tasked with creating a new brand for LACHSA and conducted deep research to define what sets the school apart from others. In that bright and airy conference room, LACHSA's new tagline was revealed: *Born to Create*.

I burst into tears.

I then recognized an ugly truth: For years, I had been resisting creativity. I thought it would make me look weak, less professional, or lacking gravitas. I remembered my fifteen-year-old self, eager to learn and ready to collaborate. Born to create. My classmates—some living under freeways, others commuting four hours each day to get to campus—taught me the power of creative confidence. I can still see them planted in LACHSA's fertile soil. Bursting with possibility and potential. *They* were born to create. And you, starting your first job out of college, taking your first team leader role, or finally ready to launch your own firm: *You* were born to create. We are *all* born to create. We just have to muster the confidence to believe it.

## THE AGE OF ENTREPRENEURSHIP

I've had the opportunity to speak about Creativity at Work to dozens of companies, firms, board of directors' groups, and universities. Among them have been several undergraduate entrepreneurship classes full of bright-eyed, ambitious, and mission-driven young people ready to change the world. And yes, many of them end up seeking (and securing) seed money or Series A investments to start the next big company. But far more, even with newly minted business credentials in hand, do not. They choose a different path.

The truth is, we live in an age where we're all entrepreneurs. Even within a mature, traditional organization, knowing how to create, articulate an idea, build a vision, and execute against a plan can make or break your career. We are all builders.

Today, our very relationship with work is changing. That's one of the big reasons I believe creativity is such an in-demand life skill. It's estimated that more than 50 percent of the US workforce will be working as freelancers by the year 2027.[2] With this shift in how workforces are assembled, we're invited to rethink traditional talent structures. Creativity enables us to spot problems and view them as opportunities—and then imagine how *we* can be part of the solution. It helps us relate to and express our shared human experience in a fresh way, whether that's to get along better with our colleagues to move a project forward, work collaboratively on a new hybrid team, or influence the shape of our career path.

In the age of TikTok, social media influencers, and Sesame Street, creative confidence can also transform a tiny idea into a multimillion-dollar enterprise. Still, beyond the potential for riches, creative confidence gives us a sense of security. It empowers us. It's what shifts our thinking from *this might work* to *I will make this work.*

You may have dreams of launching your own business or being your own boss. Maybe you want to write a book to tell your personal story or lead a high-stakes project at work. Perhaps you're interested in switching careers, ready to step into a field that you believe will bring you longer-term fulfillment. Each of these big goals requires an entrepreneurial mindset. And that translates to the need for creative confidence.

I recently served as an advisor to long-time colleague and friend Ward Hendon, who was working to get his new firm, Dangerous Ventures, off the ground. As he and his General Partners explored different impact models for a venture capital firm, one potential initiative was to develop underrepresented founders and give them tools and resources to succeed. To do that, we first had to unpack the personal characteristics (both innate and developed) that lead to successful entrepreneurship.

Through that research, I discovered that successful entrepreneurs have a few things in common:

- Resilience and grit to push through the discomfort of making mistakes
- An insatiable curiosity and appetite to learn
- A vision to *see* the possibility in their ideas
- Resourcefulness and a bias toward action
- The ability to be a talent multiplier, possessing a subtle magnetism to attract people to join in their journey (their creative confidence draws people in)

Now it's clear that one size does not fit all. I've met extroverted and introverted entrepreneurs, young and old, experienced leaders, and those with a true beginner's mindset (and a short resume of experiences to match). But they each have creative confidence and a commitment to experimenting. And if they didn't always show their confidence (and who does?), they know how to fake it 'til they make it.

## SEEING THE LINE

Faking it isn't synonymous with being disingenuous. Part of having a beginner's mind (regardless of age or experience) means being willing to admit we have more to learn. We can start a project or creative idea with a sense of wonder: *What might I learn from this? If it's successful, what could be the outcome?* But having the conviction to believe in our own idea, the gumption to navigate the rocky waters of necessary countless creative iterations, to hold on while faced with criticism, doubt, or non-believers—that's the stuff for which creative confidence prepares us.

Professional athletes often refer to the practice of *seeing the line.* They see the line before they whitewater raft down the river, ski down the hill, or make a play on the soccer field. They see the line in their mind, take a breath, and move toward a clear path to success. Creative confidence helps us envision our creative output even before it's produced. It helps us clearly imagine our own bright destiny.

Okay, time to address the elephant in the room amid all this talk about creativity. It's easy to think that creativity is indulgent, only for privileged trust-fund babies, or filled with too much navel-gazing to feel *practical*. I've had clients flat-out tell me they don't want to be creative since their work is so heavily process oriented. But creativity is one of the most useful skills we can cultivate, breaking socioeconomic barriers and spanning functional work. Creativity is the skill that binds us to our shared human experience. Regardless of our career field of practice, chances are we're going to encounter an unexpected obstacle that's not in the playbook. Overcoming it will require creativity.

One of my favorite television shows (believe it or not) is the History Channel's *Alone*. For those not familiar with this terrifying concept, a group of wilderness enthusiasts willingly get individually dropped in the middle of nowhere with only a few selected supplies, like an axe, fishing net, or snare wire. Their task is to outlast the competition and survive (enjoy?) living in the wilderness, completely by themselves.[3] They're trained to film and narrate the experience so viewers like me can sit from the comfort of our couches—armed with warm blankets and pantries full of Pop-Tarts—and watch in horror and awe.

What I like most about the show isn't the sport of the hunt or watching the emotional struggle most participants encounter after week upon week of isolation. It's the creative mindset they must adopt to face each day with positivity and curiosity. To survive, they *must* get creative. I like to imagine our ancestors or early inventors tinkering with primitive tools and materials to make something new. Being self-reliant on your creativity could mean the difference between eating that day or going hungry.

In today's age, creativity will help us solve our large, complex, existential challenges across the globe, as much as it will make our lives a little easier and more enjoyable. It might enable your business to survive through a recession so you can emerge stronger and more resilient. But before creativity can save you or your business, we must fall in love with our unique creative process.

Back at LACHSA, as a fifteen-year-old Broadway hopeful, I discovered that love. And when I joined a start-up, almost ten years later, I recognized the same creative process in business building. It felt familiar, a little like the rehearsal room: tinkering with my fellow creators, learning from their thought processes, playing off each other, watching the creativity unfold right before my eyes, taking a breath, and seeing the line before getting started.

## GETTING (AND KEEPING) YOUR CREATIVE MOJO

I don't mean to come across as flippant about how to get creative confidence. As if *c'mon folks, just attend the number-one arts high school in the country and voilà, you'll leave with creative confidence!* (If only it were that simple.) But I *do* believe we have more agency over building our creative confidence than we may think. We can put ourselves in situations that push us just beyond our comfort zone: not so far out that we panic and shut down, but enough to feel the itchy discomfort of growth. We must recognize what Alec Guettel knew so well: that creativity starts with us.

Getting our creative mojo takes effort and a willingness to adapt. After years of wrapping up my identity in the performing arts, I took a sharp left turn into the world of business—and specifically the business of law. I had to learn a new language. I made new habits of reading business and legal articles. I studied the resumes of people who had grown progressively in their careers and learned the lingo of what enabled them to rise. And I asked a ton of questions about what mattered to the executives in the room. *What does success look like? What are you worried about most? How do you track and measure your goals?*

After reinventing myself as a business and sales leader, I readied myself for the next challenge: stepping into the world of people, learning, talent development, and company culture. Here, I learned yet a whole new language, and a process to create interactive learning experiences and measure a return on investment in developing people. With that came the awkward, unstable feeling of being completely out of my element. But I knew creativity would help me stay curious, experiment, and adapt to discover a path forward.

Rod Lathim also knows a bit about creative reinvention. To know Rod is to love him: His broad smile, sparkly eyes, and big infectious laugh feel like warm hugs from an old friend. He grew up around theatre and music. But before he found success as an actor, director, and producer, Rod tried his hand at visual art. As a child in Sunday School, he was instructed to draw Jesus on a donkey. Obedient and respectful, he tried to follow the directions. He focused. He imagined what Jesus on a donkey might *actually look like*. He carefully sketched it out. After getting up the courage to finally share it with the teacher, her response left him cold.

"Nope," she said flatly. "That looks *nothing* like Jesus on a donkey."

Rod was devastated. Defeated. One offhanded comment was enough to shatter his creative confidence.

After studying theatre briefly in college, Rod received a flash of creative inspiration that nudged him in a different direction. He went home to Santa Barbara to launch what would become Access Theatre Company, a premier home for productions that included deaf, blind, and differently abled performers, producing works of theatre accessible to all audiences. His many successful productions toured across the United States, Canada, and England. He's partnered with creatives like Anthony Edwards, Brad Hall, Julia Louis-Dreyfus—all the way down to yours truly as a twelve-year-old actress.

Once retired from Access Theatre, Rod led the board of the Marjorie Luke Theatre, a theatre he founded and named in honor of his junior high school drama teacher. And in the dark days of COVID, Rod used his creativity to produce a virtual concert series that streamed live to over 600,000 viewers, surpassing its fundraising goals and saving the theatre.

I could easily stop the story here. After all, Rod clearly got his creative mojo and found success with his path in the performing arts. But later in life, Rod's creative path diverged. He transformed his creative mojo into visual art.

When Rod's beloved Labrador Emily passed away, he commissioned a good friend and artist to create an assemblage piece in her memory. By then a well-established leader in the performing arts community, his friend gently pushed back, suggesting that he create the piece himself. Rod ruminated: *Jesus on the donkey. Jesus on the donkey. It's going to be horrible.* But he made it anyway. He set aside the self-criticism that so easily bubbled up. He focused on his sweet dog and what she had meant to him. This piece of art wasn't for others to appreciate or purchase. He made the piece for himself, which became a creative catalyst. And his confidence began to bloom.

Now in his sixties, Rod's visual artwork has been featured in premier galleries from Santa Barbara and Palm Desert in California, to the Kate Oh Gallery in New York City. After selecting assemblages (found objects) as his medium, he shifted to working with glass neon sculpture and mixed-media pieces in collaboration with painter Chris Gocong. At first, this choice of neon took even Rod by surprise. He had no knowledge of how to work with the material. A self-taught sculptor, Rod learned all he could about neon's properties to make the desired color, shape, and movement. He leaned into curiosity and discipline to help bring his visions to life.

I'm struck by Rod's commitment to a creative life path and the many ways it applies to the world of business. First, Rod focuses on what brings him joy and energy. His creative choices have been influenced by his passions and heart, flowing from the relationships he's formed and the stories he wants to tell. Next, despite his expertise in many creative endeavors, Rod has an insatiable appetite to learn new things. He's deeply curious. Knowing nothing about neon (in fact admitting to being intimidated by it), Rod tackled the fear head-on, devoured research, and expanded his comfort zone.

"Neon is just energy," he told me. "It transforms based on how you use it. It's completely adaptable, which might be why I was drawn to work with it."

And finally, while the application of his creativity has evolved, he's maintained the core belief that to make something of value, it must start with your own expression and enjoyment. Having an audience matters (much like any business needs clients or customers), but what's more important is a guiding North Star. Living in accordance with our values can ease decision-making that can leave many of us feeling paralyzed.

You may be considering: *Should I keep practicing as an attorney or finally follow my passion to start a nonprofit? Can I make ends meet by working part-time so I can finish writing my novel? Am I ready to risk leaving my stable job to start my own consulting firm? Should I pick the college major that my parents think is a reliable path or take the classes that are of real interest to me?* When we filter these decisions through a lens of what we value, where we're finding joy, and how we're making an impact, the angst surrounding them dissipates. Our choice comes into sharper focus. We can take the leap and find our light.

## THE POWER OF CREATIVE CONSTRAINTS

I launched my own business in February 2020, a month before the world hit pause. What was envisioned as a consultancy focused on in-person team building, and creative thinking workshops quickly morphed into something much more . . . virtual-friendly. Like many of us, I soon became a Zoom super-user, adept at breakouts and chats. (I also became much more self-conscious of the elevens deepening between my eyes—*don't be so cruel, webcam!*)

My daughter, mid-year through kindergarten, was thrust into virtual school. As these remote-learning five-year-olds figured out how to unmute themselves, it required a heavy lift of involvement from my husband and me. We carefully choreographed our day (I worked on client business in the mornings, and he taught his college students remotely in the afternoons), each of us negotiating for a little extra work time around the edges of our prescribed schedules. My newly-turned-three-year-old son was also home, putting good use to the trampoline we had purchased only months prior. Owning a trampoline with small children during the pandemic was like being ordained a prescient being—as if we had somehow predicted our playgrounds would soon be wrapped with yellow caution tape.

At the time, my son was also still of napping age, yet rapidly resisting it. (Days without naps were hellscapes. IYKYK.) I wasn't above bribing him with cookies, stuffed animals, and his favorite music to coerce him to Just. Sit. In. The. Stroller. I walked the same ten blocks around the neighborhood, familiar with each lemon tree, barking dog, and garden gnome along my route. Between doom-scrolling, scrambling to buy toilet paper, and wringing our hands for the announcement of a vaccine, his hour-long nap was the brief calm in what was often a very ugly parenting storm.

The trouble was, I couldn't escape the pressure of wanting more time to *build a business*. It often felt like the weight of the world. Amid the constraints of this pandemic, how was I supposed to feel remotely creative? And here I was, advising businesses on how to cultivate *creativity?!* Most days I wanted to scream, cry, or run away completely. Okay, usually it was a combination of these things. And sure, we all experienced those moments. (You might even be experiencing them now—no judgment!)

Let me be the first to admit: I was terribly skeptical that I could produce anything creative during that time. My uninterrupted work time was often limited to what felt like five precious minutes during the day. If I was lucky, I might also get a twenty-minute stretch right before collapsing from exhaustion at the end of the day. But I was ruthless about protecting the little time that I had. It was my time to think, to write, to somehow *will* the creativity to come. I resisted the urge to say, "But the conditions aren't quite right; I'm not *feeling* creative today; I'm not *rested* enough; it isn't *Tuesday*, etc., etc." I simply blocked off the time I had. I gifted it to myself. And I committed to the discipline.

Sometimes the creativity came when I finally got a shower in.

Or when I was stirring tomato soup on the stove.

Or building a puzzle with my kids.

But it (almost) always arrived.

And I seized that moment to capture it, writing it down long-hand in my notebook.

It's true, we can't always control when creativity comes, or exactly how. But we have to be ready to receive it when it does. There are no log cabins awaiting our stay for a summer-long retreat, replete with a woodsy yet modern home office ripped from the pages of *Dwell* magazine. I don't always wake up bursting with fresh ideas, ready to innovate on command. These fictional moments likely won't come, no matter how long we wait for them or how many fir-scented candles we light.

Instead, we must make space for creative moments or daily Creativity Boosters. We squeeze them between childcare drop-offs and pickups. They live in the cracks of status-update meetings and budget-planning conversations. What I often see with my clients is how creative, deep work is easily pushed to the side or deprioritized. Maybe we feel guilty or self-indulgent about scheduling it into our lives. Maybe we fear it—*What if nothing magical occurs?* Or maybe we simply don't know what to do with the time we set aside, feeling aimless, without a map or directional device. (Stick with me: The tools are coming!) But we need to be intentional about letting this creative time in.

## CREATIVITY BOOSTER:

Write down three words that reflect your creative energy. Circle the one that feels most unexpected. Write three more words that relate to the circled word. Circle the one that surprises you most. Take your final circled word and see if or how it shows up in your daily work.

## CREATIVITY BOOSTER:

Build-your-own crossword. Start by writing down one word that represents a creative challenge in your work today. Build other words connected to those letters. Keep building on that crossword throughout the day and notice if a solution emerges related to the problem word.

## CREATIVITY BOOSTER:

Go outside (or look out the window) to see nature. Maybe it's a tree outside, a cloud in a patch of sky, or a blooming flower. Imagine the lifetime of that plant. Personify it in your mind. Spend five minutes imagining its story.

## CREATIVITY BOOSTER:

Find sensory material. (Putty. Play-Doh. LEGO.) Carve out five minutes. Close your eyes and breathe deeply. Feel how the material sits in your hands. What words would you use to describe it to someone who's never felt this material before?

Whether you're living with the creative constraints of a pandemic or stuck in the confines of your current life or job experience, you, too, can tap your creativity. You may not have as much creative time as you'd like, or feel as creatively supported as you deserve, but *your ideas* are a buried pot of gold. Your job is to build the confidence to get that creativity to the surface.

# SCENE DIALOGUE FOR CREATIVE CONFIDENCE

**SETTING:**

(MARIA, twenty-three years old with jet-black hair and dark eyeliner, sits quietly in her team meeting. Her colleague ALICE, twenty-eight and oozing confidence, finishes her presentation and turns to the group for feedback. As the clock reaches the top of the hour, team members scatter to their next meeting. ALICE turns to MARIA before she reaches the door.)

ALICE

Hey, what'd you think of my campaign idea?

MARIA

(looking away)

Yeah. All good. Everyone really liked what you came up with...

ALICE

What about *you*, though? You're a big part of this team so you've got to speak up if you think we can make it better.

MARIA

Well, I've been giving it a lot of thought, actually.

(MARIA closes her eyes and takes a deep breath.)

I wonder if we might want to rethink the order. Like, maybe we should start with your strong ending moment, which is such a powerful visual. So we tell the whole story in reverse order. Flip it on its head.

ALICE

Huh. Tell me more...

MARIA

The moment she discovers how we helped her get there—*that* could be the closing beat. It feels fresher to me. That way the audience is in on the secret from the start. The big reveal is our company at the end. It feels more memorable that way.

**ALICE**

That's pretty cool, Maria. Let's play with it.
I'll set up a meeting for us to rethink things
tomorrow. And hey, next time, it's totally chill
to share these ideas in our team meeting, okay?

**(END OF SCENE)**

In this scene, Maria is test-driving her creative confidence. She has a clear vision for her idea but isn't feeling completely safe yet to share it. Notice she didn't criticize Alice's initial concept, but instead found a way to build on it. Next time, Maria can work on speaking up earlier to contribute her creative ideas.

## KNOW YOURSELF

Knowing what makes us tick is an important first step in developing our creative confidence. That self-awareness can emerge from challenges like the one Leslie Odom Jr. made to return to the moment your heart first opened, or from regular reflection and gathering feedback from others. Creative confidence on the face of it may feel like an obvious step in the creative process. How can you communicate an idea effectively if you don't fully believe in it yourself? How do you innovate or try new, unheard of, and off-the-wall ideas without standing up and walking with a little confident pep in your step? But truly knowing yourself can be deceptively difficult.

You may be in the early stages of figuring that out, or you may already have a deep appreciation of what conditions help you get creative. We're all remarkably different: Some prefer to work with the background hum of a busy Starbucks, while others need silence to channel our creative thoughts and ideas. Some of us love to riff with others—a group brainstorm gets our wheels turning. Some value time on our own to process connections. Your job is to discover your preferred environment. You might be thinking, *I have no clue when I'm at my most creative. How in the world am I supposed to know that?* It's okay if you don't already know. But you do need the curiosity to learn.

I invite you to run an experiment on yourself. Over the next two weeks, at the end of each day, take five minutes to reflect on the moments throughout the day when you felt your creativity flowing. Maybe you had a solid thirty minutes of deep work time after lunch when creative ideas bubbled up. Maybe you spent fifteen minutes after work painting with your kids or jammed on a Peloton first thing in the morning when fresh, creative thoughts emerged. While making dinner, maybe you tried new combinations of flavors to flex your creative muscles. List out the moments—the seemingly small and satisfyingly big. Note the amount of time spent in each creative burst.

Your next step is to write them down. Capture those moments on paper. Take note of the time of day and how long you stayed in a creative flow.

Next, as you look at your list of creative moments, note the conditions around you. Get detailed with it: What was the temperature in the room? What did you hear? Was there music playing? Where were you sitting (or standing)? What visual cues did you take in? Note the details of your environment. Write down how you were feeling in each of these micro or macro creative moments. Don't feel tempted to judge your creativity logs. Simply gather the data. Observe, like a scientist.

| DAY # | WHEN WAS I CREATIVE? | WHERE WAS I CREATIVE? | HOW LONG? | HOW WAS I CREATIVE? | PAINT A PICTURE, INCLUDING EMOTIONS |
|---|---|---|---|---|---|
| 1 | 8:30 a.m., 10 a.m., 8:30 p.m. | At my desk; walking in my neighborhood; in the shower | 45 mins. 10 mins. 5 mins. | Wrote some of my book; developed new ideas for our offsite at work; thought of new ideas for my son's b-day party | Wearing my favorite cozy sweater, quiet, calm, no interruptions, sitting at my desk, enjoying my hot tea. Right after my workout. |
| 2 | | | | | |
| 3 | | | | | |
| 4 | | | | | |
| 5... | | | | | |
| 14 | | | | | |

Finally, at the end of two weeks, reflect on your responses. What patterns do you notice, if any? Are there common themes when you had a burst of creativity? Did certain conditions yield longer stretches of creativity? Or maybe shorter stints generated more satisfying creative output? This method to knowing how to access our personal creativity is a bit like cracking a code: We get curious, experiment, observe, learn, experiment some more, and we may discover an insight about ourselves. It may not be as predictable as a go-to recipe, and that's okay. But it helps to recreate situations when we know (with some level of certainty) that the *opportunity* for creative thinking can occur. Maybe it helps for you to be in nature. Or in the shower. Or mid-sweat in a yoga class. Knowing ourselves better is our engraved invitation to more creative thinking. We're priming the pump. Fertilizing the soil. Creating a welcoming space.

Now let the creativity flow.

## FOR YOUR TOOL KIT: YOUR CREATIVITY SELF-ASSESSMENT

Throughout this journey, I'll share different assessments, exercises, tools, and templates you can carry with you. Here's the first. One quick general note about assessments. I realize some of us are tough graders: on ourselves, or on others. In that spirit, these tools are highly subjective. Try not to overthink it and remember the intention behind the practice—it's a chance to reflect, gain insight, and potentially adjust behavior going forward. I recommend taking this self-assessment to gauge where you may be on your journey *right now*. Remember, it's not an IQ test! And we all have room to improve.

*Read the following statements and answer with the numeric value (1 = rarely, 2 = sometimes, 3 = usually) that corresponds with your assessment of yourself at this time.*

- I consider myself to be a creative person.
- I actively seek out learning new things at least three times per week.
- When confronted with a challenge, I see it from at least three different perspectives.

- I am quick to spot emerging patterns in the work I do.
- I enjoy the generative process of developing new ideas with little guidance.
- When I get immersed in a project, I can lose track of time.
- It's easy for me to see multiple approaches to solving a difficult, complex problem.
- If given the choice between tried-and-true practices and trying out untested new solutions, I choose the new at least 90 percent of the time.
- I routinely seek out a variety of feedback sources on my ideas.
- When I discover an idea doesn't work, my first instinct is to adapt my approach and try again.

Total Score: 10–15 **Emerging creative**. *You have a growth opportunity to stretch and expand your creative mindset in new ways through practice, discipline, and effort!*

Total Score: 16–27 **Evolving creative**. *You are well on your way to developing your individual creativity. Stick with it! With additional practice, discipline, and effort, you can continue to strengthen your creative mindset.*

Total Score: 28–30 **Expert creative**. *You have likely developed a strong capacity for creativity. Keep up the great work! You can continue to improve your creativity through dedicated practice, discipline, and the application of your creative mindset.*

## SCENE ONE SHOW NOTES

- We are all **born to create.**
- **Creative confidence** can be strengthened with practice.
- **Entrepreneurial thinking** requires a beginner's mind.
- **See the line** before you start your creative act.
- **Creative mojo** can be developed by trying things that scare us and being adaptable.

- **Creative constraints** can lead to sharper creative output.
- Make time for **Creativity Boosters.**
- **Know yourself**, including how, when, and where your creativity shows up.

In Scene One, we set the stage for creativity by examining creative confidence—what it is and how we can get more of it. At work, this creative confidence helps us raise our hand for the next challenging project, share an idea that's been bubbling up inside of us, or authentically connect with our teammates without needing to be a know-it-all. In our next scene, we'll explore how activating our imaginations can prepare our brains for even more creative thinking (and creative output) at work.

# STRENGTHENING YOUR IMAGINATION AND PUTTING IT ON ITS FEET

*"We have a lot of power in building our own narrative life story. That's applying creativity. It's about finding new connections from things that already exist."*

—Kris Bowers, composer and filmmaker

**N**ow that you've reflected on where, when, and how you express your individual creativity on a daily basis, we'll take a closer look at ways our brains strengthen creative thinking, like any other muscle. It's time to imagine.

I've always loved using my imagination. As a kid, I'd spend countless hours playing with Fisher Price Little People, acting out their relationship dramas. In kindergarten, I was the last to be excused from the rug because I was adamant that the yellow and green Crayola markers were married, and therefore *must* be complementary colors. (I'm still flummoxed that my kindergarten teacher disagreed.) These inanimate objects very much had an inner life, at least to me.

Back in Santa Maria, my older sister, Kristen, and I would often escape to play in the undeveloped fields behind our tract housing. The blank canvas of the dry brown grasses would transform into odysseys to a different land. Kristen, usually leading the way, would fashion a sword from discarded scraps of wood from nearby houses still under construction. The passage between my ordinary life to the extraordinary world of imaginative play was the gateway to inhabiting different characters.

We would hide out in the grove of eucalyptus trees, not far from the 101 freeway, where we'd discover other kids' discarded play props: a rusty, empty soup can, boards stacked up as a makeshift kitchen countertop, an old, deflated football. We'd act out scenarios of *hiding from the bad guys*, our hearts pounding when real teenaged boys would zip through the empty field on their motorbikes. The smell of eucalyptus still brings me back to that space. Sunlight filtering through the leaves. Sand filling my Velcro shoes. We were the heroes in that story, even as the plot changed from day to day.

Accessing my imagination has always felt effortless. But I never knew it could be a superpower in the workplace. When we activate our imaginations, we're creating a possible path forward. We're building a vision. The good news is, even in navigating our adult worlds, there are ways to strengthen our creative thinking by putting our imaginations to work. Techniques can help us bring the intangible fragments of experiences into fleshed-out human stories. As we sharpen our imagination with detail, we can transform the seemingly banal to richly descriptive, captivating, and meaningful emotional journeys. Then comes the fun part: We get to bring our ideas to life.

## TAKING A DIFFERENT PERSPECTIVE

Trained actors are skilled at getting into the heads of imaginary people. They transport themselves to a human experience separate from theirs—different life circumstances, personalities, likes, and dislikes. Using that new lens, they then filter the world in a new way.

Between my junior and senior years of high school, I spent the summer in New York at the Strasberg Institute studying acting at NYU's Tisch School for the Arts. We studied human behavior and psychology: what motivates people, how they physically move, the distinct sound of their voice, and the unique way they express themselves. The work of developing a character involved journaling a detailed backstory of key experiences in that person's life. It was more than imagining a different point of view; it was embodying a walk in their shoes.

At work, we're also called to imagine different perspectives. We get to tap diverse colleagues and customers to help us better understand motivations, buying behavior, likes and dislikes. Through surveys, listening-tour interviews, and focus groups, we can seek out opinions. Look under the hood. Data in hand, we can then analyze common behaviors or sentiments to (hopefully) spot trends.

To bring this to life in the workplace, imagine that you're at a company and tasked with growing the sales of your product or service. There's power in dreaming up how your buyer experiences what you have to offer. We can apply the acting journaling exercise to this work by imagining different buyers' interactions with your product. Imagine + Journal:

- Why does your customer need your product?
- Describe the moment when your target customer initially hears about your business.
- What are some specific experiences your customer has with your product?
- How does engaging with your product make them feel?
- In what ways does their life improve?

This exercise helps us become more empathetic, curious, and compassionate about how a fellow human might interact with your company. This applied creativity (taking different perspectives) sharpens your customer value proposition.

## THE ART HANGING ON THE WALLS

Imagining different perspectives is often best brought to life through the practice of improv. There's a clear connection between improvisation on the stage and the skill of imaginative adaptability in the workplace. When I was at Northwestern University as a theatre major, I was privileged to share the stage (and green room) with future Tony Award winners like Katrina Lenk and celebrity comedian Billy Eichner. In acting class, we'd often work a scene first without using the script.

We'd start by learning the layers and behaviors of our character to inform how to respond in certain situations. Then we'd improv.

Improv professionals embrace the phrase "yes, and." If I'm on stage with a partner, I might start a scene by saying, "Pepperoni or veggie?" It's a quick way to establish the setting. It would be very uncool for my improv partner to reply, "I don't know what you're talking about. But my bus will be here in five minutes." Instead, the "yes, and" approach urges us to accept what our collaborator gives us and build on it. You may reply, "Pepperoni, but make it vegan." And the scene evolves.

In the workplace, our ability to take a colleague's idea and build on it stretches our skills of collaboration, as we observed from the dialogue between Maria and Alice in Scene One. Maria saw the potential in the campaign Alice had created, but she had the creative idea of sharing the character's journey in the reverse order. Sure, our inner monologue might be thinking, *Well, that idea would* never *work . . .* But when we accept it, take it in, and find a way to improve and enhance it, a better and stronger idea moves forward. Yes, we may need to tweak it, or see it from a slightly different viewpoint, but we may just discover (and help co-create) a diamond in the rough.

Improv teams are adept at doing this at an accelerated pace. They take one-line openers as invitations to quickly build out the details of the scene. And they do it fast. They paint a full picture of what's happening with rich description, multilayered characters, and story with heroes, villains, conflict, and resolutions. They can build a whole reality from one short line.

When I was starting to tell colleagues about my future plans to launch my own business, I connected with David Angelo, fellow LACHSA board member. We stood on the backyard patio of Julia Sorkin's home (I promise I'm not that fancy), sipping wine at a fundraising event. David is someone whose career journey I admire; he built his successful brand agency, David & Goliath, out of nothing. While scaling it over twenty years, he artfully balanced serving clients and staying true to his core ethos and mission: Be Brave.

Back at the cocktail party, I summoned my creative confidence and got up the nerve to share the sketched-out idea of my business, and how passionate I was about my nascent idea to help leaders strengthen their corporate cultures through applied creativity.

David urged me, "Before you start your business, think about what you want the experience to *feel* like. Take time to see it. Three years from now, what kind of chair are you sitting in? What's the art hanging on the wall? Write down every detail."

I nodded, taking it all in. It's a gray fabric chair with a high back. In front of me is a clean white table with a laptop, facing a window. My favorite notebook is on my right. Breeze is blowing the sheer curtains, softening the afternoon light. The vibrant painting on the wall beside me feels personal—perhaps from a fellow LACHSA grad or close friend.

"Does it feel right?" he nudged.

"Yep. And I can see it."

"That's how you know you're on the right track," he told me. "That's how you start."

To bring this to life for you, think about something you'd like to happen roughly three to five years from now. Maybe you hope to be in a job where you're making a big social impact on the world. Or you may want to have enough money saved up to finally make a down payment on your first home or travel the world. Perhaps it's more about a relationship you'd like to have, or the family you hope to start.

Next, take a few minutes for a Creativity Booster. Journal—in great detail—about a day in the life of this future version of you. Be sure to jot things down in the present tense, as if they're happening *now*. What is your typical routine? Who's in your life? What projects are you working on that light you up?

## CREATIVITY BOOSTER:

*Journal:*
*In the morning I wake up and . . .*
*By mid-morning, I'm doing . . .*
*It's lunchtime and I see . . .*
*By mid-afternoon I . . .*
*In the evening, I'm doing . . .*
*By nighttime, I see . . .*

Finally, reflect on the day-long story you just created. What surprised you? Maybe you're no longer at your current job and your day starts with a long neighborhood walk with your dog. Perhaps you've been promoted within your company but are leading a team and function that has yet to be formed. What would need to change in your current reality to start to influence this future version of yourself? Be sure to capture a few insights in the moment. Notice how you feel. Aim to commit to one micro-change that can help move you closer to that future.

Memory plays a powerful role in creative thinking, too. Harkening back to that moment our hearts first opened, we can draw on the details of past experiences to inspire more specificity in what our imaginations are creating. This value of using detail to activate our imagination is backed by scientific research.

Dr. Roger Beaty, professor at Penn State University and leader of the Cognitive Neuroscience of Creativity Laboratory, has done extensive research on creativity in our brains. His research reveals that allowing our minds to wander and activating our imaginations are powerful tools to kickstart our brain's neural networks to produce more creative thoughts. It's the strength of our brain's connections between the default, control, and salience networks that serves as a strong predictor of creativity. The technique we can use is waking up our episodic system, the method of *remembering* things in great detail, which stimulates the same brain region that activates our imaginations.[4]

What David Angelo, Roger Beaty, and dozens of skilled acting teachers confirm is the power of specificity in our vision. By being specific about the physical environment and emotional experience of a future state, we're able to focus, zero in on details, and wake up pathways in our brain to make new connections. It's CrossFit for our creative thinking.

During some of my guest visits to the University of Southern California Marshall School of Business, I've delighted in guiding students to activate their creative mindsets. The room full of student energy is as electric as it is diverse: young star athletes donning sportswear, tattooed trend-setters with large Instagram followings, and studious type-A's sporting blazers, eager to maintain their unblemished academic records.

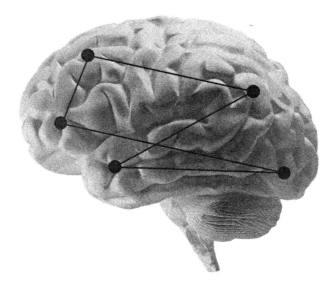

Creative Thinking in the Brain

I usually invite two students to come to the front of the class for an exercise I call *Sell Me on It*. One student is identified as the Seller and the other is the Buyer. Next, I toss the Seller a spherical wooden ball roughly the size of a plum with one flat side. The flat side reveals a drilled-out hole about an eighth of an inch in diameter. The Seller's singular job is to make the business case to the Buyer to buy the product. The Buyer's singular job is to ask questions about the product.

## SCENE DIALOGUE FOR STRENGTHENING IMAGINATION

SETTING:

(SAM is nineteen with a patchy five-o'clock shadow, wearing gym clothes for his evening work-out. CARLA, also nineteen, wears ripped jeans and lime-green earrings. They raise their hands among their chatty classmates and are picked as volunteers to stand at the front of the room. SAM holds the wooden spherical ball in his palm and tosses it casually up in the air.)

                              SAM

Let me tell you, you're gonna want to get yourself one of these.

                             CARLA

Why? What is it?

                              SAM

Believe it or not, you can throw this little
thing in your backpack, and it can store energy
as you move through the day.

                             CARLA

Really? How does it do that?

                              SAM

      (Looking around the room for clues.)
It senses energy sources through a magnetic
field.

                  (STUDENTS giggle.)
It detects that energy as you move through
a room or walk down the street. Windy day?
Energy. Sunshine? Energy. Your kinetic movement? Energy.

                             CARLA

What can I do with it then?

                              SAM

It can charge your phone. It can charge your
e-bike. See this hole right here? That's where
you connect it with your other devices. It's so
powerful, it can even run your car.

                             CARLA

      (laughing along with other STUDENTS)
Okay...

                              SAM

So the real question is, *how many* of them do
you want to buy?

                    **(END OF SCENE)**


   At USC, we've done this exercise a few times, and I'm always amazed by the
students' courage to get out of their comfort zones, as well as their in-the-moment

creative thinking. Some ideas are practical and analog in nature, like using the ball as a massager to ease back pain. Others promise digital technology solutions embedded within this device, like the fictional scene we just observed.

I'm often left wondering what would happen if a student in the seller role flipped the script and started *asking questions* of the buyer. Maybe it's not about *selling* at all. Maybe it's about *listening*. Here's the chance to tailor a business solution and move in virtually any direction their imagination will allow. They could get curious and ask, *"What are your biggest challenges? What are you struggling with these days? If you could fix one problem in your life right now, what would that be?"* Then that wooden ball can magically transform into the solution. After all, there are no rules, no boundaries around what this object can do.

Instead, even with endless possibilities in front of us, we often revert to what we know. We go to what feels familiar and safe. We choose what's practical. But creative thinking invites us to dream up what isn't yet in front of us. It gives us permission to inhabit the world of the unknown.

By the end of class, as I wrap up and summarize the impact that improv can have on our creative-thinking process, I usually turn to the students and hold up that spherical wooden ball. I pass it around so they can hold it in their hands, feel the weight of it, and trace their fingers across each smooth and rough part.

"Your final challenge," I propose, "is to tell me how this object was designed to be used."

Many shout out that it's part of a bed post or stair banister. Some suggest it might be a board game piece. But one night, my jaw dropped when the right answer was revealed.

"A doll's head?" the student pondered.

I stopped in my tracks.

"Bingo," I said. "This plain wooden object was intended to replace a broken doll."

Activating our imaginations and putting things on their feet can help us in the workplace, too. You may get tasked with building a pitch deck for your boss to flesh out a new product idea. Maybe a pile of data landed in your inbox that needs to be analyzed and conveyed with a story. Perhaps you're on the hook for developing a communications plan for your team. If we perceive our creativity to be lacking, it's easy for these projects to feel overwhelming, uninspired, or rote; in reality, these are each a personal invitation to get creative. Much like the improv example at the pizzeria, you now have your setting. It's up to you to engage a "yes, and" approach and build on it. Stand up, shake off the inner monologue of *it should look like this*, and use your imagination. *What could this look like? What do I want the audience to be left thinking and feeling? How would someone in a different department approach this?* Take a risk. And let your wild ideas roll.

## TAKING THE SHOT

Imagine 14,481. This is the #1 NBA record for missed shots. It's currently held by the late great Kobe Bryant, who also currently holds the record for the most NBA All-Star MVP awards. Growing up, my family rarely missed watching a Lakers game on TV—my love for the game runs deep. In fact, before going off to college, I worked the graveyard shift as a hostess at the Kettle, a 24-hour diner in Manhattan Beach. At around 3:00 a.m. one night, in strolled Shaquille O'Neal, who ordered about seven items on the menu (one of which was 86'ed, so the sous chef ran out to buy more ingredients). Even given my brush with Shaq, there's a reason Kobe is Mamba forever. As an Angelino, I find it difficult not to admire the legacy he's created.

That's why, when reflecting on this #1 record for missed shots, it's impossible to separate the spirit and effort of Kobe from his noteworthy number of failed attempts. Imagine for a minute being the leader in failure ideas in your work. Does it make you want to hide under your desk? Be more cautious in sharing your next idea? Quit all together?

To earn a record like Kobe's, tenacity is required.

An indefatigable growth mindset.

Belief that it's worth taking the shot.

I'm no basketball player, but I've pored over stories of athletes who psych themselves up before games, imagining the shots they'll take, and seeing the line. To keep taking our shots, we've got to set aside the fear of missing it. We've got to be more interested in *learning* than winning. We've got to persist in finding our spark and taking the risk.

Kris Bowers learned a lot about creativity from Kobe Bryant. A fellow LACHSA alum, Kris is humble and approachable, with a (dare I say it) creative confidence that oozes from every pore. Perhaps best known for composing the music scores for the Oscar-winning *Green Book* and the television hit *Bridgerton*, Kris also produced an Oscar-nominated documentary short, "A Concerto Is a Conversation," about his grandfather's life journey from Jim Crow Florida to urban Los Angeles. With a deep connection to his roots, Kris readily makes links between his artistic expression and the creative ingenuity of his family.

Kris and I first met as our LACHSA foundation board was prepping for our annual fundraiser in February of 2020. Given the timing, the gala had an air of "this-could-be-the-last-time-we-hug-for-a-while" vibe about it. It was there that Kris debuted a piece he wrote in collaboration with Kobe before his passing; it's a reverent, soulful work that left the audience bathed in serenity. Kris's music tells a story with knowing intimacy.

When Kris and I later talked about his creative process, I was immediately struck by his contemplative and engaging demeanor. Bursting with charisma, Kris can be lovingly described as a borderline perfectionist—someone who takes great pride in his work ethic and quality of creative output. With an unwavering commitment to excellence, Kris starts each of his pieces with a feeling.

## CREATIVITY BOOSTER:

Before tackling your next creative project at work, write down three to five emotions that describe what you want your audience (internal or external customer) to feel.

"Piano helps me eliminate my inhibitions," he shared. "And film scoring is very intentional. I work on the feeling first. I do my own orchestrations, and the instruments come to me like dominos. I might start with the violin line, or something that's very clear to me, then work on the counterpoint. The sounds just build themselves."

In our own creative processes at work, we can think about each instrumental component of the piece we're working on. We can unbundle each part of the collective experience. For example, we may be working on a team presentation that will require a story, meaningful data, compelling visuals, and end with a clear call to action. It helps to start with what the customer or employee is meant to *feel*. Once we're clear about that, many of the other components will start to fall like dominos. But by intentionally starting with the human emotion like Kris does, we can allow the rest of our work to build from there.

Kris fondly remembers Kobe's obsession with learning: He'd listen to the rhythm of people's footsteps before recreating them, and he improved his balance on one foot by watching how a cheetah uses its tail to run.

"Few people were on his level," Kris told me. "Kobe pushed me forward. It's a mix of work ethic and drive, discipline, talent, and dedication to the craft."

Kobe demanded this level of insatiable curiosity from those he worked with across all disciplines. He compared the legendary work of composer John Williams to basketball great Michael Jordan. He expected that level of excellence from Kris. And it became a creative dance between them.

We may not all have the athletic or musical gifts of Kobe Bryant or Kris Bowers. But these two transcend raw talent. At their core, they both demonstrate applied creativity to their respective disciplines. Our time here is limited. Living creatively calls us to keep taking the shot.

## What's My Motivation?

Sitting on the floor with my fellow sixteen-year-old acting class members at Tisch, we were directed to close our eyes and *be* an animal of our choice: a cat, a dog, a pigeon (no doubt our parents were so proud). Our job was to think through how each feather or hair was positioned, how we moved, the feelings we felt, the embodiment of this animal. After class, we all had a good laugh about what may have been motivating the creature we selected. I get it: *What's my motivation?* is a common jab at the acting profession. But it turns out motivation is a highly relevant factor in our professional and personal lives, too. Knowing what drives us can have a big impact on our creativity.

Neuroscientists also care about motivation. Dr. David Rock, founder of the

NeuroLeadership Institute, breaks down social motivation into the following categories, known as SCARF:

- status
- certainty
- autonomy
- relatedness
- fairness[5]

We each care about these things to different degrees: Some of us strongly value the feeling of being in control, so we may rank high on the scale of autonomy and certainty. Others may value the feeling of being socially connected, so relatedness may rank higher. Regardless of where we fall on the spectrum, when we raise our awareness of these factors and see how they may play a role in our lives, we can start to understand why we behave a certain way in situations—or why others in our lives do what they do.[6]

Another common link to motivation is purpose. Knowing our purpose at work is an increasingly important component to feeling engaged. Amid the foggy pandemic years, many of us were confronted—potentially for the first time in our careers—to consider defining our purpose at work. You might ponder:

- *Beyond a paycheck, what do I get out of my working experience?*
- *Do I miss my time in the office working with colleagues, or do I feel more productive and fulfilled working remotely?*
- *Does my work align with my values and what I care most about?*
- *Do I regularly find meaning in my work?*

These questions may feel like an existential swirl for you—they certainly do for several of my clients. But how we address them may impact how well we can activate our creativity.

For many of us, finding joy in the work we do is easier said than done. We might have a humorless boss (sorry), or a highly stressful career. We may experience pressure or difficulties outside of work that spill into our work lives. Or we may not feel supported to play, express joy, or be creative in our work culture. (We'll dive more into these organizational culture questions when we get to Act III of this book.) But let's first try to better understand our individual relationship with work and our reason for being.

Let's discover our *ikigai*.

Ikigai is a Japanese philosophy around our life's purpose. A quick Google search will yield dozens of visual frameworks on ikigai, but here's my take on it:

Ikigai is the intersection of:

- LOVE (What I love doing)
- TALENT (What I'm good at doing)
- COMMERCE (What I can get paid doing)
- DEMAND (What the world needs)

Now, let me be abundantly clear about something. I don't think work should define us. We are not our work, and our worth should not be solely derived by what we do. That said, our ability to lead creative lives can be significantly impacted by the harmony and balance among these four dimensions. For example, feeling free to be creative may improve if or when we feel more financially secure. And when we're doing work that we enjoy and that others value, we may find greater success in it. All of this leads to an upward spiral of growth. We want to do more of it, which leads to better mastery of it, and therefore yields stronger financial benefit, and so on.

Remembering back to the brain science, when our amygdala (at the base of the brain) is triggered and we sense a threat, we go into fight or flight mode. Cortisol (the dreaded stress hormone) floods our brain. The problem is, we can't successfully function creatively when this happens. It's as if the brain's creativity highways are blocked and under construction. Think about it: If you feel like a bear is chasing you, do you run away? Or do you creatively think up ways to train the bear to avoid you? (In case there's a question, I'd run.)

As Dr. Roger Beaty's research shows, to optimize for creativity, we want to engage multiple pathways of our neural networks. Therefore, finding this sense of equilibrium—a sense of purpose and ikigai—can help us make our brains more relaxed and in a creative state. That's when we can unlock our individual creative potential.

## TIME FOR CREATIVITY

With the backdrop of knowing the benefits of using our imagination and taking the shot, how should we spend our *time* to optimize for creativity? When we add up the tiny moments of our day, they soon become our weeks. Then months. Before we know it, years have passed, all comprised of tiny moments strung together. If creativity is important to us, how do we choose to spend those moments to support the development of a more creative life?

Okay, I know what you might be thinking. *Yeah, it would be nice to have limitless time to be creative all day . . . but my boss is pressuring me to get this creative project done TODAY, and I can't find my spark!*

I get it. I really do.

To get into a more creative state of mind, especially when we may be feeling blocked or under the pressure of a deadline, Creativity Boosters can often relax our nervous systems and enable our brains to be more receptive to creative ideas.

## CREATIVITY BOOSTERS:

- Step away.
- Return to work in a different physical space—a different room or facing a different direction.
- Meditate for five minutes to clear your mind.
- Take a power nap.
- Create a starting ritual, like pouring a cup of tea (or stealing a handful of chocolate chips—who, me?).
- Use the Pomodoro technique, where you set a timer and work for 25 minutes, then take a break for 5 minutes (equaling one Pomodoro).
- Commit to three Pomodoros, then gift yourself a longer break.
- Indulge in a brain break. I'm a fan of Drop 7 (careful, it's addictive) or Candy Crush.
- Chip away at the *New York Times*'s Spelling Bee or solve Wordle.
- You write a haiku:

    Or a kindergarten rhyme

    See how well you did!
- Build with LEGO.
- Work with Play-Doh.
- Start (or finish?) a puzzle.

Imagine challenging your team to each write a haiku at the start of your Zoom meeting to sum up what everyone's working on for the week ahead. Forcing succinct clarity might reveal more than a rambling 10-minute update. Try giving your team a lump of clay and inviting them to create an award for other team members that symbolizes their contributions to the group. By applying creative techniques that get you out of your own way, you can start to invite a mindset of play. Shifting the energy (even if for a short amount of time) can free up our minds to be more receptive. Creativity needs space to breathe.

Creativity's relationship to time can be a complicated one. As a recovering overachiever, I now see how my urge to excel-excel-excel may have inhibited moments of creativity. If you start to feel the overwhelming itch of needing to produce something before your creativity is flowing, try practicing mindfulness. Instead of judging and criticizing yourself, try silently observing. What do you see? What do you hear? What's the temperature in the air or where are the pressure points in your body? What smells are present? What's the last thing you ate or drank, and how did it taste? Be present. Hold on to that awareness. And begin again.

## CREATE A LIFESTYLE

Each of us has limited intimate exposure to how people move through the world. You may have schoolteacher parents, so you've observed the lifestyle of nightly grading coupled with a bit of downtime in the summer. Perhaps some family members are firefighters or nurses, where several long, intense days of work are followed by days to recover. Maybe your aunt is a freelance art director. Or your cousin is a public company exec who jets around the world. Our imaginations can be limited by what we've observed growing up. When we have a limited set of lifestyles which we've observed up close, we can get trapped by these finite exposures.

Next, imagine for a moment that there were no prescribed rules around where and when you worked. You were able to design a life of what works best for you. Instead of adhering to a specific job's requirements for how you choose to live, you get to design how you prefer to live *first* and mold a job to *those requirements*. This is the mindset of creating a lifestyle.

No stranger to this principle is Shedrack Anderson III, a fellow LACHSA classmate and friend. Even in our teenage years, Shedrack had an air of wisdom and boundless confidence. He found early commercial success in the arts, appearing in movies like *Hook* with Robin Williams, and stealing the show of the LACHSA Dance Department, effortlessly performing back-to-back straddle leaps (called Russians) that brought the audience to its feet.

Shedrack's creative path has taken him from dance major at Juilliard to producer, real estate investor, and business entrepreneur. Years later, when we caught up about creativity and the habits that support it, I asked him how he decides what creative projects or endeavors get his time and attention. With so many talents, connections, and potential creative pursuits, along with his myriad businesses and projects in flight, I wondered how he never looked frazzled.

"It's about the lifestyle you want to create," he explained. "Don't think about how much money you have in the bank or the title you want to have. Keep the focus on your *lifestyle.*"

In other words, as you're designing your creative life, is it important for you to have dinner at home every night with your kids? Do you want to be able to travel frequently, exploring new places? Do you value having chunks of free time or the freedom to continuously expand your learning? Maybe you want to be surrounded by deep thinkers and academics, or you thrive in the fast pace of a growing tech start-up. Think about what motivates you. Know your values. Picture your purpose, or ikigai. Then creatively build your life to support that journey.

I'm not suggesting we all quit our jobs, abandon our responsibilities, and move to Indonesia (although I hear it's lovely there). But we likely have more power and control over designing our lifestyle than we imagine. You might start by considering if the work that sustains you can be done at least part of the time remotely. Or perhaps you'd find more fulfillment by working fewer than forty hours per week to make space for other creative passions. Maybe there's a career path that would enable you to travel more and explore more of the world. It's out there. You, too, can reclaim more ownership over your life's creative direction. It just might take a little imagination.

## FOR YOUR TOOL KIT: PIE CHART OF YOUR TIME

I've been doing this exercise for about a decade, usually a few times per year. It always seems to unlock an insight. The purpose is to break down how you're currently spending your time over the course of a typical month. Then, with a clean slate and open mind, create a pie chart of how you'd *prefer* to be spending your time (in a perfect world) across the month. For example, you might want to spend less time doing housework and running errands and more time on creative projects.

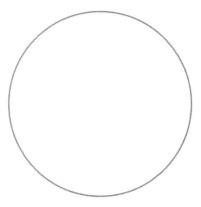

Current monthly time breakdown

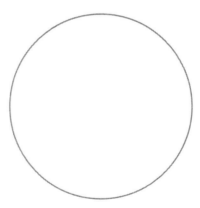

Preferred monthly time breakdown

Finally, when comparing the two pie charts side by side, observe any surprises around how you currently spend your time and how you'd prefer to be spending your time.

*How can you expand the time doing what brings you energy and fulfillment?*

*What items can you outsource, do less of, or let go of completely?*

What *changes would you need to make to create space for new activities that are important to you?*

Today, my pie chart looks a little like this:

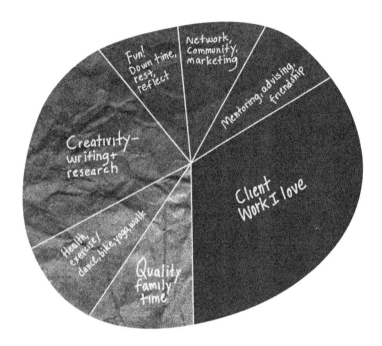

This is expected to change over time (after all, life priorities shift!), but the exercise usually reminds me to consciously make changes in how I spend my time to support the lifestyle I desire.

## FOR YOUR TOOL KIT: WORK CATEGORIES

Many of us blindly go through our workday without much attention to how we're spending our time. In this exercise, think about how you would optimally be spending your time while you're *working.* I usually categorize work into four big buckets:

- **Deep work** (creative development, thinking through ideas, research, reflection, and highly focused tasks)
- **Admin work** (responding to emails, submitting expense receipts, catching up tactically on the flow of company information)
- **Collaboration** (meetings, discussions, human relationship–building)
- **Process work** (the meat of what you do in your job that already has a predefined path, playbook, or established operating rhythm)

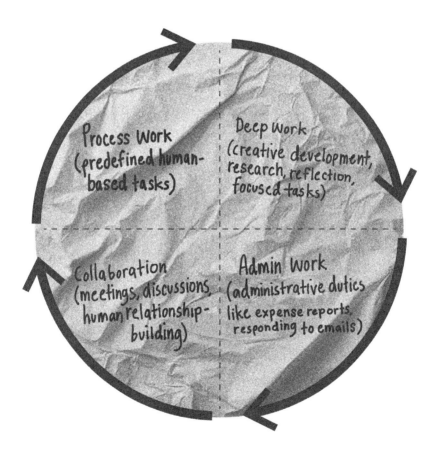

Similar to the previous exercise, first think about your current state. Keep in mind, this might require a bit of time-tracking to have an accurate picture. For example, you may think you don't spend much time on admin work, but after time-tracking for two weeks, you may discover it takes a surprising 30 percent of your time to sift through and respond to emails throughout the day. I also recommend noticing how each category of work makes you *feel*. You can use a log like the one that follows and download a digital log for yourself. You can find a link to one in the Recommended Resources section at the end of the book.

| DAY | DEEP WORK | ADMIN WORK | COLLABORATION | PROCESS WORK |
|---|---|---|---|---|
| 1 | 2.5 hours/fulfilled (25%) | 2 hours/frustrated (20%) | 3 hours/energized (30%) | 2.5 hours/ accomplished (25%) |
| 2 | | | | |
| 3 | | | | |
| 4... | | | | |
| 14 | | | | |

After you've conducted some self-research, think about how you'd *prefer* to be spending your time at work. What is the impact of reallocated time to different categories of work?

The final step to this exercise is to consider the *time of day* where each category of work is best suited. By scheduling the *type of work* we do at optimal times throughout the day, we can harness the creative energy we have, focus it, and ensure it's put to good use. For example, you may be responding to emails throughout the day, haphazardly shifting your focus from one task to the next. By consolidating that time into a chunk of your day that requires less brain power, you may protect and even expand that valuable deep work (typically the domain for creative thinking) time that gives you more energy. That's when the spark will appear.

## SCENE TWO SHOW NOTES

- **Activate your imagination** with detailed memories and descriptions of a future state.
- **Gather different perspectives** to discover new insights about a problem.
- **Experiment, improvise**, and get out of your comfort zone.
- **Take your creative shot.**
- **Find** your **motivation and ikigai.**
- **Make time to be creative.**
- **Create a lifestyle** that supports your creative journey.

In Scene Two, we got a closer look at how details from memory and future vision can lead to more creativity in our present moment. This can help us better understand our purpose or ikigai and build the lifestyle that supports our creative journey through the world. In our work, we need to think big *and* small. We can be bold visionaries, dreaming up ways a small wooden ball will soon power the earth, but also make space to imagine the intimate details that are meaningful to us.

In our next scene, we'll look at how the feedback process shapes the creative process. We'll dive into brain-friendly ways to make our creative ideas even stronger and transform criticism into the power skill of adaptability.

# THE ART OF SEEKING OUT FEEDBACK (TAKING THE NOTE)

*"In a growth mindset, challenges are exciting rather than threatening. So rather than thinking, oh, I'm going to reveal my weaknesses, you say, wow, here's a chance to grow."*

—Carol Dweck, Stanford psychologist and author of *Mindset*

S o far, we've explored some big rocks in the foundation of personal creativity. We've danced with the idea that it requires confidence to show up creatively. We've examined motivation and purpose that guide us in our creative acts. The big leap of faith for any creator, the one that requires being vulnerable and open to judgment, is the process of asking for feedback on our creative idea. (Cue the foreboding music.)

I'll admit it. Early in my career, I sucked at getting constructive feedback. Any mention of how I could improve felt like a personal attack. I once had a feedback conversation that reduced me to tears—so if this is you, there's hope! When I shut down in that moment, I now realize I was blocking any creative intervention. I was limiting my chance to grow.

More recently, during a virtual team workshop I led on Discovering Purpose at Work, I started to have an almost out-of-body experience. I felt *off.* I had planned and prepped and conducted this workshop before with great results. But this time, it was the *absence* of any feedback from the workshop participants that left me swirling. Without the ability to see anyone on camera and next to nothing in the chat feed, my audience's reaction was an unknown. I felt the back of my neck getting hot and sweaty. A lump grew in my throat. After the session, I did what I couldn't have done earlier in my career. I reached out directly to a few of the attendees and asked for feedback.

"I'd love to hear how that session landed with you," I bravely queried. "Specifically, when we did the exercise about linking values to purpose, what did you like about it, and what could I have done differently?"

I was specific in my ask. I requested something positive and something constructive. The surprising thing? Many of them shared new insights they discovered from the workshop. They appreciated the prompts for reflection. The silence I was experiencing may not have been critical judgment or a lack of understanding, but rather the space to process what I was offering. And yes, I did receive some constructive pointers, too. Areas where I could have offered specific examples or been clearer. But it turns out, I hadn't bombed my performance as I'd expected.

It's easy to get wrapped around the axle when it comes to evaluating ourselves. Anticipating feedback from others can be stressful. A person's feedback is simply that: one person's perspective, full of bias and subjectivity. Unsolicited feedback can easily put any of us on the defensive. *Seeking out* feedback, on the other hand, primes us to learn. It's more brain friendly. We can take it in and put it in its proper place, hopefully tear-free.

One of my clients and I worked closely on orchestrating an enterprise-wide roll-out of their refreshed Code of Conduct. In a cross-functional planning meeting, I watched a member of the team offer constructive feedback to the other collaborators. It was delivered in a way that was supportive, clear, specific, and actionable. I wanted to pass along my positive feedback of their approach in real time, so I wrote an email with the subject: *Some unsolicited feedback.* They later confessed that upon simply reading the subject line, they panicked, heart palpitating. Their brain flew into a threat state from getting an unexpected note on their performance—even when it was all positive praise!

Being aware of our brain's hardwired fear when facing feedback underscores the importance of actively seeking it out to regain some control. We can develop techniques to prepare ourselves to move through it: deep breaths to manage the physiological reaction, self-talk to remind ourselves that it's only one person's perspective, and the active reframe that any feedback—regardless of its accuracy—can be used as fuel to improve.

## FINDING "LOVE NOTES OF RESISTANCE"

In the theatre world, there's a well-worn phrase between actors: "Just take the note." The notes process is a sacred part of the theatre ritual. After a rehearsal, the breathless (and often still-costumed) cast gathers with the director to get feedback on their performance. Character by character, the notes are read. Missed your cue? Expect a note. Flubbed a line? Note. Thought you gave the performance of a lifetime? Not so much, it turns out—tone down the melodrama. Note.

As a child actor, I was desperate to be professional, but the notes process gave me a cold pit in my stomach. Yet while I sat there in the house seats, releasing hair from pin curls under my Little Orphan Annie wig, dreading my turn, I also watched with awe as the grown-up actors got their notes. They were attentive and receptive, nodding, even writing down notes of their own, and sure enough, in the next run-through, they'd be right on cue. And on the rare occasions they argued with the director, or pouted, or passed the buck on their mistake?

*Just take the note.*

This process wasn't just formative for me as exposure therapy for receiving criticism—although it certainly was that!—but it also served as a kind of model for a functional feedback system. We all knew, amateurs and pros alike, that "getting notes" was a given. It was going to be public. It was going to have something for each of us—because nobody's perfect. And, ultimately, it was a gift—an opportunity to learn, improve, and support each other. Witnessing this process also prepared me for my eventual role as a leader, where I'd be on the hook for *giving* the notes.

We can learn a lot from the notes-giving process in theatre. Feedback may be (ironically) the biggest unspoken challenge facing our professional lives. How to strike the right tone, deliver messages through the right channels, and provide criticism that's genuinely constructive takes a lot of social and emotional calculus. But by the same token, of all operations, feedback—and communication in general—has arguably the greatest impact on culture. No matter how awesome your team's work is, or how much customers and clients gush about your company's services, if those triumphs aren't communicated to any and all interested parties, they might as well not have happened.

Even mentioning feedback can have a high emotional charge for many of us. We might clam up, feel judged, and slip into defensive mode. We suddenly feel *less than,* even though subjective feedback from one person is likely not a universal truth. Still, it tends to feel that way.

At the risk of coming across as a little woo-woo, we must first learn to seek out feedback from ourselves. What's the feedback in our own body telling us about this experience or work? What feedback might we give someone else in a similar situation?

These "Love Notes of Resistance" are a form of self-feedback that I've learned to heed. They often pop up when I sense myself avoiding a creative project, or when I'm not quite sure I'm on the right track. If I'm procrastinating or putting off working on something that requires deep creative thinking and attention, there's usually an underlying reason for it. There's a story there. A subtle message whispering in my ear. Maybe I'm not yet clear on what the work product should look like. Maybe there's work that feels uncomfortably new and I'm feeling a bit out of my depth. Or maybe I'm getting bogged down in the details and over-engineering the process. Love Notes of Resistance might help me pivot in a completely new direction, or they may simply serve as speed bumps on my creative journey, reminding me to slow down. Either way, they shouldn't be ignored.

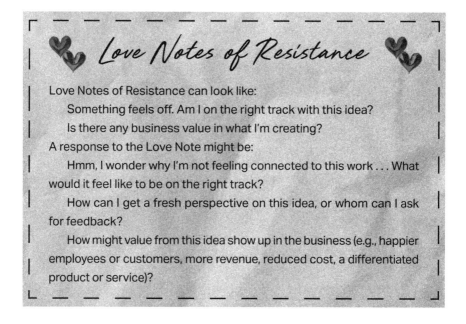

Love Notes of Resistance can look like:

Something feels off. Am I on the right track with this idea?

Is there any business value in what I'm creating?

A response to the Love Note might be:

Hmm, I wonder why I'm not feeling connected to this work . . . What would it feel like to be on the right track?

How can I get a fresh perspective on this idea, or whom can I ask for feedback?

How might value from this idea show up in the business (e.g., happier employees or customers, more revenue, reduced cost, a differentiated product or service)?

The best way to overcome or respond to Love Notes of Resistance? Ask more questions. Be objectively curious. Then do the hard stuff first. A task you're dreading? Tackle it first thing in your day. Eat the frog. We need more psychic energy to get difficult tasks done, so tackling them when we're fresh and feeling sharp helps build momentum for the rest of the day. It clears the deck for more creative thinking. Once we act, we can reflect on the new information we discover.

## KEEPING THE FEEDBACK PROCESS CREATIVE

There are tons of articles and books about how to give and receive effective feedback. There's also no shortage of opinions about how the feedback process, when done well, has the potential to drive higher performance. But I rarely come across feedback tips that actively support the creative process. The following few apply the filter of bringing our best creative selves to work.

**Start with self-feedback.** This allows us to recognize and celebrate our growth and reflect on where we'd like to continue to develop. Notice the moments in your work where you're fully immersed and find your flow. What are the conditions that set you up for creativity? When you discover those Love Notes of Resistance or sense yourself getting stuck, maybe tell yourself, "I can do the hard things" or another phrase to boost your confidence and keep creating.

**Seek out peer feedback.** This can help raise awareness of our blind spots and identify our superpowers. We can learn how we're showing up for others—what's working, and what's not. Rather than worry how our peers are *evaluating* our creative ideas, consider how they're building on them, like the dialogue between Maria and Alice in Scene One. Do you take that feedback and adjust? How easy is it for you to evolve your creative idea to make it even better after getting peer feedback?

**Be specific in asking for manager feedback.** By taking more control over the areas where you'd value more guidance, you can boost your level of autonomy, owning your development. You may ask for concrete examples where your creative contributions are making an impact on the business. To limit the potential for overwhelm, ask for one area where you're doing well and one place to grow and improve.

**Connect feedback from work to other parts of your life.** Maybe you learned you could be a better listener. Or you've been told you come across as overly critical of yourself, which is limiting your executive presence. Maybe you've heard your creative ideas are helping people to rethink business processes, leading to new efficiencies. Where might these bits of feedback show up in other parts of your life? How might they be influencing your creative process and effectiveness? How could you use that feedback to grow creatively?

Now that you have more tools for receiving feedback to facilitate creativity, consider how you might deliver feedback to others.

## Effective feedback is:

- Delivered directly in real time. (Don't wait for that year-end performance review!)
- Clear and accompanied by specific real-world examples. ("Hey, remember when you chimed in during our call yesterday to help with Sara's project?

I really liked how specific you were about ways you'll contribute, and how you committed to a timeline for the next deliverable.")

- Tailored to the recipient. (Know and adapt to your audience.)

- Shared with empathy, care, and thoughtfulness, in the spirit of making someone better. (Imagine sitting shoulder-to-shoulder with someone, rather than across the table from them.)

- Delivered in private when constructive. (Unlike the theatre world, it's best to avoid giving critical notes in a public setting.)

- More frequently positive than constructive. (Research suggests high-performing teams receive six times more positive feedback than constructive feedback, and praise goes a long way with creative thinkers!)

- Contextualized within external and internal circumstances.

## WHAT THE DATA ARE TELLING US

Gathering and analyzing feedback often requires thinking like a scientist. And scientists rely on data.

Dr. Glenn Fox and I first met at the National Association of Corporate Directors' Symposium in downtown Los Angeles. With a PhD in neuroscience from the University of Southern California, where he now serves as assistant professor at the Lloyd Greif Center for Entrepreneurial Studies at USC Marshall, Glenn knows a thing or two about brain science. At the symposium, he presented his research findings on the neural correlates of empathy, gratitude, and neuroplasticity—and we became fast friends.

I've had endless conversations with Glenn about creativity at work and was curious to learn how he believes the creative process relates to analyzing data. Many of us (at least I do) think of the scientific process as somewhat sterile, emotionless, and cold. It's about objective observation after all, and we don't want to color the scientific process with a bunch of feelings. But, since we're all human, I thought it was worth better understanding how science and creativity intersect.

"The deeper I went into science and the *process* of science," Glenn shared, "the closer I realized it was a creative process. It takes acts of synthesizing a lot of information to arrive at a method and conclusion, and that is a creative process to see how things are connected—you're creative in making *links* in the same way that you create *things*."

Picture, for a moment, the brain of a process-oriented engineer engaging her prefrontal cortex. Maybe in addition to those linear thoughts, information-processing, and decision-making, there's room for engaging the neural pathways to creativity. Maybe that's all part of the big scientific consideration of "What if . . . ?"

Glenn's research on neuroplasticity reveals how our brains are always changing based on what we feed them. For example, you practice gratitude and get more gratitude. You practice pessimism and get more pessimism. The same goes for creativity. If we value the act of being creative and want to lead a more creative life, we need to practice it and feed our minds. When we create that feedback loop with creativity, we get more of it.

I wanted Glenn's take on how creativity comes up in data analysis and, lucky for me, he had a compelling story about it. During one of his experiments, he was curious to understand the connection between levels of gratitude and the practice of perspective-taking. His hypothesis was that people with higher perspective-taking end up having higher levels of gratitude. So, he and his research team ran the experiments and analyzed the data, gathering levels of perspective-taking correlated to levels of gratitude. Surprisingly, when analyzing the averages, they kept finding the oppositive was true. The *more* people took perspectives, the *less* grateful they were.

Glenn described the moment of throwing his laptop against the wall, thinking, *What have I been doing with my career? Was this all just a big waste? I've ruined everything!* But his research assistant Cheryl, a brilliant mathematics, economics, and psychology triple major, asked a powerful question:

"How are we defining and applying the calculation of 'average'?" she wondered.

When they adjusted their analysis to account for the range of responses to the gratitude prompts, they recognized that people higher in perspective-taking were not just putting full marks for every gratitude stimulus; instead, they had a wide range of responses, bringing their average down over the experiment. When they correlated between the perspective-taking and the standard deviation of their gratitude ratings, that's when they saw the significant correlation. The takeaway is this: People who are good at perspective-taking did not necessarily see more gratitude overall, but instead saw more varieties and overlapping *types* of gratitude, which yielded a new scientific insight.

Glenn learned a meaningful lesson through this process.

"The way you interpret a piece of data can be very wrong," he told me. "You have to think, *What if I'm wrong?* What's the *opposite* interpretation of the data? What else could it be? And say, 'If I changed one element, would I expect a drastic change in the data?'"

The need for curiosity and creativity within the scientific process feels evident. Without that human interpretation and peeling back the layers to fully understand what's happening with the data, results can be thrown out of whack. We need to not only be the observer but also the storyteller. We take the feedback we get and interpret it. And that requires creativity.

## FIND YOUR BLIND SPOTS

Imagine for a moment you're an early career professional at a large, successful, and rapidly growing tech company. You have an idea and would love to pitch it, but you're not quite sure how it'll land. Finally, you get up the courage to share it. It falls flat. What do you do? If you have the right mentor, you may just find a way to try again, adapt your idea, and get it to stick.

Aaron Mitchell is often that mentor: a creative entrepreneur who rapidly ascended his HR career at Netflix. Credited for ideas like Netflix's transfer of $100M to Black-owned banks following the killing of George Floyd, he knows a thing or two about idea generation, as well as pitching it and persuading decision-makers to act.[7]

Aaron and I bonded over pandemic parenting. We shared many a Zoom catch-up stunned in silence from our shared struggle to get our kids to sleep through the night or resolve their sibling rivalry, all with the backdrop of a world in social unrest. Our chats offered the empathetic feedback I desperately craved.

We connected over "I see you" moments of frustration and uncertainty that got us to the other side—at least that day. Both graduates of arts high schools, Aaron and I carry a keen awareness that our MBA journeys and corporate lives are continuously influenced by those early experiences in the creative arts.

One story Aaron told me about creativity in his work hit me by surprise—although not because I couldn't imagine this creative idea taking flight. What struck me was the *process* by which this creative idea was birthed—which is rarely discussed. We forget that creative ideas travel through zigs and zags, painful missteps, embarrassing swings, and misses. Having a mentor or coach to point out our blind spots and forge a path forward can sometimes make the difference between an idea taking flight and flopping.

Aaron recalled a powerful example where the Black Employees @ Netflix Animation, the precursor to an employee resource group, came together to brainstorm ways to celebrate Black History month. One of the early career members sparked an idea to highlight a story of a Black animator's journey through Black character design, including nuanced cultural expressions captured through personal lived experiences.

Although Aaron helped coach her to pitch the idea to business leaders, it was initially rejected by the studio head due to a concern of not being celebratory enough. With Aaron's help, she persisted in researching, refining, and developing an irresistible story called the Unlearn Series, an effort meant to highlight what must first be unlearned in order to create an environment of real inclusion and belonging.

"She helped the studio to see all of this authentic work that we're doing to try to create authentic stories," Aaron reflected. "But the real story is how she asked the right questions, did the research, and connected with the right people. Telling *that* part of the story—that's where people think, '*Oh, I could do this, too?*' We wanted people to change the way they look at their own career development. 'No' doesn't mean it's not a good idea. It means that maybe I need to do it a bit differently."

The studio head later green-lit the idea, publicly and humbly sharing that he had originally been against it. He also highlighted he was glad to have been initially wrong.

In our work, we can share an idea that's a gem yet hasn't been polished enough for others to appreciate. Especially early in our careers, it's easy to not have the years of lived experience or full context to know how a new, creative idea will land with leaders. We get distracted by the initial rejection and feel bruised and too dejected to move our idea to the next phase of refinement.

Rather than discard a creative idea, consider your potential blind spots. Respond to Love Notes of Resistance with curiosity rather than defeat. Sure, this approach won't work in all instances—we do sometimes need to pull the plug on our ideas, even when we're still in love with them. But how many times have you discarded an idea too early? Maybe you gave up, only to find that months later your core idea is reflected in someone else's, simply modified, remolded, or repositioned? Chances are you've tossed more than a few good ideas into the dumpster before their time.

## DIALOGUE TO SET THE STAGE FOR A FEEDBACK CONVERSATION

**SETTING:**

(LAKSHMI is waiting for her boss to join a Zoom feedback session on the creative proposal she shared yesterday. She fiddles with her bracelets as JEREMY enters the virtual room on the screen.)

**JEREMY**

Hey, Lakshmi. Sorry I'm a few minutes late.

**LAKSHMI**

No problem.

**JEREMY**

We're here to talk about the big proposal—wow, there was a lot in there.

**LAKSHMI**

Yes! I really want to hear what you think. I know Section Two was a complete miss—

**JEREMY**

Wait. Why do you say that?

**LAKSHMI**

I don't think it was customer-focused enough.
And Section Three could be punchier... I just
think—

**JEREMY**

Okay, hold up. I'm stopping you right there. I
haven't even shared any feedback yet and you're
already second-guessing yourself.

**LAKSHMI**

You're right, no, I just want it to be as good
as it can be.

**JEREMY**

Me, too, Lakshmi. And it'll get there.

(pauses)

I'm going to share two specific pieces of feedback today. The first is what I think is working
really well in the proposal—where I wouldn't
change a thing. And the second is where I think
you have room to push the boundaries a bit. How
does that sound for the rest of our chat?

**LAKSHMI**

That would be great.

**JEREMY**

As I share this feedback, do your best to take
it all in, and jot down any clarifying questions you might have. At the end, I'd love to
hear what lands with you and where you might
even push back. Who knows, maybe I got something wrong. Or maybe you can refine things
just a smidge, which would shift my perspective. But I'd love to see you take the feedback
I share and do a second pass of the proposal.
We can then regroup after that. Is that all okay
by you?

**LAKSHMI**

Absolutely. Let's get started.

**(END OF SCENE)**

In this scene, Jeremy is navigating Lakshmi's creative vulnerability. He's preparing to share two concrete pieces of feedback for her to digest (it's tough for us to take in much more than that at one time), and also outlining the process for her to integrate it. This feedback partnership is a common way that creative ideas at work are formed.

When ideas are rejected, finding a trusted ally, coach, or mentor may help reveal potential blind spots. With a little objective emotional distance, we can start to see how the idea *could* land differently if elements of it were changed. Think about ways the idea may look more compelling with additional pieces of data or information—then work to gather those data points. Build a story for the audience member: who they are, why the idea matters to them, what action it inspires them to take because of your idea. In Aaron's example, this meant bringing to life the Black animator's journey of character design, integrating memories of family growing up, rich with cultural expressions and personal emotions. Those vivid details helped paint a full picture of the idea—and inspired others to see themselves in those stories. The process of refining and refreshing our ideas often shines a light on what's magical about them in the first place. It helps others finally see the potential of our creativity. Consider the following phased workflow:

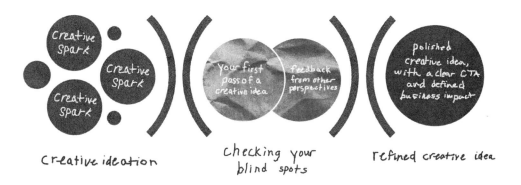

You start with the raw sparks, the bits of creative ideas not yet shaped. Next, feedback and context are incorporated. You check for blind spots. Finally, your refined creative idea is molded with a call to action (CTA) and clearly defined impact on the business.

## BEWARE OUR CREATIVITY KILLERS

As I write this, my daughter, Caroline, is eight and my son, Parker, is five. If you're a parent (or spend time around little ones), you've likely observed how young humans can effortlessly let creativity flow. They fill the inner lives of Calico Critters, build LEGO dungeons that transform into flying spaceship pods, and cast themselves as grown-up characters: *the tired mom, the exasperated teacher, the busy shopkeeper, the fearless Superhero.* As their creativity is expressed, a feedback loop is formed. Playmates (both young and old) either accept, validate, and reinforce this creativity, or it's rejected, discouraged, and snuffed out.

Self-feedback also bubbles up during these early creative expressions and bursts of curiosity. As a toddler at a vacation rental, my son stumbled on a small box labeled *GOTCHA! RODENT TRAP*, which he shook with delight, squealing, "It sounds like there's somethin' in here, Mom!" (I'll admit the feedback he got from my reaction may have squashed some curiosity there.)

In addition to his imaginative play, one of Parker's creative outlets is drawing. Thanks to YouTube Kids, endless streams of videos spark his imagination, guiding his creativity onto the page. A couple of years ago, before he was as dexterous as he is today, he routinely reached a boiling point in creative frustration. Mid-drawing, he'd break down into tears. The crux of it was his creative *inspiration* and *abilities* were not yet matched. He couldn't get his hand to produce the image of what he pictured in his mind.

You might be familiar with these moments of creative frustration. Maybe you're not able to bring something to life in your work the way you envision it. Perhaps you're working on your craft in the arts, and your proficiency isn't yet where you'd like it to be. Or maybe your business idea is clear to *you*, but no one else at work understands or shares your vision . . . yet.

It's possible that from an early age, you weren't supported to be creative. Perhaps you didn't have Grandma playing along with your pretend-teacher lesson plan, or a caretaker who tolerated dozens of barrettes in their hair. Even worse, maybe your family harshly judged your creative expression, rejected it, or even discouraged it.

These moments of frustration can be Creativity Killers. We start internally judging, becoming self-critical, and we spiral. The feedback loop we're giving ourselves isn't affirming or reinforcing. Instead, it's prohibiting us from trying again, persisting, and finding a new way in. Instead of a gentle Love Note of Resistance, Creativity Killers can prompt us to temporarily shut down, lash out, or give up completely. What we may need most in these moments is the same loving patience you might offer a small child. Briefly step away. Put your pencil down. Grab a snack and some fresh air.

## COMMON CREATIVITY KILLERS:

Here are some common patterns that can easily stop creativity in its tracks.

- Overthinking
- Judgment about our creative product too early
- Lack of sleep
- Hunger
- Fear
- Perfectionism
- Overvaluing the status quo
- Encountering those with a fixed mindset (e.g., "This will never change")

In Parker's case, he needed to keep producing. He would discard one drawing and do it again. And again. Until finally, the artwork on the page more closely resembled what he had in his mind. Sometimes we need to get misshapen expressions out in the world before our true creative vision can be set free.

Even during the creative process of writing this book, I often feel the Creativity Killer of self-judgment creep in. It's as if I'm standing on a ledge, staring into a large chasm, and shouting into the abyss. *Are these stories going to resonate with anyone? Is this any good? Am I connecting?!* For me, what often helps is taking a moment to pause. I process the structure, stories, and core creative output in my mind. I replay them as I'm falling asleep. I try to observe: *What feedback may I have gotten (either from myself or someone else) that is putting me into this negative frame of mind? How might I shift the perspective?* I reflect. Take a rest. I commit to beginning again.

## THE ANTIDOTE TO IMPOSTER SYNDROME

So far, a big theme of Act I's spark to ignite individual creativity involves getting out of our comfort zone. *Doing the hard things.* We build our creative confidence, strengthen our imaginations, put things on their feet, and ask for feedback on our creative output. Through that process, we may receive a few Love Notes of Resistance. We stand face-to-face with Jesus-on-the-donkey ruminations that outline all the things we might be doing wrong. We may even encounter Creativity Killers that threaten letting our creative spark go out completely. Sure, we're in the position to do bold creative thinking, but somehow, a big hurdle blocks us (or mocks us!), causing us to question whether we even deserve to be here in the first place.

These signs of imposter syndrome plague many of us. We feel we haven't earned the right to hold a position, role, or title, even amid myriad qualifications that would indicate otherwise. Imposter syndrome causes doubt that we've got *the stuff* it takes to shine. And unfortunately, it's what stops many people from fulfilling their creative potential.

When I was still early in my career at Axiom, I helped shape the Engagement Management function for the company. I defined the process and created the playbook. Around that time we hired our first Engagement Manager leader, a fantastically accomplished lawyer with an abundance of emotional intelligence to lead conversations with our Chief Legal Officer clients. Engagement Management was all about gathering feedback. It required asking insightful questions and being an effective listener. It needed the gravitas to have a peer-to-peer conversation with legal executives with the EQ to pick up on what *wasn't* being said.

Sitting at my desk in our Spring Street loft office, I replied to emails, enjoying my first coffee of the day and dutifully prepping materials for our Engagement Manager's high-stakes meeting at Goldman Sachs. Then she called me. Out sick. And she asked me to go in her stead.

I panicked. What?! I hadn't yet been in a room with our clients without a safety net. Okay, I had corresponded by email and taken the occasional phone call to confirm logistics. But this felt different. It felt important. And I didn't want to fail.

The antidote to imposter syndrome is assuming the role and playing the part. We've got to be the zebricorn—unabashedly ourselves. Heart pounding, I suited up and took the train down to Wall Street, the closest stop to Goldman's building at 85 Broad Street. Putting one unsure foot in front of the other, I rehearsed the conversation in my mind. After being whisked up the elevator, I waited in the pristine investment banking lobby. Nerves continued to build. And then the moment came. I was escorted through the glass doors and settled into the senior attorney's office. I took a breath, ready to discuss performance feedback on our employee. Showtime!

And you know what? It went fine. I held my own. There were nerves, to be sure, much like an opening night performance, but I channeled the energy. I played the role and executed the task. And it actually felt . . . fun. Empowering, even. After that trial by fire, I had newfound confidence that I could fill those shoes without the world coming to an end. Sometimes the nerves still came in the form of a tiny caterpillar egg versus a flock of butterflies. But I knew I would only improve from there.

It would be only a few short years later that I was running the entire Engagement Management program for Axiom, launching new offices across the country, engaging in strategic conversations with Chief Legal Officers about their legal spend, business operations, and organizational structure. Time is funny that way. What feels daunting and completely overwhelming one minute soon becomes old hat. It requires taking a leap of faith and parking our self-criticism. You might begin to recognize your own little Love Notes of Resistance in your work. Maybe you hear whispers of *am I on the right track?* After a brief pause, keep going. You belong here. Take the imposter syndrome antidote and assume the role.

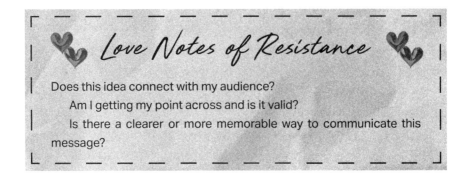

## DROPPING IN

A few years back, I sat on a panel comprised of creative entrepreneurs who were either alumni of arts high schools or highly trained artists who had pivoted to corporate life. Among us were a classical-musician-turned-venture-executive, a Juilliard-prodigy-turned-music-producer, a Broadway-performer-turned-serial-entrepreneur-and-philanthropist, and an African immigrant and business leader recently named to the Forbes Next 1000. I was struck by the common energy across the group: We each brought a passion for the arts along with our current professions. But I also noticed a pattern. Most of us were college dropouts.

I'm not particularly proud of having dropped out of Northwestern. I left for what I felt at the time was the right reason: I was booking work in the theatre, I had a significant professional opportunity that required my leaving school for a quarter, and I abhorred the idea of accumulating more debt than was necessary. Would I do it again the same way? Maybe not. But I live with my choice and am grateful for where I am today.

One panelist, now a senior vice-president (SVP) at a major entertainment studio, shared a personal story about sitting in the audience as a high school football player. By the end of the performance, he had fallen in love with ballet. He dropped everything and dedicated his life to it, taking forty hours of ballet classes each week. Within eight short months, he was quietly tapped on the shoulder by Baryshnikov, who said, "You need to join my company." What he learned from that experience transcended his undeniable talent. With discipline, focus, and passion, he could break down just about anything and master it. He developed creative confidence.

Another story came from a man who admitted to being a troublemaker in his youth. His moment of transformation happened after seeing the musical *STOMP* at age ten. He was hooked. He dedicated his life to music and dance, stopped getting into trouble, and was eventually cast in *STOMP* only ten years later. Now a serial entrepreneur, he travels the world teaching kids the power of dance.

As I sat (virtually) alongside these highly successful leaders, I recognized that each of us had experienced a moment of spark. But instead of using that spark to complete the path we were on, we dropped out. Another panelist noticed the same pattern.

"Maybe it's not about dropping out," she reflected. "Maybe it's about *dropping in*."

When we discover a love or passion, something that draws us in and lights the spark within us, we want more of that. We discard the traditional, more familiar path. We follow the energy.

Dropping in today takes courage. It means being open to the feedback—both internal and external—that might lead us in a different (and more creatively fulfilling) direction. Many of us are burned out at work. We're overloaded by information, distractions, and competing demands for our attention. We're weighed down by responsibilities, financial pressures, and to-do lists a mile long. Even the thought of following your passion and getting creative might trigger overwhelm.

In a quiet moment this week (if you can steal one), think about your spark. Reflect on what lights you up and gift yourself that personal feedback. Think about the thing in your life that is not only deserving of your focus but invites the metaphorical tap on the shoulder, reminding you of the moment your heart first opened.

Think about what you're *creating* in your life, even if you never thought about it that way. Maybe you never imagined you would know anything about artificial intelligence, and suddenly you find yourself among the experts. Maybe time with your aging parents or young family brings you deep contentment (even when it's difficult), and you want to create a lifestyle to spend more time with them. Or maybe you're still looking for that spark that might forever change you—that's okay, too. But when you discover it, I hope you see it. I hope you fiercely protect it. Breathe enough life into it to create a flame. And let it burn.

## FOR YOUR TOOL KIT: REFLECTION TREE EXERCISE

It can be hard to get perspective on how others perceive us. This exercise is intended to help you see yourself as others do.

First, pick three to five people whose opinions you value. These might be trusted colleagues at work, a friend who knows you well, or a family member who has a good view on how you show up in different environments.

Next, ask these people to pick three to five qualities that best describe you, three to five of your biggest strengths, and brief stories when they've observed you exercising creativity. You can set it up with something like, "I'm doing an exercise to gather different perspectives to learn more about myself so I can bring more creativity to my work. In a few words, if I were about to start a work project with a new team that didn't know me, how would you describe me to others? What are three to five of my biggest strengths or hidden superpowers that you think I should integrate into my work? Finally, can you think of a specific situation or two where I've applied my creativity?"

In the roots of the tree, write down all of your values and strengths. In the trunk and branches, write down the situations or lived experiences demonstrating creativity. In the leaves of the tree, write your personal qualities and characteristics.

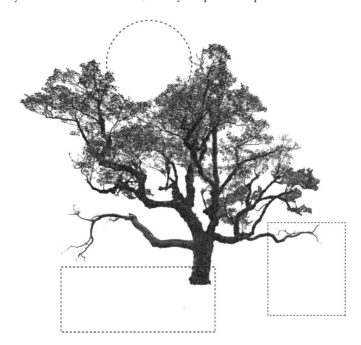

Finally, think of this tree not as *who you are*, but as a reflection in a lake. It doesn't define you—reflections are often different from the real thing. But it may indicate how you show up to others.

In your roots, how can you continue to build on your values and strengths so the tree stays steady, even in big headwinds? How can you demonstrate creativity in different parts of your life (on the tree trunk) so that how you're described in these stories can show up more in the leaves? What parts of this reflection make you feel proud? What would you like to change, and what's within your control to develop?

Feedback is about perspective and reflection. We can take it in, learn from it, and move on from what doesn't serve us.

## SCENE THREE SHOW NOTES

- **Love Notes of Resistance** can indicate where we might want to pause or gather feedback.
- **Feedback** is merely a perspective that can come from many inputs: ourselves, peers, managers, or what the data are telling us.
- **Take the note**, incorporate what's helpful, and then move on—don't take feedback too personally.
- **Imposter syndrome** can keep us from being open to feedback to shine; the antidote is to assume the role and play the part.
- **Beware the Creativity Killers** that might be blocking your creative expression.
- **Dropping in** to follow our passion is a form of self-feedback.

In Scene Three, we dove into the sensitive process of giving and receiving feedback. We can now recognize that gathering feedback (even from ourselves!) is part of the creative process. By seeking it out, we can make our creative work product even stronger.

Enjoy a brief intermission—grab that handful of M&Ms and a cup of coffee—before we begin Act II.

[HOUSE LIGHTS RISE.]

# ACT I. INTERMISSION

*"Then, one day, something amazing happened. My idea changed right before my eyes. It spread its wings, took flight, and burst into the sky."*

—*What Do You Do with an Idea?* by Kobi Yamada

iscovering your personal creative spark is now within reach. Sure, you might encounter a Jesus-on-the-donkey moment here or there, but you're able to manage your own creative energy by building creative confidence. We've learned the science-backed value of activating our imaginations, along with the benefits of carving out time to do it. Finally, we've explored the art of gathering feedback (from ourselves and others) to continue to create, ideate, and move an idea forward.

If there's one message that landed in Act I, I hope it's this: You have a limitless capacity to create. Our world is cluttered with distractions. Our brain feeds on patterns. We like to put things into categories. We're often seeking more of the same because it's comfortable, low risk, and seemingly safe. But what if you found out a secret? Things are going to change regardless. And the way to gain more agency over the life you dreamed of living, the one integrated with your values, the one that reminds you of when your heart first opened, that rush of beauty and life-giving energy and awe all rolled into one, is to know how to cultivate your own creativity.

Act II will reveal the skills of creative leadership. Maybe you're a new manager of people and don't want to slip up. Perhaps you've led teams for years, but are now tasked with a new creative challenge, thirsty for innovation. You might be an executive who's considering how creativity can be applied as a leadership skill across your team.

As we swim in these creative leadership waters, I'll share techniques to help you foster your creativity, but also challenge it. You might bring the skill of creative leadership to unlikely places in your work as an accountant, lawyer, engineer, or project manager, creating new techniques for you—and for those you inspire. I believe you can do it. You have the spark and it's growing. Now let's help the creativity burn even brighter.

# Act II.

# The Blaze: Cultivating Creativity in Others to Innovate

**N**ow that you've explored how to build more confidence to express your ideas, apply more of your imagination at work, and gather feedback on your creative work product, let's take a closer look at strengthening your *creative leadership* in our new world of work. Working creatively is rarely a solo journey. Act II is about how you can cultivate creativity in others to innovate.

In December of 2018 at a Nashville, Tennessee, boot-scootin' bar, I gathered with colleagues after a full day of leading breakout sessions at our company's Global Management meeting. We promenaded to the live band's music, showing off our country dance moves and exchanging hugs of appreciation—after all, it had been months of careful planning to successfully pull off this 600-person event.

"Don't tell me you're leaving the company," my then-boss said, kicking her boots and shuffling in lockstep with the group. I don't remember saying anything back. I didn't have to. She already knew.

There's a lot of noise about people leaving companies because of bad bosses. We hear horror stories of toxic work environments and the *I've had it!* moments that lead to resignation. But sometimes, people leave *because* of great bosses. Though it sounds counterintuitive, I left my last in-house job because my leader believed in my creative potential. She believed enough in me that I was able to see it in myself. A blaze was building that I could no longer ignore.

Liz Dick, that boss at the time, served as a role model for creative leadership. A Deloitte alum and leader in the Los Angeles business community, Liz was as generous with her connections as she was enthusiastic about helping people develop professionally. A social magnet with deep business acumen, her leadership following was almost cult-like. In return, Liz was ruthlessly loyal to those on her team. I left my initial interview with Liz feeling a comfortable familiarity, like I'd somehow already worked with her for a decade.

We quickly developed a shorthand. Often huddled around the small table in her downtown Los Angeles office, our brainstorms led to the rebuilding of our company's Learning, Development, and Culture group before I transitioned to leading the function. Liz and I were attached at the hip, spending hours collaborating, co-building, and co-creating. She gave me the autonomy to invent, design, take risks, experiment, and apply my creativity in new ways. With some reflection, I now see how those hours were the incubation phase of my professional reinvention.

Liz believed in me. Because of her positive reinforcement and encouragement, work didn't feel like work. On many an hour-long bus commute home from downtown LA, I tuned out the chatter of surrounding conversations and worked away, laptop open, typing at a pace that could send smoke fuming from the keys. Abuzz with ideas and filled to the brim with possibility, I felt fueled to bring a new vision to life. Liz wasn't putting pressure on me to work during this hour; she effortlessly fostered the creativity within me.

Her confidence in my potential and trust in my ability to run with things only accelerated my drive. She gave me explicit permission to try new things—*for example, instead of a newsletter,* I thought, *why not try a leadership podcast?* Liz trusted me to fearlessly experiment to discover insights—all making way for reimagined learning programs. In this phase of my career and life, I yearned for the combination of creative freedom and rock-solid job stability, what with juggling new parenthood, intense travel (with a carry-on breast pump!), and the steep learning curve of a new professional focus. Liz made it safe for me to stretch out my comfort zone in all the right ways. This is creative leadership in action.

By the time I found myself at the Grand Ole Opry in Nashville, Tennessee, the hard work of building a new function culminated into an *aha* moment I wasn't expecting. As I practiced my presentation on a growth mindset to soon share with 600 colleagues, a powerful feeling took over. It wasn't nerves or stage fright, but something much bigger, rooted in what I was seeing in my work: that strong cultures, those consisting of happy, engaged, and productive employees, all cultivated creativity.

I recognized that creative leadership enabled—even demanded—employees to bring their best ideas to work. These leaders designed spaces and time for people to play, connect, experiment, and fail together, all with the goal of discovering new, better ways of building and delivering their products and services. Creative leaders value each person's unique perspective and humanness. They bring out the best in their people, and in return, their employees just seem more satisfied with their work and lives. Creative leadership is what lit a spark within *me*; I knew it had the power to change the lives of many more. I just had to figure out how.

As we scoot into Act II, you'll soon discover practical tools to foster creativity in others. We'll address the great need for psychological safety and providing the optimal environments for more creative thinking at work. We'll share examples of what creative leadership looks like in action—and how it results in tangible business innovations. Regardless of whether you're a leader of people today, this style of creative leadership can enable you to shape not only your own creative path, but also the journey of those whom you're in the position to inspire.

Creative leadership may call you to speak up for others who struggle to get their ideas seen and heard. Perhaps it'll prompt you to empower those you lead, even with the awareness that they may stumble. Rather than simply generating your own new ideas, this style of leadership will move you to ensure your work environment supports the creative process to co-create with others. You'll become equipped to serve the team's shared mission and collaborate to bring the best new creative idea to life.

So, as my then-colleagues enjoyed the electric slide at the Nashville bar, Liz saw the spark in me. She knew I was imagining a new professional chapter, perhaps even before I fully knew it myself. Creative leadership makes space for the intuition that may reveal your team member is ready for the next creative challenge.

I eventually told Liz what was calling me so strongly. I confessed my intent to help others access their creativity to build thriving workplace cultures. I assured her I'd only leave when the team was ready—after all, she modeled loyalty and integrity, and I took that to heart. And then Liz did what any creative leader would do. She had my back. She encouraged me to go create. Then it was time to innovate.

# TRUST FALLS: WHAT'S REQUIRED TO BE A CREATIVE LEADER TODAY

*"My job is not to have the best idea in the room*
*at any given time, but to identify the best idea."*

—Thomas Kail, director, *Hamilton* and *In the Heights*

worked with Thomas Kail (whom I know as "Tommy") back in the early 2000s in one of my last professional musical theatre performances in New York City. He is now a world-renowned, Tony-award-winning director best known for *In the Heights* and *Hamilton,* but with a long list of accomplished credits to his name. In his career, he's walked red carpets, accepted award statuettes, and gotten standing ovations.

But those aren't everyday occurrences. In the day-to-day, Tommy's a manager. A boss. A leader whose sophisticated emotional intelligence is hard not to admire, but whose day-to-day style is relatable—even if you're outside the theatre world.

Take the afternoon where he was catching up on email and got a chat from a colleague who was away on a trip: it was mostly catching up, talking a bit of logistics, but also mentioning a book he was reading, something that really piqued his interest for a new project. So Tommy, always one to take initiative, typed back that they should get together as soon as they returned from their trip to discuss—and then made good on the plan.

The colleague was Lin-Manuel Miranda, and the book was Ron Chernow's *Hamilton.*

Of course, the smash-hit status of the musical can't be directly attributed to one meeting scheduled from a G-chat session. But that little moment of mundane calendar management shows how seriously and consciously Tommy approaches his work as a director, manager, and colleague in every interaction—and it's not just because of his collaborative personality.

"I made a musical about leadership and what it means to lead, and what's effective," Tommy told me. "And I spend a *lot* of time in the work thinking about it."

Tommy has developed an industry reputation for his creative genius, and deservedly so: even if you're not tapped into the performing arts, odds are good you've heard of at least one of his projects. But despite his status in the theatre world, Tommy doesn't see his leadership approach as exclusive to theatre.

"Running a theatre company and being a freelance director is basically being an entrepreneur," Tommy said. "I go in and launch start-up companies. If I do my job well, then they can exist without me; if I have to be there for them to succeed, then I've failed. But my job is to take a group of people whom I've never met, unify them, and see if I can create an environment where they can do their work once I'm gone."

In fact, if anything, his even-handed, thoughtful leadership is the polar opposite of what we'd expect from a theatre director. The cultural image of the director is one who's temperamental, irresponsible, single-minded, even abusive—something that Tommy, as producer of FX's series *Fosse/Verdon* about the notoriously destructive and exacting director/choreographer, is only too aware of—and pushes back on.

"One of the things I try to dismantle, show by show, is that great art comes from great pain," Tommy said. "Or that you need acrimony or this cauldron of intensity colored by some of the darker arts to make something. I think that's completely mythologized. Safety is the number-one thing I try to provide. An environment that is devoid of acrimony and tension."

Not only that, he's also a living, breathing, Tony-winning refutation of the idea that successful creatives are born, not made. He entered the theatre world as an adult—fairly late for the industry—and even in the way he talks about his career in the arts, he shows how intimately connected the work is to a sense of leadership.

"I took one theatre class in high school but didn't start really doing it until I was 21," he told me. "I've always thought of myself as more of a craftsman than I think of myself as a creative person. I know that I have creativity, but I like shaping environments and people as much as I like shaping the story."

The reality is, being a theatre director isn't some wild bohemian experience driven by impulse. Of course, there are the occasional monomaniacal directors, but no industry is immune to bad managers; and they're the exception, not the rule. *Creative* leaders aren't so different from *business* leaders: they still have to hire and train, manage and troubleshoot, budget and brainstorm. They can study their craft, but still need to roll up their sleeves.

Three things in particular stand out to me about Tommy's leadership. First, he leans into a sustained sense of incremental progress, even when the end feels far off.

"I try to create an environment of being comfortable *not* knowing for a while," he said. "When we're on Day 3, we don't need to be anywhere else but there. We need to be beyond Day 2, but we don't need to be on Day 7 or 8."

In your work, you may be at an early-stage start-up (or a mature organization that acts like a start-up!) that doesn't yet have fully baked processes for delivering performance feedback. Perhaps career paths aren't established because things are changing so quickly, or your industry is experiencing disruption, so strategic priorities are often in flux. There's no stasis. In these real-world examples, you're still very much on Day 3. You don't need to be on Day 7 or 8, and in fact, living there would make little sense. Can you find ways of celebrating your team's incremental progress? Are you able to heed those Love Notes of Resistance and come up with a short feedback guide, rather than venture to launch a complex, multilayered performance-review process?

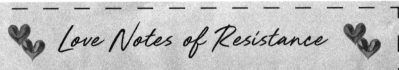

*Love Notes of Resistance*

"I feel like I should have a more sophisticated work process developed by now—I'm going to fail because I'm not further along."

Remind yourself: I don't need to be on Day 7 or 8. Today, I'll work on making Day 3 as good as it can be. I'll reflect on what I learn. I'll plan ahead but enjoy the creative process of building *today*.

Second, Tommy is hands-on, and lets that experience dictate his approach rather than some abstract theory—or, as he puts it, "I'm not the product of an academic process, but I've certainly spent a lot of time sitting in dark theatres solving things with really smart people who spent a lot of time thinking about the problem."

In your work, think about how being hands-on might cause you to rethink your approach. Sometimes *best practices* simply don't apply—they may not resonate with your business culture or company situation. To bring this to life, imagine you have advisors (perhaps pricey experts) urging you to centralize functions like sales and marketing, but you know from experience that the business responds better to a decentralized approach. After thinking creatively about the problem, be prepared to experiment to find what works for *your* team or organization. Don't be afraid to try something new, but *just because Google's doing it* doesn't mean it's best for your business.

Third, Tommy is at home with the unknown-unknowns of the creative process, and balances feedback with intuition.

"For three or four years, when I described *Hamilton*, this hip-hop musical about our first US treasurer, a lot of people looked at me like, *Why are you wasting your time?*" he recalled. "The reality is you get a lot of nos. You hear, *No, this won't work*. Sometimes getting a 'maybe' from one person is good enough to move forward."

This final insight is reminiscent of the process Aaron Mitchell described at Netflix Animation in Act I. Consider how best to give your team members the time and space to share ideas in the rough, gain perspective, and then polish up their idea. A *maybe* might reveal a blind spot—and you, the creative leader, can start to provide more visibility. You can hold up the mirrors.

What Tommy underscored for me is his relentless focus on creating an environment of trust and safety with his fellow collaborators. As a leader in your work, this skill is table stakes for nurturing creativity. We can all have a good laugh at referencing trust falls during kumbaya offsite learning experiences, but there's a reason these practices stick. Deep down, we know that without trust, we can't create. We can't build. We can't be part of an effective, high-performing team. And we can't be a leader who brings out the best in the people we lead.

## SCENE DIALOGUE FOR IDENTIFYING THE BEST IDEA

**SETTING:**

(SUE is mid-brainstorm session with her TEAM—some around a conference room table and others logged into a virtual room displayed on the monitor. All TEAM MEMBERS are logged on to their laptops, using the chat feed to share and reinforce ideas.)

**SUE**

Daria, you bring up a good point. To recap our goal for this working session, we want to come up with the *best idea* for making our new interns feel welcomed, but we're somewhat limited by what we can do since they're working remotely around the globe.

**DARIA**

Yeah, I just wonder if there's a way to integrate them more somehow. Especially since they won't have any physical connection to our offices—

**BRAD**

(chiming in on the screen)

I like that. Maybe we can do a series of master classes, so they can learn about different parts of the business?

                              WILL

Nah, we did that before. It was a ton of work
and low impact—

                              SUE

Can I gently push back on that, Will?

                              WILL

Sure thing.

                              SUE

I'm curious how we *could* redesign a learning
series so it didn't fall to one person to orga-
nize. And how might we drive greater impact?

                             DARIA

I bet we could invite some of the other business
heads to do a fireside chat. That's usually a
pretty light lift on us... and what if...

                              SUE

Keep going with this, Daria.

              (SUE monitors the chat feed.)

And yes, Brad and Will. The master classes
could absolutely be done in different cohorts
to accommodate different time zones.

                             DARIA

Ooh, I like that, too. And what if we had a
scavenger hunt of some kind? Filling up a bingo
card? Some way of inviting them in to learn
different parts of the business and get curious—
but with some structure...

                              WILL

That'd be fun. Gamify it.

                              BRAD

And maybe some of their work projects could
also be gamified.

                              SUE

Nice job, team. Let's keep refining from here...

                       **(END OF SCENE)**

Sue is in the process of shaping the best idea while inclusively gathering multiple inputs across the team. She's careful to spot the fixed mindsets and gently call them out, steering the group toward the possibilities. By guiding the creative process, she can help nurture the best idea.

## STORIES OF BELONGING FROM A TROUPER

In our last act, Act I, we examined how the creative process is an act of courage. It requires getting out of our comfort zones and risking the wounds of criticism. When teams are *led* with creativity, they're shielded from those wounds and instead can experience higher levels of belonging.

Belonging is a key driver of employee satisfaction in today's world of work. Perhaps attributed to our evolutionary need to be part of an "in-group," belonging at work is influenced by workplace behaviors, as well as governing structures. We can examine what leads to greater belonging at work (like passing the ball, having an ally at work, or being asked for feedback and noticing adjustments being made) while pressure-testing any cultural norms that could be standing in the way of it. Unfortunately, it's not a check-the-box exercise; cultivating belonging requires continuous effort. Even organizations with high levels of belonging know they can't take it for granted.

I got my first taste of belonging back in my theatre days. When a production's cast and crew come together, they bond over the shared identity of the show, all working toward the vision of opening night. As an eight-year-old Thumbelina in *Hans Christian Andersen*, I was swept up by the community that's formed during costume fittings into wooden shoes, the blocking of musical numbers, and the downtime of rehearsal breaks—that grown-up feeling of putting in a full day's work, playing a card game of Spit with fellow young cast members, and running lines in preparation for showtime—this is where belonging got cemented.

At work, that sense of belonging is formed through similar moments that matter. Your opening night could be your product or new initiative launch—and the run of the show is the journey of delighting customers, reaching revenue targets, and creating a unique employee experience. Maybe you feel the support of someone who has your back at work or you get asked to provide input on an important project. These micro-moments, in the aggregate, are what enable us to feel part of the tribe. When we belong, we're safe to be vulnerable. We're able to be the zebricorn without worrying what others may think. We can be a *real trouper* when the going gets tough, because we know our community is there for us.

"There was a long time in my life where I couldn't get off the couch."

That common expression of *being a trouper* was brought to life as I led a client's Belonging at Work session. It was summertime, the height of vacation season—and perhaps not the kind of day you'd look forward to spending in a company culture meeting—when this young man volunteered to share his story. He was known to his colleagues as an army veteran with a good work ethic—a solid coworker, easygoing, but not open about much else.

He went on: Back in his lowest days, his life felt meaningless, like he'd hit a dead end too early in life. He was depressed. Stuck on that couch. Needing direction, he enlisted in the army, where he learned discipline, but also started specializing in technology work that eventually led to his current job. He finished his moment of sharing by expressing gratitude for the company and how much the work, as well as his work community, meant to him. He was emotional—and so were the rest of us.

This young man might not have ever set foot on a stage, but he was undoubtedly a trouper. In the most strictly theatrical sense, *troupers* are those who can persevere through anything, from thunderous applause to a hailstorm of rotten tomatoes. They can put aside discomforts and distractions to get the job done—not because they crave the limelight, but because they're part of the troupe. And—crucially—afterward, they know the rest of the troupe is there to support them. By that same token, a good ensemble cast shines onstage in a way that just can't be faked. There is a trust and openness that radiates right out into the audience.

That trust and openness isn't just key to theatre troupes, however. According to research by Google's Project Aristotle, the top factor in creating effective teams is a sense of psychological safety.[1] Dr. Amy Edmondson, Harvard Business School professor and author of *Fearless Organizations*, has helped raise awareness of the importance of this dynamic. She shares that beyond trust, which is more of a person-to-person relationship dynamic, psychological safety is a dynamic found across the entire team. It's what makes you feel okay about asking a seemingly silly question in front of your peers, being fully yourself with your teammates, and even feeling okay about challenging the team strategy and approaches in a respectful way.[2]

Building psychological safety in teams takes work and effort. It doesn't equate to a "nice culture"—Dr. Edmondson is clear about the need for teams to address conflict directly—and psychologically safe teams aren't devoid of friction. Instead, psychologically safe cultures invite debate. They have a high degree of self-governance, where team members hold each other accountable to shared high standards of conduct. And they enable people to take risks, fail, learn, and keep creating.

Psychological safety is more than just trust; it's a sense of being safe to take risks without the fear of embarrassment. This has an obvious application in the theatre world—where the work regularly demands you get vulnerable, silly, or emotional in front of your colleagues—but it's relevant for us in knowledge work, too. It all comes down to a shared sense of purpose, and that shared sense of purpose starts with storytelling.

As a creative leader, you can invite your team to share experiences to organically build belonging rather than institute values from the top down. Stories that exemplify your cultural values can transform employees into ambassadors, empower them to do the right thing, and make them feel like they can bring more of their whole self to work—as this young veteran's example shows, even colleagues we think we know well have stories that we'd never suspect.

Knowing those stories—and making space to share them—connects us to each other and to the values we have in common. It shifts the focus to the *how* as much as to the *what* of your team. It makes us all into troupers.

## A CREATIVE LEADER'S ROLE TO SET THE TONE

Tommy's leadership philosophy—and his success—is the kind of example I've always wanted to share with business leaders, since at *least* that initial calling back in Nashville, and long before I'd ever heard the word COVID. What I've observed creative leaders bring, perhaps in contrast to other styles of leadership, is a commitment to the discovery process that transforms the seemingly impossible into a reality. They often see things that others cannot. They are master connectors and reconnectors—of people, of information, of insights. They believe in the possibility of overcoming obstacles when many others don't.

Creating that culture of possibility is up to everyone, but the leader sets the tone. Let's imagine for a moment that an existing team has a track record of success. They inspire each other to produce innovative ideas from disciplined experimentation, dedicate time to reflection, incorporate lessons learned, and celebrate incremental improvement.

Suddenly, a new team member is introduced—someone without history and context of what's been tried before. A few weeks in, the new team member gets the courage to present a new idea, which falls flat. As we observed in the scene dialogue, you may get the knee-jerk response of "Nope. That won't work. We've tried it before." It's then up to the creative leader to intervene. You may explore:

- *What variation of this idea could we consider?*
- *Was the failure in execution a function of timing, stakeholder buy-in, or other adjustable variables?*
- *Is there a component of the idea that could be applied to a different, new solution?*

Rather than discard the idea entirely, it may need a reframe. A creative leader sets the tone to live in that state of possibility. If employees—especially the more vulnerable junior professionals, newer hires, or underrepresented colleagues—don't have their ideas fully considered, recognized, and appreciated, it's tough to build a team culture of creativity. That responsibility falls to the leader.

## CHAMPIONING CREATIVE IDEAS TO DRIVE CHANGE

Responsibility is a heavy word. But it's also the byproduct of building trust. Tommy Kail reminded me of the specific responsibility creative leaders carry.

"Manny Azenberg would say something like this: 'When you start to get known and win Tonys, you tell the same jokes, folks just laugh harder.' When you have some success, people start to listen more deeply. They're a little more attentive," Tommy shared. "The fact that you have people's attention asks for a large measure of accountability. I have a responsibility not to take advantage of others if I'm put in a leadership position."

Leaders are often in the unique position to either be the gatekeeper or the gateway to creativity. They can go along with the status quo or champion necessary change—sometimes facing strong headwinds. Big creative ideas require a leader to bravely step up, even when it's difficult.

Jen Brewer is that shining example: guided by her moral compass and steered to champion change, Jen embodies the courage required to speak up and do what's right. I've been lucky to have a front-row seat to Jen's career ascension and rise to Chief Ethics and Compliance Officer at Activision Blizzard; as a client, she's shaped my perspective on creative leadership, resilience, and the responsibility of care that comes with positional power.

Once comprised of three compliance professionals, Jen's team has quickly expanded, adding 26 individuals in 2022 alone. It was her creative leadership that spawned Activision's first companywide employee program called the Way2Play Heroes—a peer-nominated group of colleagues across all business units, championing ethics everywhere in the world they do business. The origin story of the program is significant. Sometimes a creative leader's job is to fiercely advocate for an idea that isn't immediately implemented.

"I knew it had to be a grassroots effort," she told me, reflecting on the early stages of her Way2Play Heroes program vision. "This program has been an absolute game changer. Seeing it come to life has been the highlight of my career so far."

It hasn't been an easy journey. Jen has scaled her Ethics and Compliance team with the backdrop of changing leadership hands, a pending merger with Microsoft, and an enterprise-wide culture-change initiative. Comprised of a creative workforce that publishes some of the world's leading interactive entertainment, fostering an ethical, speak-up culture is table stakes for Activision Blizzard. Without it, talent suffers. Work product suffers. It risks not only reputational damage, but also the lost trust across the workforce that thriving organizations work so hard to engender.

Jen's leadership style is heart-led and direct; she shows up to her team as wholly human. Mid-pandemic, she and her family moved to Ojai, California, to be surrounded by animals, a community of other families, and an organic, what she calls *unscripted* lifestyle—nearly unrecognizable to the urban life they left behind. It's that counterpoint that offers Jen the much-needed perspective from her role's intense pace and high stakes. As the leader of the Ethics and Compliance function, Jen and her team hold the daunting responsibility to investigate all workplace concerns, drive policy development and enforcement, and educate a global workforce of over 13,000 employees on workplace integrity.

With all the essential ingredients of an effective enterprise leader and a family history that shaped her resilience, it's Jen's *creative* leadership style that sets her apart. Much like Liz Dick, she's a connector: artful in bringing people together, persuasive in communicating and repositioning situations in a new light, and indefatigable in her pursuit to get things done.

This ability to blaze through obstacles enabled Jen's idea of the Way2Play Heroes program to be born. Starting with a concept to equip ethics champions to be a voice for all employees, she carried the weight of responsibility that director Tommy Kail described. By leading creatively—finding out what each unique stakeholder cared about, demonstrating trust with decision-makers, and painting a clear vision—Jen connected the dots between the kernel of a creative idea to tangible business outcomes.

Creativity in the workplace is nearly impossible without a sense of safety, trust, and openness. But it flourishes when there's respectful connection among colleagues. Jen's people-first approach encapsulates the belief that focusing on ethics and doing the right thing doesn't hamper creativity—it enhances it.

The Way2Play Heroes program has now expanded to nearly 140 dedicated employees across the globe. After years of educating Way2Play Heroes, building community, and expanding the Ethics and Compliance program, Jen has empowered the broader workforce to speak up—and scaled her team's infrastructure so those voices can be heard. One creative leader's idea may start small, but it has the capacity to inspire meaningful, transformational change.

## CREATIVITY IN TIMES OF CRISIS

Jen Brewer demonstrates what's possible when obstacles are transformed into opportunities. As she dances in the moment with her work and family life—frequently pausing on a Zoom call to respond to her daughter's new business invention or her son's question about one of their animals—Jen has helped me realize how creative leadership calls us to show up as unapologetically *human*. It's a combination of authenticity and trust, but also grit, ingenuity, and tenacity. To a creative leader, a *no* may land more like *not yet.* After all, they can see what others cannot.

Much like Jen, Chelsea Grayson is a leader who fearlessly stares down challenging situations. A successful chief executive and board director whose formative years were spent in a white shoe law firm, Chelsea once prided herself on *not* being creative.

"For sure, I'm creative," she told me. "Although I wouldn't have admitted to that word early in my career."

In Chelsea's early law firm life, she and her 21 fellow associates hired a psychologist to give them what she called the left-brain or right-brain test. Setting aside what we now know are myths about these generalizations, the test was intended to reveal a dominance in either the brain's left hemisphere (considered the domain of an analytical, strategic, linear thinker) or right hemisphere (more likely activated by a creative, abstract, divergent thinker). Sweating bullets, Chelsea worked to game the system to avoid positively responding to test questions that might lead to (God forbid!) a right-brained result.

Like Chelsea, her peers also gamed the system. Out of the 22 lawyers who participated, only one attorney displayed the right-brained result, henceforth labeled the abstract creative thinker. Snickering at the attorney's ill fate, the associates figured this *creative* wouldn't cut the mustard at the firm for very long. (Chelsea reports that while this lawyer *did* eventually leave the firm, she went on to become a successful federal prosecutor and was recruited back as an equity partner, where she still works today.)

Now in the prime of her career, Chelsea readily admits the storied evidence of her applied creativity at work. While serving as General Counsel at American Apparel, Chelsea was the Swiss army knife: problems of all shapes and sizes would cross her desk, to which she'd quickly find a new tool, strategy, or approach to get the job done. By the time she was swiftly elevated to CEO during a time of crisis, there was no corner of the organization she hadn't touched.

Chelsea describes her creative thinking during that time as the byproduct of high stress, high stakes, and necessity; she was fearless in her creative approach to survive.

"Nothing is irreversible," she reflected. "Knowing that you can pull out a tool and say, 'Whoops, that one didn't work. I guess I'll try another.' That's another thing you learn. That's creativity."

Chelsea now recognizes how her creative leadership sets her apart. Approachable and relatable, Chelsea advocates for team collaboration, as well as the structure and clarity of specific roles.

"Communication is key," Chelsea reflected. "Regular, frequent, transparent communication." Much like parenting, Chelsea recognizes how the structure a leader provides is also what enables creativity to flourish. That safe, trusted working environment is what's necessary to push the boundaries and explore the unexpected.

When serving as CEO of True Religion, another apparel company, Chelsea was pressured to find novel ways to reduce expenses and knew a cookie-cutter solution wouldn't work. There had already been judges, legal counsel, and banks who'd weighed in to cut costs, restructure, and fix. At this stage, she knew a radically different perspective was required; a positive outcome needed a novel approach for an extra jolt. Locking herself in a quiet room, she considered, *What hasn't been done here? How can I rip this company down to its studs and reconsider what's sitting on my P&L that no one has bothered to look at?*

And it came to her. They could completely rethink the life cycle of the supply chain. This previously untouched and sacrosanct process had been overlooked. Chelsea thought, *What if we could experiment with on-demand manufacturing?*

"I could come up with a bunch of design ideas that I think my customer might want," she brainstormed, "prototype it, put models in it, put it on the website, make it available for sale, but it's only *made* once the customer orders it."

**CREATIVITY BOOSTER:**

When facing a thorny challenge, find a quiet hour all to yourself. List all of the common solutions that may have been tried before. Next, look for hidden parts of the problem. What hasn't yet been examined? Are there areas where no one has looked or re-examined? Start there. Aim to see the problem in a different light.

Chelsea's creative idea changed the business model. By eliminating inventory risk, the company could experiment with the customer to gauge and calibrate what they really wanted. When everything else has been tried, creativity is born out of necessity.

You may be in the position of leading creatively through challenging economic times, and much like Chelsea, are looking for untapped revenue streams or eliminating waste in expenses. Or, like Jen, perhaps you have a kernel of an idea that requires a bold vision, persuasion, and indefatigable tenacity to become a reality. Maybe you simply want to create more belonging across your team and are inviting more open sharing of stories. In all cases, your foundational skill as a creative leader is to build trust—with your team and broader organization—to bring these creative ideas to life. You may see what others don't yet see. You may need to go after the sacred cows. This is where creative value is often found.

## FOR YOUR TOOL KIT: CREATIVE LEADER SELF-ASSESSMENT

If one of your goals is to lead more creatively, the first step is to gather a baseline for how you're *thinking* about creativity. Learning more about your mindset and held beliefs will help you design the best creative approach with others. It'll inform where to get started and invest your energy.

Carefully read through the following statements in each column.

| TRADITIONAL LEADERSHIP | CREATIVE LEADERSHIP |
|---|---|
| I am focused on efficiency across the team, making sure everyone is productive. | I am focused on psychological safety across the team, making sure everyone belongs. |
| When my team completes an initiative, we quickly move on to the next priority. | When my team completes an initiative, we take time to reflect and integrate learning. |
| I activate my imagination in specific tasks, but it's not explicitly discussed. | I dedicate time for our team to activate our imaginations to continuously improve. |
| My team's North Star and values are typically discussed about once per year. | My team's North Star and values are integrated into the flow of work, regularly discussed in work projects and feedback conversations. |
| I rely heavily on what's worked in the past to determine my go-forward strategy. | I rely heavily on experimentation to determine my go-forward strategy. |
| Innovative ideas are typically owned by a particular department or person. | Innovative ideas are shared and woven into my team's core operating rhythm. |
| I gather feedback on a quarterly, semiannual, or annual basis. | I gather feedback on a continuous basis. |
| I rely on traditional office workspaces to foster creativity. | I consider and curate my team's physical work environment to foster creativity. |
| Creative output (if implemented at the company) is what's rewarded and celebrated. | The creative process, as well as the output, is rewarded and celebrated. |
| When a misstep occurs, my focus is on negative consequences and not repeating mistakes. | When a misstep occurs, my focus is on curiosity and learning. |
| When faced with a business problem, I seek out expert guidance. | When faced with a business problem, I seek multiple perspectives at all levels. |
| I typically follow a specific defined process to get things done at my organization. | I typically consider the best path to get something done, even if that means going outside of the defined process. |
| After I build a vision, I hold others accountable to execute the plan. | After I co-create a vision with my team, I empower the team to play their respective roles and we share accountability. |

Consider the leadership style you currently adopt in each row. Next, consider what changes you could make to shift your leadership style to foster more creative thinking and behaviors, and whether that creative leadership style could better serve you, your team, or your organization. Remember, context is everything! Not all creative leadership techniques may apply or serve you in your situation. Finally, think about using this framework as a conversation starter for an upcoming team meeting or a 1:1 with someone you lead.

### SCENE FOUR SHOW NOTES

- **Creative leadership starts with a mindset** of believing in your team's limitless potential to be creative.
- **Building trust** and **psychological safety** is the foundation to a creative team.
- **Belonging at work** leads to greater work satisfaction, including the social permission to create, experiment, and be imperfect.
- Creative leadership requires **tone at the top.**
- **Creativity** in times of crisis is often **born out of necessity.**

Creative leadership starts with trust. In Scene Four, we've learned lessons from theatre icon Tommy Kail to corporate executives Jen Brewer and Chelsea Grayson; when building safety and trust is the focus, creativity can flow. In our next scene, we'll build on the psychological safety that shapes your workplace environment, exploring the *physical* workspaces that influence our creativity.

# CREATIVE PHYSICAL AND PSYCHOLOGICALLY SAFE WORKSPACES

*"There's credibility behind the argument that if you put people in spaces where they are likely to collide with one another, they are likely to have a conversation. But is that conversation likely to be helpful for innovation, creativity, useful at all for what an organization hopes people would talk about? There, there is almost no data whatsoever."*[3]

—Ethan S. Bernstein, Associate Professor,
Organizational Behavior Unit, Harvard Business School

**W**ith the trust of your team, you're now ready to lead creatively, but does your work environment support or detract from your team's creative process? In this scene, we'll explore the physical and psychological attributes of creative workspaces.

People don't normally leap at the chance to walk through the bitterly cold streets of Chicago in winter. But at the tail end of 2008, that's what I did. And it lit me up.

## OFFICING LIKE A SET DESIGNER

On the heels of completing my MBA while juggling full-time work at Axiom, I found myself hungry for a new professional challenge. I itched to get out of my comfort zone. Our company was about to scale to new regions across the United States (and potentially around the globe), so I threw my hat in the ring to help launch new satellite offices. Still living out of my shoebox sixth-floor walk-up on Mulberry Street, I reveled at the idea of *also* living in Chicago, the Second City, in what I considered the peak of high luxury: corporate housing.

Turns out I'm not cut out for the glamorous, jet-setting life, but that's a separate story. I picked a corporate apartment in a high rise right off Lake Michigan. The furnishings were bland at best: neutral maple wood coffee tables, utilitarian lamps, an innocuous black-and-white cityscape hanging on the walls. I landed in O'Hare the night of the 2008 US presidential election. Newly elected President Obama was making his acceptance speech at Grant Park, only a few blocks away. Change was in the air.

At that time, part of my job was to help hire and train the founding team members in the new region, but also pick the office space where we'd work together. While we got our footing with the first few local client engagements amid headwinds of a financial crisis and recession, we selected temporary office space in Chicago's downtown loop. Still considered a start-up, we wanted a spot that felt credible and accessible; sharing an address with a white shoe law firm near an El stop felt like a safe bet.

This was just the first of many office hunts on which I'd embark. By this point in my career, I had visited hundreds of corporate office spaces to check on client engagements. From sparklingly modern financial institutions in Hong Kong and London (where tea and biscuits were served at business meetings, to my great delight), to the gritty, no-frills creative spaces at the Apollo Theatre and Blue Man Group, to large media conglomerates at the landmark 30 Rockefeller Center, each space had a uniquely defined energy.

The character of each office typically reflected its culture. I walked through the open floor plans of high-growth tech start-ups decked out with ping-pong tables, beanbag chairs, and stocked with limitless snacks and energy drinks. There, the T-shirt–wearing CEOs spontaneously pulled working groups into huddle rooms with Post-its and dry-erase marker covering the walls—a colleague's laughter heard from an impromptu celebration in the next room. Other clients had me wandering through a maze of muted colored carpet and rows of cubicles, accompanied only by the slight hum of fluorescent lights and echoes of robotic keyboard tapping. I sat waiting for clients at heavy mahogany tables blanketed in a thin layer of dust and flanked by the few unbroken roller chairs from the 1980s. You can sometimes tell a lot about a team by the office décor.

Some banks and insurance companies showcased modern interior glass-walled offices across Wall Street and Midtown Manhattan overlooking sweeping views from 100-story floor windows. The world was at these colleagues' fingertips, poised for progress and exploration, yet bound by the institution's traditional hierarchy that left them trapped in a glass cage. And now here I was, exploring new clients' offices across downtown Chicago. I roamed new sets of corporate hallways, lobbies, and meeting spaces, many of them brandishing old-timey photos from their 100-year-old legacies.

These intimate glimpses into others' workspaces left me highly sensitive to the *feeling* you get when you walk into an office. Almost like reading an energetic frequency on a monitor, I could sense if its colleagues worked in fear, harmony, creativity—and everything in between. My job was to skillfully match human talent to these diverse environments, so I became tuned into the specific work-style and presence that might mesh.

Since client visits often occurred over lunch, we found ourselves touring the corporate cafeterias of the world, joking about authoring coffee table books to highlight the wide range of corporate culinary offerings. Some touted private sushi chefs and 100 percent subsidized meals throughout the day—small-batch ice cream, custom coffees and teas, and freshly baked pastries, nursing their employees' sugar highs with the latest treat to lure them back to work.

Other offices created family-style spaces where colleagues microwaved leftovers from home. These shared lunch spots were humble, yet the culture of the team was often strong and familial. I would spot half-eaten plates of homemade cupcakes for the beloved accounting manager's sixtieth birthday, or a coffee tin donation container for the office coordinator's sick dog. Across all of them, I detected a rhythmic heartbeat to these workspaces. Sometimes vibrant or quirky, other times on life support, these were not much more than a transient worker community within a sterile shell.

Back in Chicago, winter had come early. I zipped up my black-leather heeled boots, fastened my flowery wool coat, and ventured out from my corporate apartment. Only six or so blocks to the high-rise building with our temporary office space, a cab made no sense, so I hoofed it. The cold wind lashed across the lake. I passed crowds of people exiting their El stop. The bagel shop with the best hot coffee. The tourist-attraction popcorn factory.

Each time I walked up our building's exterior steps to push my way through the revolving doors, cold wind whipping at my back, I got a rush of warm energy. It felt official and grown up. Maybe it was the newly elected Obama, the hometown win. Perhaps it was living in a corporate apartment among furniture I never picked out, as if secretly living someone else's life. It could have been the eerie, looming uncertainty of the financial system's meltdown. But each day felt like a new invitation to create an experience in space, not unlike how a set designer might approach their work. It was a chance to shake things up. A new moment to invent and create. Those foundational spaces were ripe for creative leadership, even though I was years away from articulating it like that. We were building. Set designing. It marked the early scaling of what had started as a humble, creative idea.

## PROVIDING CHOICE IN WHERE
## TEAM CULTURE IS FORMED

In a short couple of months, the Chicago team was in place with an established operating rhythm. Bouncing between Chicago and New York was wearing on me; I longed for more stability, a home base, and the comforting proximity to family. With a hub-and-spoke growth model, I was relieved it was time to launch a Southern California presence.

After building the initial presence in a Century City high rise in Los Angeles, we moved west; this far hipper Santa Monica office in Dog Town better reflected the fresh, innovative culture we aimed to create. It was the perfect landing pad for my rescue dog Teddy, a lab-mix with separation anxiety, whose best life was spent lying on the office's concrete floors, sleeping most of the day away, only occasionally waking to enjoy the presence of his humans.

In our work lives, the *being around humans* part used to be a given. Team culture used to mean showing up in the office first thing in the day, sitting alongside your colleagues and co-creating. Together. That's not to say in-office culture always leads to collaboration—in fact, the opposite happens all the time. But the human togetherness used to be part of the deal.

Back then, I clung to the idea that a thriving team culture necessitated a shared workspace. How else would we develop our unique team energy or openly share status updates on client matters in real time? How would we develop our early career team members, come up with a short-hand language to get stuff done, or socially bond and connect?

I'll admit to holding a strong bias for in-person teamwork, believing it would magically drive better business results. And to some extent, those hours in the office together did facilitate relationship building. We knew each other's work-styles and passions outside of work. We integrated into each other's lives, sharing professional wins and setbacks, idiosyncrasies, and areas for growth. Our holiday party was a planned neighborhood scavenger hunt and tour of our favorite haunts, celebrating that shared physical environment: the restaurant with our favorite chocolate chip *fleur de sel* cookies, the coffee shop with the barista we befriended, our highly frequented YogaWorks studio.

Months into this new team operating rhythm and marveling at the community we had co-created, telecommuting started to creep in. I found myself negotiating with my team for more time together in the office. I romanticized the idea of all of us coming together, sharing insights, eager to work in a communal space. In reality, the burden of requiring everyone to be in the office at the same time simply wasn't realistic. It put a strain on people's energy and their other responsibilities outside of work. It likely bred resentment.

Creative leadership isn't about holding tight to what you think it *should* be. It's about offering choice, designing exceptional employee experiences, and letting go. It's both push and pull. A creative leader knows that spaces can inspire the freedom to create, but they can also hamper it.

We now live in a new era of work. My beliefs about the team culture benefits of working together in a shared office have shifted by living through the personal trade-offs that it often requires. With the right creative leadership, remote teams can still achieve thriving, innovative cultures. It might just look a little different.

Since the grand experiment of moving knowledge work online, initiated by the early days of COVID, we've all learned a lot. We've collectively saved millions of commuting hours, reduced our environmental impact from less frequent travel, and shown up more for those we care for—even if that means ourselves. You may have incorporated more exercise into your daily routine, eaten more economical and healthier lunches at home, or savored pausing work to be present with your family. Remote work has benefits aplenty.

Luckily, technology has kept up too. We default to Zoom at the drop of a hat, which enables more visual cues that build connection (and often more inclusive) forms of engagement. We've embraced tools like Jam Board, Miro, and Google Docs as digital collaboration spaces. And (if we're lucky), we now recognize that team belonging is not one-size-fits-all. It's not as simple as putting a ping-pong table in the room and beer on tap. People want different experiences from work, likely at different phases of their careers and lives. We're still motivated by autonomy, mastery, and purpose, but those elements may be obtained differently today. Perhaps most important is recognizing we can't go back to what was. Now is the time to look forward, rethink, and rebuild the experience of what work can be.

I'm not advocating for a particular work structure. There are some businesses that lend themselves to more (or less) time in co-located spaces. Creative leadership can be expressed through remote-first, hybrid, or in-office cultures, just as much as it can be absent in any of these work structures. But being mindful of the work environment (both physical and psychological), work flexibility norms, leadership cultures, and operating rhythms can all influence a team's creative potential. Creative leadership calls us to listen to the stories of your team members, get curious about what environments help them to co-create and collaborate, and continuously ask, "How can we do even better?" so that all can thrive.

Perhaps we're all a little like my rescue dog, Teddy. Our environment matters. We need a sense of safety and connection with the people around us—whether physically or virtually. As humans, we've evolved as a species by working cooperatively in our tribe or community, knowing what role to play, experimenting, and communicating to accomplish a goal together. In this new era of work, co-building a creative work environment takes intention. Thankfully, there are practices to help get us there.

## SETTING THE WORKPLACE SCENE

I have a deep appreciation for my clients' decisions around *where* to work. My career has taken me from swanky European hotels to packed Midwestern conference centers to all those corporate cafeterias. (Seriously, I will write that coffee table book someday.) But until that sunny California morning, I'd yet to set foot in a rocket factory.

I didn't quite know what to expect when I arrived to tour the campus of a company dedicated to disrupting space travel (!) by using 3-D printing techniques to drastically reduce manufacture and R&D time. Maybe something sleek and serious, or sterile and efficient—part Jetsons, part Star Wars, all business. Instead, what greeted me at every turn was art. The company had decked out its headquarters with artwork made from the same 3-D technology that built its high-tech products. The overall impression wasn't so much "concrete bunker" as it was "funky museum."

Of course, there were more business-focused aspects, too, but even those had a vibrance and personality to them. A dynamic display showed company goals and blinked merrily with live progress updates, the antithesis of a mean-spirited, Glengarry Glen Ross–type leaderboard. Displays showcased not just triumphs and milestones, but flops and missteps, putting out visual reassurances that failure was an expected part of the innovation process. In fact, I realized, every aspect of the company environment tied back to its North Star, whether it was the cheekiness of using space-grade technology to make colorful doodads or the positive energy of seeing colleagues hit their targets in real time.

For leaders who aim to inspire a creativity culture, the environment—the office décor and physical structure—reflects the people and company mission within it. Yes, the aesthetics of office environments matter. But creating the right environment is about more than just *looking creative*. Spaces for work—be they traditional offices, flex space, or home offices—also need to be functional. Collaborative teams need both shared office space and places to have private conversations. Remote employees need both the requisite tech setup and the feeling of being "at work" for the company when they sit down at their desk (or kitchen table, or beachside hammock). And for spaces to be truly functional and creative, they must be built in a continuing dialogue with the values of the people who work there.

You may be considering how your physical structure or operating rhythm can build more connection across your team. Does your work environment promote connection and a feeling of psychological safety? Maybe the open-office layout needs to get swapped for private workspaces, so people don't feel "on display" and have their sympathetic nervous systems constantly on guard. Maybe you need a dedicated space for socializing and catching up (and not just the two-foot radius around the water cooler!).

As a team leader, perhaps you're on the hook for driving innovation. What physical environment inspires your team? What space do they need for their best creative thinking and deep work? Maybe it's quiet, "do not disturb" zones for people to buckle down without traffic noise, colleague chatter, or buzzing fluorescent lights. Maybe it's boxes of Trivial Pursuit cards scattered around the common areas for a quick, stimulating brain break.

Finally, since we know belonging at work leads to higher levels of work satisfaction and engagement, you might be examining how to practice more inclusive behaviors. What signals (even if unconscious) might be contributing to your team's *unbelonging*? Even a seemingly mundane change in environment can bring out the best in a team—or the worst. Try moving workers from private offices to cubicles, and you, too, might pick up on some *Who Moved My Cheese?* grumbling.

It's also essential that we expand our definition of "work environment." While leaders can dedicate hours of thought to designing and setting up a "hub" office, the offices of remote or hybrid team members are left as an afterthought—if they're thought of at all! The fact is, the "workplace environment" now includes home offices, and as more workers opt to do work remotely for part (if not all) of their work schedule, leaders should consider the form and function of those spaces just as much as the in-person, communal workspaces.

And since these home offices can range from makeshift spaces in closets to revamped spare bedrooms, leaders will also have to think creatively (surprise!) about how to give remote team members the best environment possible. This doesn't mean barging in and redecorating someone's private home, and it doesn't mean bankrolling thousand-dollar ergonomic setups, either. There are plenty of ways to bring the company brand and mission into people's home office environments in a way that's personal to them. Maybe some opt for a framed team photo, while others choose a branded coffee mug or a comfortable logo sweatshirt. (And providing remote employees with a quality webcam and lighting can help them feel less like they're working out of a cave when on a Zoom call.)

Much like a director is mindful of the scenery, set, and props, creative business leadership requires knowledge and interest in the work environment that's being created. After all, it influences the actors and informs what messages they receive throughout the day. Consider these approaches:

- Asking your team what equipment or materials would make them more comfortable and effective at work, ranging from an office chair, improved lighting, standing desk, or ergonomic keyboard setups.

- Offering a visual inspiration board that includes workplace equipment and artifacts you're able to provide; this could be as simple as a mobile whiteboard with colorful markers, or a corkboard with team pictures, handwritten cards, and printed values.

- Holding the space to talk about, well, *space*. Invite team members to share what environment helps them to focus and share best practices for technology (and analog!) tools. Not only may it help others to try out and adopt new, effective habits, it's a great way to learn more about your team's individual preferences and unique work styles.

Your physical environment at work matters. It can directly influence your team's ability to create, develop new ideas, and feel comfortable enough to share them. As a creative leader, you're helping to dress the set, reinforcing the collective vision of your team by visually telling the story of how team members experience their day-to-day. The creative leader doesn't miss this opportunity to curate a unique shared experience.

## SCENE DIALOGUE FOR AN UN-OFFICED TEAM

**SETTING:**

(The TEAM assembles in a large hotel board-room. Doors open to an outdoor patio aglow with late afternoon light, ocean in the distance. LILY, the team leader, stands with a marker in hand as she prepares to jot down notes on the flipchart.)

### LILY

What did you enjoy most about our offsite this week?

### BEN

Finally connecting in person has been amazing. Since we all work together on Zoom, it's like we wake up and start a video game together—you miss the casual in-person moments of talking through your day and sharing the hard stuff that happens.

### SHEILA

I'm with you, Ben. These moments to just learn more about each other have been incredible. The funny thing is, I feel closer to my team now than I did at my prior company where we all worked in the same space. Here, whenever we connect—even virtually—it's intentional. But I do love this time when we can be together.

### KATE

Maybe when we all go back to our virtual spaces, we can do more of that informal connecting. Not just game nights, which are fun, but really learning about each other.

>                          **LILY**
>
> I'd love to hear if people have feedback on the
> physical space of this offsite... What worked,
> what didn't?
>
>                          **KATE**
>                (standing and pointing outside)
> I'd like to request an ocean view for every
> offsite.
>
>                       (TEAM laughs)
>
> Seriously, though, it was nice to take breaks
> and get out in nature together. Walk and talk.
> That's where some of the real deep strategic
> thinking happened—
>
>                          **BEN**
>
> I agree! But also the structure of the offsite
> made a difference. This U-shaped table, our
> breakout groups that mixed us up across func-
> tions—we all got a chance to listen and learn
> from each other. Now we're ready to go build.
>
>                    **(END OF SCENE)**

In this scene, Lily allowed her remote team to reflect on how the in-person offsite brought them together to deepen connections. When we miss spontaneous moments that build relationships, it's up to the creative leader to intentionally create them.

Let's be real here: not all companies have the resources to whisk their teams away to a four-star oceanside resort. Whatever your budget, un-officing requires creativity. In some cases, it means making the implicit more explicit. It takes dedication from the leaders to invest in the moments when the team can come together—be it virtually or in person. A creative leader seeks out these moments. That may mean pulling in external help to ensure an offsite is executed flawlessly or giving internal team members the time and space to craft a meaningful experience. What I've found from leading dozens of retreats, summits, and offsites is the common desire to build memorable experiences that last well beyond the few days the team is physically together. When teams are open, committed to growth and learning, and in sync with the organizational purpose, that's when the magic happens. A creative leader understands the potential (and desire) for that level of impact.

## LEADING CREATIVELY IN A NONLINEAR DAY

Kim Rohrer, Principal People Partner at remote-first company Oyster, lives the challenges of bringing out creativity in others. A fellow theatre kid, Kim and I bonded early in the pandemic as she was heading out on maternity leave with her second child. Years later, Kim's home office is multipurpose: primary colored building blocks, board books, and a tiny play kitchen are often spotted in her Zoom background. Given a spare thirty minutes in her day, Kim relishes the chance to clean under her desk where toys mingle among laptop cords.

On the topic of creativity at work, Kim shared an early-career story when she interviewed for her role at Twitter circa 2009, back when it was roughly twenty people.

"I sat down with Biz Stone," Kim told me, "and he gave me a big speech about why it's useful to hire theatre people into tech. '*They're resilient and creative and think outside the box. At the end of the day, it's about delivering the show. You need to collaborate and rely on other people in the community. Theatre people know how to navigate different personalities and work under pressure.*' That blew my mind."

At the time, Kim hadn't yet connected the dots between her success in handling administrative work in high-growth tech companies and navigating interpersonal dynamics within tightly organized schedules in the theatre. Yet the two environments eerily resembled each other. Now a people executive at Oyster, a global outsourcing services firm that's scaled from 75 people to 650 in a mere eighteen months, Kim designs people-first experiences within a fully remote team that's distributed all over the globe.

With a caffeinated, no-bullshit energy, Kim openly navigates modern-day challenges: working full-time in a fast-paced career while parenting two young children. Leading creatively in a high-growth company across international cultures takes intention. There's effort behind crafting asynchronous brainstorms. Kim's emphasis is on enabling people to contribute their creative ideas at a time that works best for them.

"Maybe our scheduled meeting is right when the kids are coming home, so there's a lot of chaos. Or maybe it's the middle of your night, or during your lunch hour, so you're not in a receptive state," Kim elaborated. "It's not that there's no value in live or in-person collaboration. But I like to use synchronous collaboration as an *un-blocker* rather than creative ideation work."

Kim's day is decidedly nonlinear. She might use a free hour to fold laundry or take advantage of no-meeting-Fridays to visit her friend with a new baby. With a perk that many call radical flexibility, her work always gets done. This level of trust and autonomy at work must be coupled with a high degree of personal accountability. It's common for her to log on to tend to work for a couple of hours after the kids are in bed or catch up with her counterpart in Australia at 9 p.m. with a glass of wine, since that's a better time to align their calendars. That nonlinear day (at least for creative leaders like Kim) breeds loyalty and work-life integration.

Kim's preferred creative process involves a specific cycle:

This creative leadership process requires a high degree of empathy and listening. She's constantly flexing based on how her style is being perceived. Proudly introverted and neurodivergent, Kim has learned to allow time and space for people to contribute in the way that is compatible to their unique workstyle; often this means contributing to a shared document rather than relying only on live conversation. She's adapted her approach so different workstyles, personalities, and cultural backgrounds can come together and thrive—across regions and time zones. Most of all, she's a fierce advocate of the Messy Middle. A concept we'll explore more deeply in Act III, the Messy Middle can sometimes feel like a muddy slog nestled between the fresh energy of a newly started project and the closing momentum you may experience at the end.

"A lot of people are afraid of creativity because of the messy process to get there," she mused. "But if you want to be more creative, you have to get comfortable in the scribbly zone."

Not every creative leader will bring a background in the theatre or the arts. But by recognizing the experiences and skill development that occur in these spaces, we can start to replicate that training ground's environment to help build more creative teams. As Biz Stone shared with Kim, it's those environments that get you ready to deliver the show.

## BEYOND THE PHYSICAL

So far, we've explored the importance of designing an optimal physical space to foster creativity across your teams. But what about the environment that has nothing to do with the physical? The psychological climate, perhaps even more than one's physical surroundings, heavily influences the creativity of a team.

"We knew we were getting a gold mine when we hired Frances," Joe Kucera told me. "What we didn't know was that when you moved the gold mine, there was also an oil well underneath."

I met "Texas Joe" Kucera on a bus ride to a Pure Storage Legal Team offsite I was facilitating. When Joe talked about his team members, his body language came alive. He enthusiastically explained the company's patent and innovation program, which his new team member Frances Winkler had elevated as part of the Legal team (internally branded the Best Legal Team on the Planet) at Pure. The goal of the program is to provide the "easy" button for engineers, inventors, and more recently, any innovative thinker to submit a creative idea.

It was Frances who brought her fresh thinking and magnetic energy to think bigger—and more inclusively. By shifting the request from desired *patentable* ideas to *any business improvement* idea that added significant value (regardless of their technical design), they widened the funnel of innovators. Suddenly, the program felt accessible to anyone with a novel, valuable idea.

The results have been game changing. Shortly after the expanded program approach was launched, a new employee joined the team who discovered a customer-facing license agreement business challenge. Located on the box wrapper of a product inventory, this legal agreement needed frequent modification, yet was logistically cumbersome and expensive to change. While working from her home office in North Carolina, the employee considered: *What if instead of putting the full license agreement on the packaging, we simply put a QR code? That way, as updates are made to the contract, there would be zero waste in the repackaging.* By rethinking the problem and exploring a new solution, this seemingly small, creative idea led to significant business value and the reduction of environmental waste.

Given the focus on fostering creative ideas across Pure, I was curious to observe Joe's creative leadership style around this team and how he set the tone. Following the lead of the Chief Legal Officer, Joe co-created an environment that enabled Frances to reinvent, dream big, and expand the innovation program. Joe is:

- Quick to give others credit, sometimes using self-deprecating humor to build connection
- Tuned in to knowing when to stop talking and give other people the floor to speak, as well as when to interject to give ideas more energy
- Naturally curious and eager to learn
- Seeking to understand others first
- Full of unbridled enthusiasm, building on positive momentum
- Looking for the possibility, not the roadblocks

These qualities all contribute to an environment of psychological safety, where it's safe to take risks and share ideas, even before they're fully baked. Because there's no lingering concern of ideas being stolen or falling flat, they're more readily generated across his team.

Bursting with creative energy, the team applies an inclusive approach to shaping ideas and making decisions. Different opinions are valued, considered, and integrated. Joe might say, "Frances is the real expert on this, so I'll let her explain." These subtle (and sometimes not-so-subtle) cues of affirmation, recognition, and appreciation help anchor creative ideas to the business purpose as the team holds time and space for play and ideation. Their "yes, and" approach helps nascent ideas get even better.

With the backdrop of safety and a positive work environment, creative ideas are sought after and cultivated across the team. After new ideas are generated, the next challenge for the creative leader is to help prioritize and evaluate them. This often involves inviting new stakeholders to the working team. Enter stage left: the creativity gatekeeper.

## BEWARE THE CREATIVITY GATEKEEPER

A red flag goes up when I hear about organizations with Innovation Groups, Idea Labs, or Creative Hackathon weeks. It's not that these are *bad* things, per se. But they can subtly signal that creativity is only for those deemed special enough to be creative. It puts creativity in a box. The inference is that new ideas are only for designated times during the year. Or only for specific functional groups. Creativity belongs to all of us, and as a creative leader, your job is to enable it for everyone, with the right guardrails.

### CREATIVITY KILLERS:

"We'll leave the creative ideas to *x* team."

"Let's save all of our creative thinking for our team building event."

"Let's go with what's been done before since we know it works."

Creativity gatekeepers (or blockers), especially within large, complex organizations, can have an important role to play. They're often in positions to filter out irrelevant content, ideas that may be too expensive or impractical to get done. Sometimes they sniff out those Love Notes of Resistance, recognizing the grand ideas that, for whatever reason, aren't yet ready for prime time.

Dr. Jennifer Mueller, author of *Creative Change*, is quick to share how creativity blockers often have the best of intentions but naturally resist the innately foreign characteristics of a truly creative idea.[4] In other words, if there's not a level of comfort or familiarity, it's human nature for us to reject it.

Knowing the propensity to reject creativity, it often falls to the creative leader to help position new ideas as safe, accessible, and relatable. This might require:

- Walking through a potential user experience and pulling in common fact patterns and emotions

- Outlining other successful creative leaps or incremental improvements made across the company

- Sharing breakthrough inventions in a similar industry that may have looked foreign at first, but led to new operating and consumer norms (think about the leap from horses to cars, faxes to email, or Polaroid pictures to the ubiquitous use of cameras on our phones)

A creative leader's role is part persuasive storyteller, part fearless advocate, and part passionate visionary. They're the ones connecting the dots from fragile new idea to tangible benefits and business results. They shepherd the creative thought. By anticipating obstacles and courageously navigating the narrative, these leaders give ideas the light of day, structure experiments and pilot programs, risk failure yet prepare to take responsibility, and advocate for change. They help breathe life into new ideas.

Once a creative leader is aware of a creative gatekeeper, they have a specific, yet challenging job to do. Using situational awareness and persuasion, the creative leader can harness their connections to provide air cover. By reaching out to their network and socializing new ideas early, concepts that may have appeared foreign start to become more familiar. Therefore, by the time a new idea crosses the desk of the blocker, it's already in the family of possible solutions.

It's how Jen Brewer enabled the Way2Play Heroes program to get off the ground. It's how Texas Joe empowered Frances to expand Pure's Innovation Program to reach not only engineers, but also a more diverse group of innovators. It's how you can be the gateway to creativity, rather than the gatekeeper.

## BE THE LEARN-IT-ALL

Being this gateway to innovation requires an openness to learning new things. But there's a dirty little secret about having a growth mindset. It requires us to admit that we're not perfect (er, not even close). It means acknowledging we're on the path to improvement. As someone who still identifies as a high achiever, I'll admit this can be a tough pill to swallow.

Much like my discovery that insisting everyone work in the office together was not the recipe for a thriving culture, a creative leader embraces *rethinking*. This includes acknowledging that some experiments won't go as planned. During a recent workplace culture assessment, a client told me, "When things don't go as planned, the reaction across the team is usually, 'Huh. I wonder why that didn't work?' We get curious." That leap from the disappointment of a failed experiment to one of learning and extracting insights is what sets creative leaders apart.

Kim Rohrer, Principal People Partner at Oyster, shared how they kick off each group brainstorming session with not only a reminder that it's okay to fail, but also the gory details of the entire failure life cycle.

"A big part of being comfortable with creativity is about being comfortable with failure," Kim shared. "People are not taught *how* to fail. People are taught that it's *okay* to fail, but that's not the same. They have to experience failing and being okay. What does failure look like? And if I fail, what happens next?"

Kim shared her process of giving colleagues a chance to have bad ideas, throwing out ones that ultimately aren't used, yet highlighting how generating bad ideas is the only path to get to the good ones. Later, combining discarded ideas with elements of new ones often produces more useful and creative work product. This experience of learning through safe failure is another way of fostering belonging at work.

To build more belonging, we often start with shared experiences, both micro and macro. We aim to coalesce around a shared organizational purpose, all working together to solve a defined problem. We unite around the mission of the company, how we'll get there and the vision of what we want to be in the world. And we agree on the shared core values we'll each embody, the collection of behaviors that set us apart from the company across the street, the qualities that stand out to our clients, customers, and prospective future colleagues.

Sometimes these shared experiences involve a physical space—the funky conference room setup or cozy lunch breakroom. But they must involve the psychological environment where team members feel safe, empowered, and inspired to co-create. Creative leaders are quick to recognize how teams that experience safety and support elevate their work to greater heights, because even failed experiments extract value from learning.

To bring this to life for you, think about an upcoming change in your work or life that requires you to learn or step out of your comfort zone. You may be considering a job outside of what you've done before. Maybe you're a new leader figuring out when and how to collaborate effectively with your team.

Next, consider what will happen when you fail. Not *if* you fail, but when. What's the process of moving forward? How will you reflect on what you learn and adjust your approach for next time? How might getting out the bad ideas move you closer to a good one?

Creative leadership comes in all shapes and sizes. Your job is to define the challenge at hand, note any gaps from where you are to where you'd like to be, and experiment. Resist the impulse to obsess over what *could be* and celebrate the creativity you already have within your team. Be the learn-it-all.

If your team is lacking creative ideas, get curious. Do they have the right physical environment to create? Are they able to find the time to think deeply and reflect, or are they in a pressure cooker, too frantic to feel the freedom to ideate? Do they have the right incentives and processes to bring new ideas to the table, or have they offered ideas that went nowhere, demotivated by a creativity gatekeeper? Find new ways to initiate creativity. Connect the dots from small incremental improvements that, in the aggregate, make meaningful, positive change. Provide the safe container in which your team can create. Build on small wins. Recognize and celebrate the creative *process*, not just the creative product. Then keep hunting that good stuff.

## FOR YOUR TOOL KIT: TEAM SURVEY— WHAT DO YOU VALUE?

The following team survey is a template for you to use to better understand what your team values. Especially for teams experimenting with change, it's critical to keep an open door and check in with team members on what's working and what's no longer serving the team. I recommend conducting a short survey like this at least twice per year to note any changes in the sentiment across your team and spot trends. As with all of the templates and exercises I provide here, you can tailor the tone, specific language, and survey details to your team environment.

*Greetings, team! We're conducting a short survey to better understand your work environment preferences and how you rank specific benefits at work. Although we likely won't be able to accommodate all requests that are made, your input will help us continue to create and refine our team's working experience together.*

- Where do you currently work? (A = 100% onsite in the office, B= most of the time in-office, with some time remote, C = most of the time remote, with some time in-office, D = 100% remote)

- What is your preferred way of working? (A = 100% onsite in the office, B = most of the time in-office, with some time remote, C = most of the time remote, with some time in-office, D = 100% remote)

- How often would you prefer to physically come together as a team to get priorities aligned and build relationships? (A = daily, B = a few times per week, C = a few times per month, D = monthly, E = quarterly, F = semiannually, G = annually, H = coming together in person is not a priority for me)

- Please share the extent to which you agree or disagree with the following statement: I feel supported by my leader to work in the way that's best for me right now. (1 = strongly disagree, 3 = neither agree nor disagree, 5 = strongly agree)

- Please share the extent to which you agree or disagree with the following statement: I feel supported by my leader to think, share, and experiment with creative ideas. (1 = strongly disagree, 3 = neither agree nor disagree, 5 = strongly agree)

- Please rank (1 being most important to you, and 5 being least important to you) the following benefits of your work experience:

  – Flexibility to do my work at the time of day that works best for me

  – Flexibility to work in a location that works best for me

  – Autonomy to get work done in the way that works best for me

  – Learning new skills

  – Mentorship from experts

  – Growth opportunities/upward mobility

  – Competitive salary and benefits

  – Doing work that is meaningful to me

  – Belonging and social connection at work

  – Community and service at work that are aligned to my values

  – Other: open text

After reviewing the responses, consider what small, incremental adjustments might be made to demonstrate your listening. How can you share those commitments with your team? What experiments might you run to test a hypothesis? Communication about action matters, so publicly sharing those commitments can be an opportunity to engender greater trust and build shared accountability.

`SCENE FIVE SHOW NOTES`

- **Create an office like a set designer.** Creative environments require awareness of the physical space and commitment to psychological safety.

- **Offer choice.** With creative leadership, you can listen to what your employees value and build a strong culture across multiple team structures.

- **Embrace the nonlinear workday**. Find processes that support both synchronous and asynchronous work experiences.

- **Spot creativity gatekeepers** and consider how to mitigate the risk of Creativity Killers.

- **Let go of the image of perfection**; instead, embrace a growth mindset and commit to learning to foster more creativity.

As we've explored, the physical workspaces your team inhabits may impact creativity, but you have the power to influence the creative process. By officing like a set designer or creatively un-officing with intentional relationship building, you can lead creatively wherever your team sits. In the final scene of Act II, we'll dance to the jam session of collaboration, exploring how to creatively navigate team dynamics.

# COLLABORATION IS A JAM SESSION (CREATIVE TEAM DYNAMICS)

*"Improvising with a band in front of an audience is one of the purest forms of unbridled creativity. It's a mix of how much I'm willing to risk, how much I'm willing to let go, and how prepared I am, all at the same time."*

—Bob Reynolds, jazz saxophonist, composer, educator, and 3x Grammy Award–winning member of the instrumental group Snarky Puppy

In Scene Five, we explored how creative leadership shows up in our workspaces—in an office, across remote teams, and everywhere in between. In this scene, we'll dive into the team dynamics that support a collaborative, creative process.

As a self-professed type A, I don't classify myself as a cool cat. But some of my favorite memories from the Los Angeles County High School for the Arts were formed sitting in a musty practice room around effortlessly cool jazz musicians. Even in our teenage years, these skilled improvisors were adept at listening, adapting, building on themes, and yes, collaborating.

At 6:45 a.m. on the nose, I'd join my carpool buddies for the hour-long commute across the 405, 105, and 710 freeways to get to our high school on the campus of Cal State Los Angeles. Among the riders were a visual artist, dancer, percussionist, and me, a vocalist. We'd pass the time with the Smashing Pumpkins, Cranberries, and Oasis creating the soundtrack of our lives, spontaneously bursting into four-part harmony (as arts kids do).

Our percussionist carpooler always had a beat going on in his head. It wasn't even an extension of who he was; rhythm defined how he moved through the world. These jazz musicians were a special breed at LACHSA—from the trumpeters and saxophonists to electric violinists, guitarists, and bass players—each bringing a different personality to the group, yet consistently primed for an impromptu jam session, adept at diving in mid-phrase.

As much as musicians get a bad rap for having big egos, my experience with these emerging artists was the opposite. They were the music *geeks*—usually at the top of our class in Music Theory and Ear Training, with a sophisticated knowledge of the jazz greats. They knew the math behind the music but lived for the sound, a good riff, or a new melodic line. Yes, their solos were chances to shine and showcase their craft, but none of the music worked without communication, connection, and collaboration.

One of LACHSA's premier music instructors, Pat Bass (whom we called Ms. B), brought her high energy, skill, and soul to our Gospel Choir and Vocal Jazz Group. Our goal was clear: blend our disparate voices as one—this wasn't a space to stand out. We worked tirelessly to meld and unify our sound. Demanding exceptional pitch and tonality, Ms. B kept us all in sync, not just in rhythm, but also through our shared breath control, which influenced our dynamics, or how loud or soft each tone was.

Ms. B was meticulous about where to breathe (insert check mark) and how to approach lyrical phrasing. As a routine winner of the Monterey Jazz Festival, our hard work, hours of rehearsal, and commitment to excellence paid off. With a no-nonsense style, Ms. B wouldn't tolerate a whiff of disrespect but loved us abundantly. She had a gift for bringing out the best in each of us, nurturing our unique potential, while insisting our sound was fused.

You probably see where this is going, but it's a parallel not commonly made. In your work, you may be leading a team comprised of people with different strengths, backgrounds, and work styles. As you struggle to find the perfect blend of voices to execute your organizational vision and mission, thorny work obstacles crop up that you never expected. Perhaps your team goal has been sabotaged by circumstances beyond your control (hello, pandemic or recession). Even facing these unforeseen obstacles, your job is to tap into the potential of each individual while elevating creativity across the team.

As creative leaders, *we* are the conductors. We set the tone. In Scene Eight, I'll go into more detail about how being a conductor helps strengthen your organization's creativity culture. You may find yourself leading a team full of individual superstars, but if they struggle to play off and support each other to blend their individual voices, those lofty objectives are doomed to fail. The creative leader can spot the unique needs across the team and coalesce them around a shared purpose. Your collaborative teamwork becomes the music, the soundtrack to your company's journey.

Then you can jam.

## DEATH (AND LIFE) BY ADAGIO

Collaboration isn't only about music. It's also about movement. At the start of 2022, I committed to getting my 40-something-year-old self back to the ballet studio. Mind you, it had been a good twenty years since I'd donned a leotard and tights, but I was determined to gift myself that time to reconnect with a past love.

The experience (for the most part) has been thrilling. I don't kid myself that I'm very good, but that's not the point. To make shapes with the music, shake the cobwebs from that part of my brain, and turn off the rumination about other aspects of life has been liberating.

There's one part of the class that always kills me, though: *adagio*.

Adagio means slow. It's the drippy molasses counterpoint to my carbonated pop rocks sugar. And though its goal is to appear effortless, adagio takes great strength and focus.

It's stunning how challenging it is to slow down, take a breath, and let a process run its course, in all segments of life. I'm famous for pushing the gas (now electric) pedal to reach a goal faster. But adagio teaches us to extend and savor each moment, to soak up all that good stuff—even when it's taxing and uncomfortable.

At work, you've probably heard, "You've got to slow down to speed up." Sometimes the fastest course to realizing our team goals requires taking our time and reflecting. We're urged to stay open to taking a different path entirely, rather than rushing on the road we're on. There are a few things we can do (in lieu of returning to ballet class) to help slow things down:

- **Observe**. In rushed or panicked moments, consider zooming out to objectively recognize what's happening. For example, "I notice my body is feeling stress. There's a work item I'm a bit behind on, and my kids are screaming. Plus, I'm a bit hungry. These are all playing a role in how my body is feeling, but these conditions are temporary." After sharing our needs with our co-collaborators, we can start changing the conditions (at least the ones we have control over) and observe again, like a scientist.

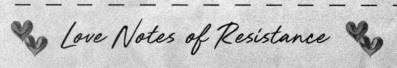

*Love Notes of Resistance*

Love Notes of Resistance often show up in my body first, where I feel itchy or uncomfortable in work I'm approaching. I might notice I'm more easily distracted by my phone, or hunger, or other physiological needs.

One way to calm this sensation is to build a ritual to move through it. I might light a candle, drink a glass of water, or pour a cup of tea before beginning the work.

- **Ruthlessly prioritize**. A boss of mine once shared there's no such thing as 10 priorities. If everything's a priority, then nothing is a priority. Look at your to-do list and circle two to three key things that *must* get done. Once those are handled, tackle another three. This process also forces us to get real about what's truly important versus unimportant (yet seemingly urgent) things on our plate.

- **Practice saying no**. For the people-pleasers among us, this isn't always easy. But saying no can also mean passing the baton to others who are ready and able to say yes! I stepped down after five years of serving on the LACHSA Foundation Board, an organization I still love to support. But in the quest to find more balance in my day-to-day, I recruited new board members to invite their fresh energy and talents. Then it was time for me to step aside. That turned out to be a remarkably positive outcome for the board, new board members, and me!

- **Get perspective**. To fully gain the benefits of slowing down, we've all (hopefully) experienced the good stuff that happens after a vacation away from home. We break up our routines and see the world through a new lens. What I find magical about those escapes is the window into other ways of *being*. In many ways, the harried tempo of our lives is a choice. Let's remember we have more control over that pace than we may realize.

When we collaborate with others, slowing down is often the best way to find our team's rhythm together. It's how we fully see the talents on the team to let them shine.

## BUILD A PHRASE

Dance is often a solo act, but Nora Brickman reminded me how it can be the ultimate collaborative process. At age 12, Nora and I met when we performed in a production of *Annie* together at the Santa Barbara Civic Light Opera. She played the role of July, the plucky orphan and friend to my Annie. After the show closed, our offstage pen pal friendship manifested into six shoeboxes' worth of handwritten letters about life, our latest crushes, and the pursuit of our creative dreams: mine in musical theatre, and hers in the world of dance.

Nora recalled a generative creative process as a company member in the Seán Curran Dance Company in her twenties. She and a few other dancers spent the summer in Maine, commissioned to create a new dance piece. Rather than choreograph the whole thing and teach it to company members, Seán Curran embarked on a collaborative journey, a process broken down into bite-sized pieces he called "Build a Phrase."

First, he instructed pairs of dancers to go away, each choreographing eight bars of music. That was it. Create eight bars, then teach it to your partner. Next, they all assembled and strung each eight-bar phrase together, smoothing out the edges so the piece felt more connected and cohesive. Then Seán gave them the next challenge. In *new* pairs, dancers were challenged to create the *inverse* of what they originally choreographed—interpreting inverse as they wished.

"Now we're doing cool lifts and floor work," Nora reflected. "Suddenly we have so much material! Plenty of choreographers head into a studio and set what they've already envisioned. But Seán's approach enabled us to feel even more invested because we had a stake in the creation of it."

The Build a Phrase process demonstrates Seán's inclusive style of collaborative leadership. We want team members to feel personally invested—that they have skin in the game. In this example, each dancer put fingerprints on the work. They personalized their responses to the challenge, collaborating to blend a mix of ideas. Slowing things down into digestible pieces ultimately sped up the generation of a longer piece of choreography. As a result, the whole company gained buy-in and ownership in the process.

In your work life, you may face large initiatives that have many complex components to them. Perhaps you're launching a new marketing campaign to acquire new clients. Maybe you're bringing a new product to market and need to develop clear, compelling use cases. You could be working at a law firm, exploring an M&A transaction for a client. Whatever big project you're embarking on, a creative leader can break things down into more digestible parts and inspire team members to put their unique stamp on it. Sure, the edges will need to be smoothed out to form a cohesive approach. But by giving team members skin in the game and inviting them to create *their eight bars*, you'll discover greater commitment, investment, and an authentic reflection of the team.

Today, business moves at the speed of light. You may have set Q1 goals that are suddenly put on hold due to a strategic opportunity emerging in Q2. New shiny initiatives quickly take the place of projects that were last month's top focus. Before your next team meeting, consider pumping the brakes to take stock of your team's top three priorities. Slow down to get that alignment. Ask your fellow leaders what *they* believe the priorities are, and fully listen. Take a breath. Get buy-in.

Then clarify expectations. Confirm deliverables timelines. Walk through who's responsible for what with a Responsible-Accountable-Consulted-Informed (RACI) framework or Recommend-Agree-Perform-Input-Decide (RAPID) decision-making process. Pinpoint where creativity is needed to think differently about a problem and find space to explore these new—maybe even off-the-wall—ideas. While it's easy to forget this seemingly simple practice, it has the potential to move your team from a cacophony of different sounds to one unified voice.

I'm not sure if I'll ever master adagio in the dance studio, and that's okay with me. Still, I'm committed to showing up and trying. You, too, can do the hard work to strengthen the muscles it takes to slow down. You can sharpen your focus, break down the components of your next big challenge, and invite others to bring their creative expression to the dance of work.

## GAINING PERSPECTIVE TO COLLABORATE

Today, most of the business challenges we face impact a diverse range of stakeholders. We're interdependent in how we operate—disparate departments and regions all influence each other. Collaboration is paramount to solving these complex problems. In Act I, we examined how perspective taking can be a catalyst to more creative thinking. Next, we'll explore how leaders who sharpen the skill of perspective taking can enable empathy and enhance collaborative problem solving.

Niki Armstrong is a client and executive leader at Pure Storage, a high-growth global technology company. Tall and slender, Niki's signature chestnut-brown bun—artfully placed on top of her head—further extends her striking stature. Throughout her career and life, Niki has embraced her flair for creativity. From dancing in her youth, to maneuvering from law firm life to in-house practice, to launching her own legal consulting practice, Niki eventually rose to her current role of Chief Legal Officer. While co-managing a busy home life with her husband, two sons, and dog Binx, she dreams of one day retiring to her farm on the East Coast, filling her days with gardening projects, miniature horses, and lazy afternoons reading.

For now, though, she embraces the challenge of bringing more creative thinking to her legal and compliance department, helping it nearly double in size in the past year to better serve the rapidly growing technology organization it supports. It's the home where Texas Joe and Frances have been empowered to expand the company's Innovation Program, amplifying Pure's core value of creativity by committing to continuous improvement. Niki instinctually knew that with the right creative mindset, her team could rethink how to get work done in a more effective way. And they could do so in a way that feels collaborative *and* builds human connection.

One of Niki's strengths is her ability to create a clear vision that leads to a positive outcome. She can see the line. By empowering talent and removing obstacles, Niki's learned how a small shift in perspective can yield a different (and better) result. At her team offsite, we included perspective-taking as one of the creative problem-solving techniques to address problem statements. Cross-functional breakout teams were given a different creative technique with which to approach or solve each problem, along with a few underlying discussion questions:

- **Root-cause analysis**. What's the potential source of the problem? What would need to change to address this root cause? Who are the stakeholders involved and what is their relationship to the root cause?

- **Divergent thinking + mind mapping**. What are the emotions and downstream consequences of this problem? How would these feelings change if the problem were solved, and what would be the business impact?

- **2x2 prioritization matrix**. List the potential solutions relating to the problem. Consider small micro-changes as well as big ambitious ones. Next, create a 2x2 grid with cost/risk on the *x*-axis, and business impact on the *y*-axis. Finally, assign your solutions to the appropriate quadrant (low cost/risk and low impact, low cost/risk and high impact, high cost/risk and low impact, and high cost/risk and high impact). Circle the solutions that are low cost/risk and high impact—do these first!

- **RAPID decision-making**. Imagine you had a solution identified for your problem. Consider a framework for deciding how to make this solution a reality.

  **Recommend**: Who will create the initial proposals and recommendations?

  **Agree**: Who must agree to the proposals from the Recommend group?

  **Perform**: Who will execute the work following the decision?

  **Input**: Who provides information and facts to the Recommend group?

  **Decide**: Who's the person who has the authority to make the decision?

- **Perspective-taking**. How do different stakeholders in your company (e.g., sales, marketing, finance, product, HR) think about this problem? Next, think of a leader you admire outside of your industry. How might *they* approach this problem?

- **SWOT analysis**. Consider a leading solution to the problem. What are the *strengths* of the solution? What are the potential *weaknesses*? What *opportunities* lie within this solution? Are there any *threats* to consider before implementing it?

This collaborative exercise rotated teams to different table stations to practice different creative thinking techniques. Across the two days, a total of six problem statements were addressed in six creative ways:

## DAY 1:

Round one: Problem Statement 1 (25 mins + 5 min break)
   Round two: Rotate and address Problem Statement 2.
(25 mins + 5 min break)
   Round three: Rotate and address Problem Statement 3.
(25 mins + 5 min break)
   Debrief the three problem statements approached six different
ways. (45 mins)

## DAY 2:

Round one: Problem Statement 4 (25 mins + 5 min break)
   Round two: Rotate and address Problem Statement 5.
(25 mins + 5 min break)
   Round three: Rotate and address Problem Statement 6.
(25 mins + 5 min break)
   Debrief three problem statements approached six different ways.
(45 mins)
   *To access more detailed instructions, check out the
Recommended Resources section.*

"I never would have thought of looking at my problem this way," one participant shared. "I usually don't stop to think how different people may be experiencing this issue."

Another leader bravely admitted, "I'm embarrassed that I usually think of myself as the smartest person in the room. But now, after going through this exercise, it's clear I have a lot to learn from others. It's changed the way I'll think about approaching these kinds of challenges."

These reflections revealed an important insight: We often get so stuck in our own lane, with our own life experience, that we fail to seek out the different stories from the people virtually (or literally!) sitting right next to us. Collaboration unlocks better creative solutions.

In your work, you may identify a shared problem statement like: *As a new hybrid team, we struggle to know how and when to communicate, which wastes precious time and creates frustration.* Maybe your business problem relates to growing a segment of your clients, or how to improve your recruitment process to efficiently attract the right talent. Regardless of the challenge at hand, chances are different people have varying relationships with the issue. By examining diverse ways of addressing the problem that incorporate distinct (yet relevant) perspectives, you can find new connections to potential solutions.

As we collaborate to solve problems, we access different parts of our brain. Rather than stay in the prefrontal cortex's linear decision-making zone, we engage our brain's imagination. While co-building a vision with others, the occipital cortex (at the back of the brain) helps us recreate pictures or images, and the posterior precuneus (between our brain's hemispheres) not only conjures up images, but also makes sense of them.[6]

Okay, before your eyes glaze over, I'm not here to give a science lesson. There won't be an anatomy quiz. As we explored in Act I, warming up our imaginations invites a detailed approach. To fully flesh out the rich layers of a human experience, we need to think *small* as well as big. Vivid details help light up different parts of our brain, dislodging potential stuck-ness. For example, if we want to imagine our customer's pain points before our software product makes their lives easier, we might empathize with their experience *before* they encounter our solution. They might think, *(Sigh), I've been wasting hours on this issue, and I'm so frustrated! It's already 5 p.m. and I'm going to be late to pick up my kid from daycare again . . .*

Imagining these micro-moments may lead to bigger insights. Who knows, maybe your marketing tagline becomes Never Be Late to Daycare Pickup Again. Creative thinking doesn't happen in a *specific* place in our mind. It's activated when different parts of our brain work *together*—and as we collaborate with others. Creative leaders can help encourage and model this way of thinking.

## CAN'T WAIT FOR PERFECT

Collaboration, in its purest form, requires imperfection. It means jumping in to contribute even when you're unsure. It requires vulnerability, an openness to truly be seen by others. Collaboration calls you to speak up before your role is fully defined, navigating the dance between building on others' ideas and fully expressing your own.

Dancer Nora Brickman's husband, Bob Reynolds, has become an expert collaborator. A professional jazz saxophone player, Bob juggles a thriving career as a musician and entrepreneur with a busy family life. Playing the sax at Bob's level requires disciplined practice; even a day of missed rehearsal can cause muscles and skills to atrophy. With a near-obsession for experimentation, Bob applies his creative discipline to unpredictable spaces with hand-picked co-creators; each live jazz performance is a bespoke expression of their love of the music.

Bob has crafted the recipe for collaboration in different spaces in his life: regular gigs at the Baked Potato near his Los Angeles home, touring with Snarky Puppy (and previously with John Mayer, Larry Carlton, and other artists), leading his own band at gigs across the globe, and partnering with Nora as Dad to their two kids. It all requires collaboration.

I asked Bob to share the key ingredient to a successful band.

"Listening," he shared with zero hesitation. "Ears wide open. Yes, there's a baseline level of faculties, but listening means the difference between floating *up here* or being heavy *down here*. It doesn't have to do with the venue or the audience—it has to do with their abilities individually and what we're able to do collectively. Is it going to match or exceed what I have? And then, are they ready to set that aside and not show off, but yield to the context of *this* night, with *this* group of people, in *this* place, with *this* audience?"

Effective collaboration isn't about finding the *perfect* outcome. It's about discovering value from a unique combination of people and places, while seizing the moment. What struck me about how Bob described collaboration was just how well it applies to the business world. We hope that our team members are focused on their craft and bringing their individual best to the table. But we also come together to be bigger than the sum of those individual parts. When that chemistry is off, it's obvious and palpable. It's like organ-rejection. And as difficult as touring on the road or building a business can be with a team, that chemistry must be intact.

"As a band leader, I'm always taking that temperature," Bob reflected. "*Where are we? Who's hungry? What's reasonable right now?* You can't make the music if the music isn't coming from a place of love."

**CREATIVITY BOOSTER:**

A lot of us fall in love with our solutions. But what does it look like to fall in love with a problem? Think about a leadership problem you have. Take five minutes to consider how you can shower it with love by thinking more collaboratively. How might you empower your team to co-build a solution, bringing in their individual talents?

That place of love is essential when leading any team—a start-up, a band, or a large company's marketing department. It's what fuels the group to tinker a bit more to improve the product before it gets released, even when everyone's exhausted. It's what allows you to engage in a difficult feedback conversation that ends with mutual respect and an even stronger relationship. That love informs your purpose, gets you through the Messy Middle, and helps move things forward even amid inevitable setbacks.

Bob shared how Snarky Puppy's band leader has mastered improving collaboration by tending to each bandmate's Most Important Thing. Everyone has a different one. For the keyboardist, it's critically important to get to the hotel room before soundcheck. Even if just to put down their bags for a quick moment, it helps him feel grounded. So the band tries to arrange travel times accordingly. For another member, the Most Important Thing is boarding airlines early to secure overhead storage for their instruments. Whereas some members aren't carrying on instruments, so it doesn't matter when they board, it matters a whole bunch to those who are! The band began flying the same airline as much as possible to accrue loyalty points, so early boarding is the default.

Another bandmate's Most Important Thing is food. Specifically, managing blood sugar levels. Soundcheck runs smoother for everyone if stomachs aren't empty, so more attention is devoted to the band's hospitality rider so that healthy snack options are available for the band and crew *before* soundcheck.

As a leader, it's our job to know each person's Most Important Thing to facilitate collaboration. Sure, it's not always possible to accommodate each person's needs. But when your team sees you go out of your way and knows you care for them as individuals, you can work more effectively. That's a great secret of collaboration: Having individuals' needs met is the foundation for everyone to operate from a place of safety and love.

I first heard Bob's track "Can't Wait for Perfect" during his late-night set in the West Village of New York City in the early 2000s. A decade later, Bob's creativity and improvisation spilled into entrepreneurship—his subscription service business offers remote coaching to other saxophone players around the world. Now with over ten years of business-building under his belt, Bob sends a different marketing email out each time he clicks send. He's constantly experimenting, tinkering, and trying something new. His business model expands beyond music instruction—Bob fosters a music *community*, which is inherently collaborative.

In the workplace, we have similar opportunities to connect, collaborate, and build community. Rather than view our colleagues as would-be competition, we can align on the shared purpose of the organization to lift all boats. We can define success not based on our individual accomplishments, but by what the team can produce as a collective. This is where creative collaboration shines.

## KNOWING YOUR ROLE

In a band, your role to play is fairly evident. The drummer keeps the beat. The bassist keeps the key and frames the song. Keyboards and horns add layers to the melody, creating the storyline of the song. In business, each role on your team needs to be just as clear—it may just take a little more effort to define it.

One client shared the dark side of collaboration. He feared that *too much* collaboration is born from a lack of structure and leads to chaos. Working in a contracts group, he described a scenario where all members of the team were invited to contribute to drafting a standard agreement in a shared document. Over the course of weeks, lawyers and paralegals jumped in to redline the document, picking apart each other's drafting styles, haphazardly commenting with no organization or direction. What could have been a relatively straightforward process was long and drawn out, frustrating all contributors. Like a jazz band, effective collaboration requires knowing your part to play. Clear structure, guidance, and swim lanes facilitate more effective collaboration.

Imagine for a minute you're interviewing a new team member. You may define roles as:

- **The Culture Carrier**—the role who represents your team culture and evaluates if the candidate brings compatible attributes
- **The Skills Champion**—the role to evaluate if the candidate has the mindset, skills, and experiences to effectively thrive in the position
- **The Seller**—the role in charge of marketing the opportunity and company experience, bringing some razzle dazzle
- **The Closer**—the role responsible for the recruiting process, managing next steps, and facilitating all communications with the candidate

Each member of this recruitment team has a defined (and distinct) role to play to drive to a positive outcome. It's true, the Skills Champion may get questions about the company culture, but the primary role is to drill down into the candidate's experience, ensuring they've got what the role requires. Similarly, the Closer could spot a red flag related to skills and experience but is primarily focused on the recruitment process. By having clear roles, all bases are covered.

What sets great bands apart from mediocre ones is communication. Through unspoken cues, they know when it's the last sixteen bars or when they're heading back to the chorus. They've practiced the structure and direction of the song but use their instincts to let the audience's energy guide the ultimate creative experience. Each band member stays attuned to the dynamics of the moment. They play off each other. That might mean letting the keyboardist continue her solo four bars longer—imagine what may emerge! With effective listening, adaptability, and coordination, they stay in sync.

As you lead your team at work, you can watch for similar communication cues. You may be facilitating a meeting where you sense resistance, and pause to invite more questions, ensuring all voices are heard. Maybe you recognize one of your team members is overwhelmed, so you take steps to load-balance and find relief—or shift a deadline to allow for more time and space to get the work done. As you each play your parts, you can celebrate the unique value each person brings to the group, along with how these talents complement each other. Staying in rhythm, the team fluidly communicates, shifting direction when the business (or team) calls for it. This is collaboration at its best.

# SCENE DIALOGUE FOR COLLABORATIVE TEAM DYNAMICS

**SETTING:**

(The LEADERSHIP TEAM stares silently at the Zoom screen. RUBEN, the leader of the team, wrings his hands, unsure of what to say next.)

**RUBEN**

Let's recap what we've covered so far. We've talked about our upcoming OKRs—

**SAL**

That's Objectives and Key Results, L.J.

**L.J.**

(rolls her eyes)

Yeah, got it-

**RUBEN**

Yes, the OKRs for Q2 are getting locked. But one of the things we committed to tackling last quarter was identifying innovation initiatives, which no one had the time and space for. What's up?

**SAL**

My suggestion is L.J. just runs with it as the Chief People and Innovation Officer. It's hers to own anyway.

**L.J.**

Whoa, hold up. We talked about how a culture of innovation belongs to all of us, right? I'm happy to be the project manager and lead the design, but this stuff isn't going to work if you all don't have some skin in the game.

**MARTA**

I fundamentally agree, but I'll also admit to struggling with how to bring some of this to life as the head of Finance.

(laughs)

Are you sure you really want innovation from my department?

**L.J.**

Okay, fair enough. And yes, I believe we do. We've all talked about the vision to automate more of our process-heavy workflows—elevating our teams to do more strategic thinking.

**RUBEN**

Where might we collaborate more effectively if you're getting stuck? Can we all imagine for a minute that the innovation projects are already underway? Think about it. It's a year from now, and we're finally seeing some of the downstream business impact. What does that look like for each of you?

**SAL**

Sign me up for that. I want my product team thinking BIG—and they need more time for that. Less in the weeds on refining what we know already works. Who knows, maybe we can finally go after that totally new customer segment...

**RUBEN**

Awesome. What else?

**L.J.**

Do you think it'd be helpful to have more defi-nition around our innovation program? Maybe our team could do a roadshow—so people can get inspired and have examples of what we're after across the org?

**MARTA**

That would be wonderful, yes. I envision my team spending a lot less time on whole categories

of work—that makes me think that maybe I can
host a brainstorming session to get my colleagues' ideas, too. I'm up for committing to
two defined experiments next quarter. Okay, I
see it now. I'll put it in my OKRs.

**(END OF SCENE)**

In this scene dialogue, a leadership team is struggling to find their rhythm in collaborating. When the leader shifts perspectives and has them envision the future state, ideas start to flow. They start playing off each other cooperatively, rather than competitively. Effective collaboration demands that we set our egos aside to move through the discomfort of unknowns and uncertainty. That's what enables creative thinking. As a creative leader, you can not only bring out creativity in those you lead, but you'll start to fan the flames for a broader creativity culture.

## FOR YOUR TOOL KIT: A VIRTUAL SESSION ON COLLABORATION

The following 60-minute exercise can help you strengthen collaboration with your team, especially if you're distributed across regions. It's designed for teams of about 8 to 20, but fewer or more team members can work by making small adjustments.

First, you (playing the role of the creative leader and facilitator) welcome everyone to the session. Clearly state your objectives over the next 60 minutes: to walk away with new tools and techniques to effectively collaborate with each other going forward. In these opening remarks, you may wish to include a story of a time your team collaborated effectively, where multiple voices were incorporated to create a positive business outcome, which you'd like to build on. If appropriate, you may also choose to reference a time when you and your team *didn't* collaborate effectively, which led to disappointment across the team. If you choose the latter scenario, be careful not to cast blame. When shared with humility, it can be a powerful way of holding yourself accountable to improvement.

With either option, aim to stay positive, upbeat, and focused on the learning opportunity ahead. (5 minutes)

Next, ask the team their response to the following prompt: *What are the core ingredients of effective collaboration?* You might use a virtual whiteboard or shared Google doc to invite different ideas, or simply use the chat feature in your collaboration platform. The responses may range from: *Listening, good communication, taking responsibility,* and *giving credit to others,* to *overcoming resistance to change.* Allow space for all voices to be heard or contribute. If anyone's contributions are unclear, be sure to ask for clarification or an example to bring it to life. (10 minutes)

Next, share a workplace scenario. I've included an example below, but you may choose to craft your own, tailoring it to your team's common situations. Be sure to clarify any confusion and address any questions before you split into breakout groups. (5 minutes)

In your breakout groups, imagine you're a member of the following team: (1) Taylor, the creative team leader who has the biggest influence and connection to other functional team leaders; (2) Charlie, the analytical subject matter expert; (3) Blair, the supportive change management coach; and (4) Danny, the junior execution-oriented doer.

Your team has been asked to deliver a presentation to the rest of the company that outlines your top three strategic priorities. These priorities should include a connection to the organization's goals, as well as specific ways you plan to measure or track whether the priorities are yielding desired business results.

Your challenge is to create a strategic approach to building this presentation that includes a vision, clear timelines, and owners.

Instructions: First define what roles you'll each play (do your best to play that part, rather than slip into your real-life role). To collaborate, first discuss how you plan to approach the challenge. Clarify who's doing what. Create a space for all ideas and voices to be heard. Play to each person's strength. By the end of the breakout, aim to have an approach to the challenge to share with the rest of the team.

In breakout groups of four, use your team's real-world priorities as material for this exercise.

If you're the leader of the group, you may choose to float, dropping in on multiple breakout groups, or you may decide to participate as a full-fledged member of a breakout group. If you choose the latter and are among a group of four, be conscious to select a role that is not Taylor, the team leader. (20 minutes)

The purpose of this exercise isn't to create an end-product. It's about building a collaborative process and practicing behaviors. Collaboration can be messy. Sometimes confusing, the goal of collaborating is to identify each person's strengths and find ways to incorporate them, so they feel invested in the process. It can feel challenging, especially if there's a looming deadline or pressure to perform. However, much like Seán Curran's Build a Phrase, it's a powerful method of creating buy-in and integrating different talents.

After coming back together as a large group, invite sharing and reflection with a few discussion prompts:

- What did you notice about how you started the exercise?
- What parts of the exercise were most challenging?
- What felt easy?
- Did you slip into your own personal style on the team or play the role as it was assigned to you?
- What insights did you gain from this mode of collaborating?
- How might your insights apply to the real work you do on your team?

Time permitting, you may invite a team to share what they were able to produce (note, this part is optional). First explore *how* they came up with the work product. Did one team member do the lion's share of the work? Was there any tension or conflict that emerged during the process? Do your best as a team not to evaluate the work product, but instead reflect on the collaboration process. (18 minutes)

As the leader of the exercise, close with the acknowledgment that collaboration can be messy. Invite any final insights about the importance of working well together as a team. Leave space for team members to follow up with you one-on-one to share ideas about what would help them to collaborate more effectively as a team. Share your appreciation for their willingness to step out of their comfort zones and practice a new skill. (2 minutes)

## SCENE SIX SHOW NOTES

- Creative leaders **set the tone** for the group dynamic.
- **Slow down to speed up** in the dance of work.
- **Observe, ruthlessly prioritize, practice saying "no,"** and **get different perspectives.**
- Know your bandmates' **Most Important Thing.**
- **Listen, listen, listen**—and know your part to play.
- **Keep practicing!**

Facilitating effective team collaboration elevates your work as a creative leader. By slowing down to empower each team member to contribute their unique creative talent while building strong chemistry across the team, your projects can transcend the ordinary. You can make way for extraordinary results.

Time to stretch for a final brief intermission before we begin Act III.

[HOUSE LIGHTS RISE]

# ACT II. INTERMISSION

Creative leadership rarely happens by accident. Like any skill, it's practiced, refined, and strengthened through painstaking trial and error. In Act II, we met creative theatre directors, CEOs, and heads of Legal and Compliance functions. We observed creativity in trust building, strengthening community, and collaborating as a team.

Creativity shows up in newly formed, fast-growing teams, as well as those that are shrinking due to business conditions. It plays a role in teams that produce creative work products (think design firms or entertainment companies), work in product development or marketing, as well as traditional corporate cost centers like human resources, legal, and compliance. The overarching commitment in these spaces is to improve the team's work process and results by engaging novel, useful ideas.

Now that we've covered the core components of creative leadership, let's set the stage for how these concepts will come to life across your organization's creativity culture.

The first principle is to build connection. When psychological safety is prevalent across multiple teams in the organization, creative ideas can bubble up without the threat of negative consequences. Connection also requires forming authentic, human relationships across teams.

The second principle is innovative thinking. Lots of people think about innovation as the invention of the iPhone or Uber. But innovation happens at microlevels within teams and organizations, too. It's what led to the Pure Storage employee's rethink of the user license agreement wrapped around a product box to be replaced by a QR code. As a creative leader, you can help drive the practices and rewards to inspire creative thinking and innovation—across all levels and functions.

Third, the principle of inclusion has a big impact on creativity culture. Feeling that sense of belonging to the team, organization, and broader community drives employee satisfaction. Without it, it's challenging to realize engagement, let alone solicit your employees' best creative ideas.

When connection, innovation, and inclusion are all working together, creativity culture can flourish. That's when colleagues feel safe, inspired, and have a strong sense of belonging. Act III will introduce more tools and frameworks you can bring to the individuals you lead, but also to your broader organization. You may not yet be in the C-suite or be ready to implement some of these strategies, and that's okay. Today's creative leadership—and culture change in general—belongs to everyone. In our new world of work, you're invited to apply these creativity principles in the way that feels most contextually relevant to you.

Get ready for more learning. As you stop and observe Love Notes of Resistance that may come up, be curious and keep asking yourself questions. Reflect on how *your individual creativity* may contribute to the broader company culture. That's creative leadership in action. That's how you take a small spark and add creative kindling and love to the rest of your team. It's time to set your creative leadership ablaze.

# Act III.

# The Bonfire: Fostering Creativity Culture across Your Organization

**B**efore the curtain call, most audiences hope the story concludes in a way that's satisfying: the Hero has wrestled with a conflict, overcome an obstacle, and the narrative transitions to dénouement. But the final stage of any creative process often looks less like an ending, and more like an invitation to a new beginning. With more knowledge and awareness than we had before, the fog lifts to reveal the daunting height of the next mountain to climb. After sparking courage and confidence to express our individual creativity, and successfully building the blaze of creative leadership, surely fostering creativity culture across our organization in Act III will be easy, right?

Building this bonfire is harder than it appears.

When you're working in a creativity culture, it can feel a bit like you—and your fellow colleagues—have been sprinkled with pixie dust. It's magical. It can also be deceptively difficult to replicate.

Back when Axiom's offices were still on Spring Street in Soho, one year-end company party was a scavenger hunt around New York City. Fun-fact trivia clues about our workmates and business history led our competitive teams to different destinations: Central Park to discover a medieval knight, up three flights for a hint in our IT director's apartment, around the corner to our local pub's jukebox.

After locating each landmark to snatch our next clue, we were led back to our office's eighth-floor loft to perform a skit complete with props and costumes fit for pirates. Fashioning eye patches and hooks, our *All-Hands* meeting got renamed to *Some Hands*, forever memorializing the abundant laughter of the special night. The celebration ended with our Soho workspace transformed to a late-night disco dance party, our group expanded to include our broader community—spouses, roommates, and friends of the company, all sharing in the social experience.

Beyond the skill of throwing a memorable big bash, back then our team's creativity was boundless. From designing themed sales spiff competitions (a way to generate a burst of activity among sales teams), and deejaying Friday after-noon slow jams, to crafting colorful Olympics garb for the global games and anointing colleagues with nicknames (Manchego the Cobbler, Fabian the Angry Curtain Maker)—we all worked hard while building meaningful experiences together. Creativity fueled our business. We invented new ways of doing things and experimented with different team structures and ways to help our clients accomplish their goals. We challenged each other, celebrated together, and commiserated when the ball didn't bounce our way.

Work didn't feel like, well, work. We usually blew through the goals we set, left basking in team wins. With the intense pace of a start-up, I'll admit it felt draining at times, but co-creating that business together was the ultimate reward. We were clear on our company purpose and primed to get our hands dirty building the company. As we delighted our clients, bonded as a team in the trenches, and took time to learn and reflect, our corporate growth felt inevitable. There was irresistibility to it. That's the business case for a creativity culture.

I recognize it may sound like I'm merely romanticizing the past. After all, many of us pine away for the time in our lives when we're building career momentum before the infiltration of many of life's stressors: aging parents, sick kids, or a mortgage to pay. Even after separating my memories from a more carefree stage of life, I can't help but reflect on the vibrant aspects of our creativity culture: a clear organizational why, a group of people who respected and helped each other learn, a shared penchant for experimenting and innovating. The ingredients were all there.

As I shared during our last Intermission, I've found creativity culture has three pillars: connection, innovation, and inclusion. If you have connection and innovation but lack inclusion, you get an *insular culture*, one that may lack perspective and create an echo chamber. With connection and inclusion but no innovation, you can find yourself with a *family culture*—not a *bad* environment, per se—but one that might stagnate or be slow to change. Finally, if your company embraces innovation and inclusion but lacks connection, that can lead to a *transactional culture*, one that's transient, with high turnover. When all three elements of connection, innovation, and inclusion are present, that's when creativity culture can thrive.

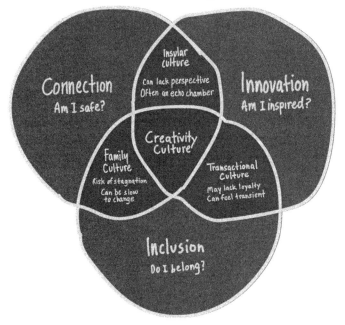

# What Is *Creativity Culture?*

**Connection** — Am I safe?

**Innovation** — Am I inspired?

**Inclusion** — Do I belong?

Insular culture — Can lack perspective. Often an echo chamber

Family Culture — Risk of stagnation. Can be slow to change

Transactional Culture — May lack loyalty. Can feel transient

Creativity Culture

## Creativity Culture

- Strong psychological safety and trust across the organization
- Alignment and communication around organizational purpose, vision, mission, and values
- Awareness of how physical space and environments impact creative output
- Emphasis on collaboration and the creative process in addition to the creative work product
- Experimentation woven into core business operations
- Time set aside for learning and conscious reflection
- Investment in authentic relationship building and information sharing
- Shared focus and accountability of behaviors that promote diversity, equity, inclusion, and belonging

## WHERE CREATIVITY MEETS PROCESS

There comes a point in a scaling start-up when each core team member is no longer doing a little bit of everything. Gone are the days when everyone weighs in on every decision and has a hand in every function. The early start-up stage of *collapsing around the ball* conjures up the image of four-year-olds playing soccer. Not yet knowing how to play positions on the field, the little athletes all cluster around the ball, which consequently goes nowhere. In business (and sports), it helps to know your position. With the aid of a playbook, you find guidance or preferred ways of operating. But too much process can be a Creativity Killer.

## CREATIVITY KILLERS:

Process that is rigid and lacking any personalization
Overengineered workflows
Roles so narrowly scoped that there's no variety of work
Obsessive time-tracking, so there's no incentive to stop and think or reflect

To be clear, I don't think process is inherently a bad thing. In fact, I love a good process; it helps avoid reinventing the wheel, offers clarity and specialization, and outlines shared expectations of performance. It enables early-stage companies to discover efficiencies of scale—a good thing to cultivate after your company gets its sea legs.

But process can also squeeze creativity out of the system. It can keep us doggedly committed to following the script, rather than improvising and dancing in the moment. It can strip spontaneous joy from our work.

If I'm hitting close to home, it may be because it's a common phenomenon; I've seen the pendulum swing between too little and too much process across multiple industries, company sizes, and maturity stages. Process is often introduced when there's a defined need to be more efficient, and I get the impetus. The pressure leaders feel to show continuous improvement and justify the investment in their team's resources can be crippling. But when a creativity culture is desired, a place where team members across the organization feel safe, inspired, and have a sense of belonging to bring their best creative thinking, too much process can throw water on the fire we've worked so hard to ignite.

As we ready ourselves for Act III, you might be wondering: *What's the process for combining my individual creativity and creative leadership skills to impact my broader organizational culture?* Soon, I'll offer you the frameworks and tools to build this bonfire. After consulting with hundreds of different organizations across industries, locations, sizes, and stages, I've seen creativity help people thrive in unexpected places. Creativity at work can benefit law firms, consulting firms, technology, design, media, and entertainment companies. It can show up in venture capital firms, healthcare, consumer products companies, and financial institutions.

You could be sitting in the C-suite, ready to green-light a big culture transformation initiative, or early in your career, ready to promote positive culture change through a discrete project; in either case, the methods of cultivating a creativity culture apply. If your organization wants to foster new ideas and continuously improve to deliver innovative business value, a creativity culture will get you there faster. Next, let's discover how.

# YOUR COMPANY'S NORTH STAR: FINDING PURPOSE AT WORK

"I have to tell you—the values workshop this morning was ENERGIZING. And, super importantly, you got us to our goal: four values statements that already feel like a comfortable T-shirt!"

This would have been a wonderful email to receive from any client, but coming from Jonathan Mueller, it was extra special.

Jonathan is the founder and co-CEO of Ascend Behavior Partners, a firm that helps families of children with autism navigate early childhood and beyond with diagnostics, counseling, and social work. But that business-card summary hardly does justice to who Jonathan is as a person. He's a generous sharer, a positive presence, a gracious storyteller of his triumphs and personal human struggles as a modern-day business leader. He's the kind of professional connection who can make you smile at your LinkedIn feed—always there to share thoughts and ideas that are as upbeat and humble as they are probing, as likely to contain deep insights as they are a sprinkling of emojis. So working with him and his team at Ascend to develop their company culture was a no-brainer, and the session— even over Zoom—was energizing and productive. I closed my computer with the happy glow of a job well done.

Of course, I'm always grateful to receive a thank you note from a client. But something about this particular email really stuck with me. But why?

Then it hit me. At the time, we were neck-deep in the pandemic. Schedules were going haywire, rules were constantly changing, and everyone I talked to seemed to feel simultaneously overstimulated and bored out of their mind. But for Ascend's clients—the families and children living with autism—the pandemic was a perfect storm shaking up already challenging day-to-day lives. Jonathan's team was providing not just services, resources, and therapy, but plain old emotional support—even comfort. A favorite T-shirt, toy, or song can go a long way.

For Jonathan, the idea of "culture like a comfortable T-shirt" is more than just a colorful turn of phrase. It's a metaphor that speaks directly and concretely to Ascend's purpose. That phrase meant something particular and special to him—and to me.

"What should we care about?" he asked me. So many questions and concerns about culture, values, and meaning at work boil down to this one question. Every organization wants—and deserves—a shared sense of purpose that fits like that comfortable T-shirt, yet standard practices for developing corporate values fall far short of what actually matters.

Indeed, the term "corporate values" gets a bad reputation. For one thing, the idea that organizations actually live by their stated values is, at this point, more or less a myth—a study by MIT Sloan found no correlation between a company's stated values and its actual work culture.[1]

But even when there's no hypocrisy in play, most corporate values seem like an afterthought. We often read generic buzzwords (e.g., sustainability, accountability), picked because they sound good—but in reality are quite disconnected from day-to-day practices. Finally, there are so many overlapping terms and definitions that it can be overwhelming not only to know what your group's values are, but whether your group needs values, a mission statement, a purpose, a vision . . .

In other words, too many organizations treat values like a stiff new blazer bought off the rack: something they wear to be taken seriously, a suit you have to grow into. But when it comes to the question of "What should we care about?" it's what's on the inside that counts—what it feels like to be living within that shared sense of purpose. In a creativity culture, I think of this as your North Star. It guides you and lights your way. It's never out of sight. It's inspiring by nature, not by focus-grouping and engineering.

Back in Act I, we explored how ikigai can help us as individuals identify our purpose. It's our reason for being. But what about a company? It comes down to one very simply question: *Why do we exist?*

Confronting this head-on can feel downright uncomfortable. After all, what if we don't like what we discover? What if it puts us in an existential crisis tailspin? Or what if we realize our company is just like the one across the street; who wants to be a dime a dozen?

Instead, discovering your company's North Star is about searching for a unique glimmer of light among a sea of sameness. A different way of solving a common problem. A new approach to overcoming a thorny obstacle. It requires creativity.

Once your purpose is clear, the real challenge is activating it across the company, inspiring your culture carriers to bring it to life. I've found the three pillars of creativity culture—connection, innovation, and inclusion—often help bring the North Star into sharper focus. You start to break the mold of what you think your company *should* be and inhabit the space of who you authentically are. Then you can shine light on the path to a creativity culture of your own.

## WE'RE NOT TALKING ABOUT PAINT NIGHT

Activating your North Star is often the first of many company practices that can help build the structure for a creativity culture. Jessica "Jess" Yuen knows a thing or two about the process of hardwiring creativity into a company.

I met Jess as a fellow advisor in our PeopleTech Partners (PTP) community, a group of leading Chief People Officers, HR leaders, Talent Partners, and consultants who lend their expertise to an elite portfolio of emerging HR technology companies. Despite having a wealth of wisdom to offer emerging companies and impressive credentials to match, I've been struck by Jess's down-to-earth demeanor: a fellow working mom who's always quick to help others.

As a junior associate at consulting firm McKinsey, Jess was handed a goldmine of an opportunity. While working in their internal learning and development group, her first project was to revisit their flagship associate training called the Initial Leadership Workshop (ILW), a two-week program that connects a cohort of forty new associates. The learning curriculum hadn't changed in over ten years, so this was a chance to reinvent and update its core components.

Jess started the project as any true creative leader would—by getting curious. McKinsey consultants, by definition, are a high-achieving bunch. What Jess sought to discover were the answers to some fundamental questions of these best and brightest early career professionals: *How do you learn? How do you think about problems?* She then asked a wide range of questions of the McKinsey partners and clients, investigating their expectations of these associate consultants.

The module she worked on designing from scratch? Creativity. And as any skilled researcher knows, sometimes the best way to start is with a good old-fashioned Google search. She pored over endless entries about how to learn creativity early in one's career. Much like my three-pillar methodology for tapping into creativity, Jess built a module on creativity with the following framework:

- Perspective of self (What are my mindset, self-motivation, and feelings about creativity?)

- Perspective of skill (breaking our assumptions, thinking about things not as step-change, but incremental, putting on different hats and engaging empathy)

- Perspective of expertise (connecting dots of knowledge to learn something new)

After building this framework, Jess designed different exercises to get people to understand what creativity is, feel better connected to their creative selves, and experience practical ways of applying creativity. It was then that she realized that creativity is most often incremental, not just demonstrated in big step change moments.

Jess has used this system of applied creativity in the myriad professional environments which she's inhabited: at Yahoo! in a product management role, as Chief of Staff to the CEO at Khan Academy in its early phase as an online educational start-up, Head of People at Gusto, a payroll processing company, and now in an advisory capacity for start-ups. She recognized that creativity was more than just a skill to put on your resume; it was a mode of operating to build a workplace culture.

While at Khan Academy, Jess saw how creativity played a role in its quirky culture and activated its value of *Fun*.

"We didn't want work to feel like work," she told me. "We had an offsite called the Un-Conference Conference. We started with the premise that you break all of the assumptions that you know." Jess shared how one coder wanted to shift her perspective, so she redesigned her physical environment and started coding under her desk. Others created board game nights to tap into creativity, where playful and inventive ritualized activities emerged, from long strategic games to short rounds of improv. (We'll dive deeper into the impact of company rituals in Scene Nine, but many of the practices that got injected into the Khan Academy culture remain today.)

Jess revealed how grassroots movements helped express the company purpose and bring culture to life. These weren't executives sitting behind closed doors and cooking up what they thought would be helpful or productive for the team. These were passionate, often junior-line-level employees who were closest to the work and energized to drive the initiatives. Much like my magic era at Axiom, they experimented together. Played together. And they were empowered to build.

The creative leader who wants to influence not only her own team but also the broader company culture has the important responsibility of asking, *What do you need from me to help bring this new idea to life?* Ultimately, the ideal execution plan is to empower the idea generators—the ones with the vision and passion—to run with, prioritize, and make time for their ideas, and then celebrate what they created.

"Supporting creativity starts small and it grows," Jess reflected. "It's not all at once. How do you get people to be creative? It's about incremental ways to build on ideas."

Starting small has its advantages. In many ways, Jess's experiences highlight how early-stage, scrappy companies on a shoestring budget can start to build the institutional muscle of creativity. It's not about nurturing your employees' artistic talents or hosting an office Paint Night (although who doesn't love a good Paint Night?). It's about finding where there are pockets of inspiration and people with a passion for doing things in a different way, and then facilitating their growth.

Maybe that means starting each meeting by playing someone's favorite song. Perhaps it's calendaring a five-minute community meditation each week where there's no content to prepare, but the team has designated a space to sit in shared silence together. Maybe it's a weekly improv game, or the ritual of ending your team huddle meeting by sharing bright spots. Creativity can be lightweight. It can be low cost. It's built into the flow of work, showing up in your meetings. It influences your hiring processes and how teams give each other feedback. It's incorporated into how different groups share information and collaborate. And it impacts your company's North Star—your purpose, or why your company exists. Creativity informs all of these, companywide.

## CREATIVITY BOOSTERS
## FOR A CREATIVITY CULTURE:

At the start of your daily standup, pick a word out of a hat to inspire fresh thinking. You might have work-related ones along with a few wacky ones:

- customer-focused
- spiky
- momentum
- flabbergasted
- people-first
- balloon
- value

## WHEN PURPOSE AND VALUES
## *DON'T* SUPPORT CREATIVITY

In our first two acts, we explored the value of strengthening your personal creativity and how your creative leadership can inspire others. But stepping into the zone of building creativity culture extends beyond your individual capabilities. It requires a conga line of similarly committed leaders and team members dancing in lockstep. And not all work environments are ripe for creativity.

"Did that meeting actually just happen?" my friend and colleague Jamie Salka asked me. We had just left the executive debrief meeting from facilitating a Spring Street workshop and stood on the sidewalk, mouths agape. The workshop was a half-day learning experience for a group of mid-level managers to explore leadership mindsets and behaviors. Part of the interactive experience included exercises that examined the company culture, allowing managers to ideate tangible ways to change things for the better. We invited their creative thinking—and they delivered. To our great delight, they were bursting with ideas, hungry to learn and share stories with each other.

More happy news for us, the attendee feedback forms came back overwhelmingly positive—a 100 percent net promoter score. Sure, there were things we could have done differently—little tweaked nuances here and there—but on balance, Jamie and I were pleased with the outcome, the level of engagement from the participants, and the next steps teed up for the team.

Then came this executive debrief meeting.

In a high-rise conference room, fumbling with technology to present our program reflections to the executives on the other end of the webcam, we weren't met with high fives or the collaborative conversation we had expected. The executive responses were chilly (at best). The exchange rattled not only us, but also our company sponsors, who, at least up until now, had shared nothing but praise and unwavering support.

The debrief took a dark turn as the execs interrogated us on each workshop micro-component. *Why did you raise the issue about company culture? Why did you spend time on solutioning ideas to make changes? Why did you reflect on what's not working here?*

The lead-by-fear tactics were on full display—frequent interruptions, public belittling; a decade earlier it would have reduced me to tears, but their behavior was so demonstrably abrasive, I felt a strange impulse to laugh (on the inside, of course), observe, and take notes. *Where's the popcorn?* It doesn't get much better than this!

It was a painful, real-world example of a company whose organizational purpose was not unified internally and whose values were misaligned to mine. These executives didn't care about learning about or improving their culture, ending their team meetings with shared bright spots. There was no appetite to peel back the onion to understand what was going well or brainstorm improvements. Rather than engage curiosity to hear what the workshop participants shared— their perspectives, ideas, and stories—it was far easier to cast blame and question our intentions. That's what felt safe to them. Clearly not accustomed to *taking the note*, I suspect that the feedback process was unsettling and threat-inducing.

After Jamie and I left the meeting, we stood in silence, stunned. But all was not lost. These executive Creativity Gatekeepers left me with a few unintended gifts that day. First, they helped me realize the importance of getting alignment of program objectives. This essential step in any creative process can save the pain (and potential wasted effort) of misalignment down the road. Second, they helped me realize that I had gained the creative confidence to live my values. Without a pang of disappointment, I recognized that our approaches to leadership and shaping culture were vastly different. Without this shared belief, my services likely wouldn't be a successful long-term fit. And third, I saw up close and personal how some leaders and environments aren't yet ready for a creativity culture.

To be fair, these executives were likely embodying what had been modeled to them: command and control at all costs, don't trust easily, and assume others are trying to get one over on you. As we learned in Act II, trust, psychological safety, creative workspaces, and collaboration are core ingredients to creative leadership. Without these fundamentals, creativity culture is likely to remain out of reach.

## MANAGING CREATIVE DISCOMFORT

When you're hardwired to delight your customers, admitting defeat doesn't come easily. But rejection and setbacks are intimate friends to many creative artists, entrepreneurs, and business leaders. We have learned to manage that creative discomfort.

Before Jamie Salka and I stood on a Los Angeles curb, dumbstruck by our corporate debrief meeting, we had met as fellow theatre majors more than 20 years prior at Northwestern University. We share a special bond: performing artists-turned-entrepreneurs, toggling between the analytical, operations-minded and the playful, spirited sides of ourselves. Speaking the language of investors, business leaders, and lawyers, Jamie and I still feel comfortable dwelling for long stretches of time in our imaginations. For us, part of the fun is when these two worlds mesh, which is likely what's kept us connected.

Jamie describes creativity as a constant yearning or an itch, the act of filling a void in our lives. One of his early lessons about creativity in business happened right after college. He and our mutual college friend wrote a musical called *All the Children Sing*. At the tender age of 21 or 22, they raised $500,000 and took the show off-Broadway, only to receive a less-than-stellar review in the *New York Times*. In an instant, they realized they had lost $500,000 of other people's money.

Following the huge discomfort of a perceived failure, Jamie spent years rebuilding his creativity confidence. The pain and disappointment gifted him a lifelong lesson about the value of humility, and how vulnerability plays a role in the creative process. Perhaps that's what made way for the birth of his company. As the CEO and co-founder of Story Pirates, a leading children's media company, his company's North Star is to inspire creativity in young people through the power of story. To do that well, he must foster a creativity culture for the adults who make it possible.

Since then, Jamie has dedicated his career to the discovery of creativity tools to manage that discomfort, building a creative team culture from coast to coast and across business units to unify their shared organizational purpose.

"If you feel uncreative, throw yourself into a new situation," Jamie explained. "First day at a new job? A party where you know no one? That discomfort of finding a solution is creativity."

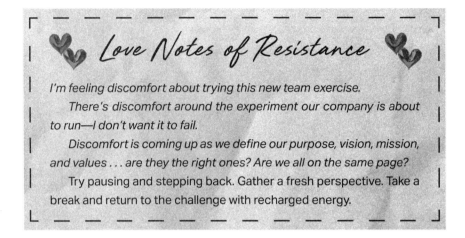

*Love Notes of Resistance*

I'm feeling discomfort about trying this new team exercise.

There's discomfort around the experiment our company is about to run—I don't want it to fail.

Discomfort is coming up as we define our purpose, vision, mission, and values . . . are they the right ones? Are we all on the same page?

Try pausing and stepping back. Gather a fresh perspective. Take a break and return to the challenge with recharged energy.

Beyond the sting of a meeting that didn't go well or striking up a conversation with a stranger at a party, discomfort is a familiar human experience. You might experience discomfort when you first try to meditate, sitting alone in stillness, observing your monkey mind swing from tree to tree among your thoughts. There's discomfort in learning a new skill, like the wobble of riding a bike for the first time or extending to arabesque, unsteady, searching for balance and stability. Building a creativity culture and business may bring up similar discomforts. *What if our team experiments fail? What if our company purpose doesn't attract the right talent or customers? What if living by our company values means letting some leaders go, which results in discord among our team?*

These moments of discomfort, sometimes appearing as Love Notes of Resistance, may be indications that you're on the right path, doing the important, deep work of defining your company's purpose. To work through that resistance, consider stepping back to be the observer. Seek different perspectives and time-travel in your imagination. That clarity of distance might bring you closer to your true North Star and company purpose.

## REVEALING THE GREEN SCREEN IN THE MESSY MIDDLE

We've now entered the part of our program that has me squirming a bit in my chair. It's the stage of any creative process that the creator usually likes to gloss over, the vulnerability of putting our creative work product out there—the Jesus-on-the-donkey show-and-tell.

Most of us struggle to let down our guard, and creativity is an innately vulnerable act. Nowadays, our lives have become curated and airbrushed—AI portraits generate images of our best, most powerful selves, Instagram filters soften the slightest imperfections. It's hard to show up as unvarnished and real. I'm about to go there. But let me first share what inspired me to remove the filter.

In the documentary *Stutz,* Jonah Hill sets up a one-day conversation with his psychiatrist, Phil Stutz, to share the tools that helped him navigate the complex and challenging parts of life. I found the film moving for many reasons, but (spoiler alert), there's a point at which they physically reveal the green screen. Jonah Hill breaks the fourth wall and admits that although they'd like it to look like only one day of shooting, they've been filming for years. Discouraged and visibly stuck, he removes a wig he's been wearing to provide continuity across years of footage. In a vulnerable moment, Hill shares his disappointment and creative block with all of us.[2]

He's honest and real. Mask off.

And that's the creative process. It's bare. It's imperfect.

My creative process with this book has felt like a verrryyyy lonnngggg birth. Sure, people warned me that writing a book is difficult. That it's a labor of love and excruciatingly challenging. That's part of the reason I wanted to do it. But in this moment, I also think it's worth openly sharing some of the feedback I got along the way.

Midway through my journey, I partnered with a book proposal coach. While initially supportive, by the end of our work together, she delivered news that I found deeply painful. She simply didn't find my book proposal compelling.

I'm often comforted by the number of rejections highly successful people receive before their breakout work. Perhaps it's my show biz or sales roots, but I don't usually bristle at the thought of a door slamming in my face. This time, though, the feedback had me swirling—*is any of this worth sharing with the world? Will anyone connect with these stories or want to learn more about creativity at work? Do I have anything of value to offer?*

Tail between my legs, I had a decision to make: Do I keep pushing forward? Scrap the project all together?

This, my dear readers, is the Messy Middle.

In your work, you might experience the Messy Middle when you're knee-deep in a project plan. That RACI you've developed no longer makes sense, what with half of the project team either on to new initiatives or gone from the company entirely. Maybe the Messy Middle for you is a business deal you thought would close three months ago, and here you find yourself still negotiating, planning, and persuading others to get across the finish line. Perhaps your Messy Middle is the half-finished creative endeavor that you've been diligently crafting outside your day-job, which you're not sure will ever see the light of day.

Creative work is messy. Feedback on our creativity can wound us. But it can make us even more determined to build something of value, figure it out, sit with the feelings, and keep tirelessly working away even when it feels like junk. You can receive the Love Notes of Resistance as they are, take them in, and keep pushing through.

So, what did I do?

I held tight to the disciplined process of creativity.

I zoomed out to see the bigger picture and get a different perspective.

I built. I experimented.

I put in the hard, uncomfortable work of creating, getting curious, fighting the creativity killers, listening to my Love Notes of Resistance, and keeping the time. Yes, it took longer than I would have liked, much like Jonah Hill's documentary. (Welcome to the creative process.) Welcome to building creativity culture.

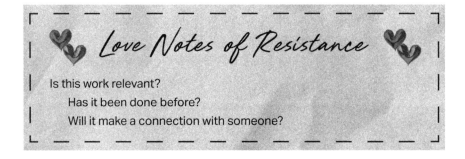

*Love Notes of Resistance*

Is this work relevant?
  Has it been done before?
  Will it make a connection with someone?

Perhaps you're facing similar internal battles with your creative ideas, or you received a piece of feedback that has your head spinning. You could very well be one submission away from finally getting your screenplay sold, landing your first job, or being tapped on the shoulder to lead a strategic new initiative. Maybe your creativity is about to take you in a completely new (and better) direction if you stick with it for one more stretch. Your next opportunity awaits—it's right around the corner—I can almost see it. Our job is to show up and keep going. Adapt. Reinvent. You are born to create.

## SCENE DIALOGUE FOR APPLYING PURPOSE AND VALUES AT WORK

**SETTING:**

(SARA, the Chief People Officer of a high-growth tech company, sits on her couch, laptop open, two braids pinned on top of her head. She listens intently as ZANE, the Chief Operating Officer, describes a challenge he's encountering.)

**ZANE**

It's not that we're not getting results. We actually are. But if I have to start another meeting with my team near tears, I don't know what I'll do.

**SARA**

Tears? What's happening?

**ZANE**

I don't know, Sara. Ever since Raj joined my leadership team, I feel like there's confusion that wasn't there before about where to focus. People don't want to disappoint him. It just seems like we're losing sight of why we're all working so hard.

**SARA**

Okay, when was the last time you talked about our North Star?

ZANE

Ah, that's a good point. I want to bring it up in our quarterly business review next week. It'll help anchor us to our big milestone in Q3...

SARA

That'll be great. *We Make Patients' Lives Easier.* Maybe pull in the story of Danielle's big product win, too, since that clearly connects to our company purpose. But first, tell me more about Raj's leadership approach.

ZANE

Yeah, he's brought in a lot more accountability, which I see as a good thing, but the team's been working around the clock on stuff that doesn't relate to our top priorities. He's been dropping some threats about cleaning house, cutting the low performers, not tolerating any mistakes—

SARA

(sets her coffee aside)

Okay, I get it. I'm glad you're feeling good about accountability, but from what you're telling me, this doesn't feel like behavior consistent with our values. How does that land with you?

ZANE

Yeah, I don't disagree. It's these side projects that really don't drive the business or support our purpose—in fact, now that I think about it, it's overcomplicating things for the patient experience.

SARA

How might you address this with him?

ZANE

Well, I just wonder if I can step in and start to simplify things. It feels like we need to focus on the core. Get the team realigned.

**SARA**

Let's talk about it. Our values are "be bold," "heart-led," "follow through," and "keep it simple." How do you think Raj is activating those values with the team?

**ZANE**

He's definitely bold—no question. I love some of the big operational changes we've made right out of the gate. He's fearless, which is what we needed.

**SARA**

That's great. What about the others?

**ZANE**

He's great at the follow-through, too. He manages up to me really well, but the rest of the team just doesn't respond to his leadership style. Yeah, I see where this is going.

(pauses)

He's just not heart-led. It's like he hasn't earned the trust of the team yet. Not to say we don't want to work hard, but the way we've talked about our heart-led value is about investing in relationships. Bringing genuine caring to our teams—I think that's what I need to coach him around.

**SARA**

What about "keep it simple"?

**ZANE**

Oh, I definitely need to address that.

(jots down a note for himself)

Thanks, Sara. I've got a lot more clarity on what I need to do. Okay if we connect again next week?

**SARA**

You got it.

**(END OF SCENE)**

In this scene, Sara was able to effectively steer Zane back to the organizational purpose and values. When questions about culture arise, applying the lens of your North Star and guiding principles can help reveal the intervention that's necessary.

## COMMUNICATING A MESSAGE THAT MATTERS

As I parachute into different organizations, it's remarkable how quickly I can sense their culture through the language used in a group Zoom chat feed. I've observed the extremes: inclusive, supportive words coupled with playful emojis, where colleagues are quick to chime in with personal affirming praise, contrasted with the chilly, standoffish, shallow, and wooden remarks that leave you doubting your every move. Culture is shaped not only by behavioral norms across your organization but also the shared language your colleagues adopt. Building a creativity culture requires a heightened focus on the words that bring your organizational messages to life.

When crafting these marketing and communication messages to best reflect your company culture, it's helpful to:

- **Start with your North Star**. Define your organizational purpose or reason for being. You can start by saying, "We exist to . . ." This is your core message, what's pasted on a billboard and printed on a T-shirt. It should be unapologetically consistent across audiences.

- **Define your different audiences**. This includes your employees, prospective employees, customers, board members, investors, community, and anyone else who may interact with your company experience.

- **List your communications channels**. How does each audience receive the message of your North Star? Do they read about it in a job description or LinkedIn headline? Hear about you from a networking group? As an employee, perhaps they have the potential for more impressions through swag, onboarding experiences, slack messages, town halls, or company newsletters. It's important to quickly grab people's limited attention and make the message land. Consider the full list of potential opportunities to communicate your North Star message.

- **Consider your timeline**. Much like evaluating your communications channels, think about the right cadence or timeline for each messaging opportunity. Perhaps you have a monthly town hall or quarterly business review (QBR). Considering the "Tell 'em what you'll tell 'em, tell 'em, then tell 'em what you told 'em" communications principle, you likely don't share your *why* message frequently enough.

- **Evaluate consistency or impact gaps**. Do your customers understand and connect with your North Star? If not, what is the value of the connection that you're leaving on the table? How consistent are you in communicating with employees or prospective employees? Much like the quantifiable value of a strong brand, the strength of your North Star message can have an impact on your ability to attract, retain, and develop talent, drive a qualified pipeline of business, or improve your investment options. The clarity of this message matters.

- **Create ongoing measurement**. We measure what matters. When it comes to your North Star or purpose for your organization, if you're not making the effort to gain data and insights on how your message is landing, it becomes difficult to make refinements when things aren't working. Learn how to (or identify someone on your team who can help) track engagement levels, evaluate email open rates, gather customer input, and solicit employee and customer sentiments about your North Star. After getting a baseline, find a system and cadence for gathering these inputs and analyzing trending data. Many platforms have easy-to-use tools for monitoring marketing analytics. By using them to their full potential, you can adjust your strategy and tactics for the marketing messages that follow.

Following these steps can help activate your North Star, where words leap off the page to engage humans who interact with your company purpose. While not exhaustive, these actions begin to paint the picture of the detailed communications plan that moves your North Star from a grand idea to a lived experience.

After starting the work of defining your organizational purpose and building a culture that encourages, supports, and develops creativity across your organization, you can connect the dots from team members' creative thinking to the impact they're making on the business. Applied creativity at work means mining for ideas that are novel and useful. Organizations with crystal-clear North Stars are primed to foster this culture of creativity because everyone is aligned on what matters most—they know what's useful, and people feel safe to try something new. When an organizational North Star includes an effective communication plan, it fuels the fire for creative thinking and output. It's the kindling we need for the bonfire.

## SAMPLE COMPANY EXERCISE— REFRESHING OUR VALUES

In the core values work I do with clients, I spend significant time listening to the stories of culture carriers to help bubble consistent themes up to the surface. The following exercise can be done within your scaling organization (likely between 15–150 people), but an outside facilitator's perspective may help you objectively spot trends.

Participants: 8–12 culture carriers, including a mix of people leaders and individual contributors

Instructions: Schedule a two- to three-hour working session to explore your company values. If possible, invite a functional cross-section of your population. In advance of your working session, circulate a questionnaire of the participating members that asks the following:

- What makes working at OUR COMPANY different from other places, including competitors?

- Which one or two values best represent who we are today and where we're headed?

- Which one or two values least represent who we are and where we're headed?

- Think of a person or two at our company who consistently demonstrates our company values. What are some stories/examples of how they live the values?

- Where in our employee life cycle do values come up? (For example, during the onboarding process.)
- Where do values fade into the background?
- From the following list, which three to five words best represent who we are and what we want to become as an organization? (Feel free to pick other words not listed here.)

| | | |
|---|---|---|
| Achievement | Fast | Listening |
| Accountability | Feedback | Love |
| Authenticity | Fresh | Loyalty |
| Balance | Future-Focused | Meaningful |
| Bold | Generosity | Ownership |
| Brave | Giving | Partnership |
| Caring | Growth-Mindset | Passion |
| Clear | Helpfulness | People-First |
| Collaboration | High-Growth | Progress |
| Committed | High-Performance | Resilience |
| Communication | Honesty | Respect |
| Connection | Humility | Service |
| Courage | Impact | Simple |
| Creativity | Inclusion | Speed |
| Curiosity | Initiative | Success |
| Data-Driven | Innovation | Teamwork |
| Efficient | Integrity | Thoughtful |
| Effort | Inventive | Togetherness |
| Energy | Irresistible | Trust |
| Enthusiasm | Kindness | Worthwhile |
| Excellence | Learning | Write-It-Down |

After picking your values and aggregating your responses, as a group, map where they all sit on this grid.

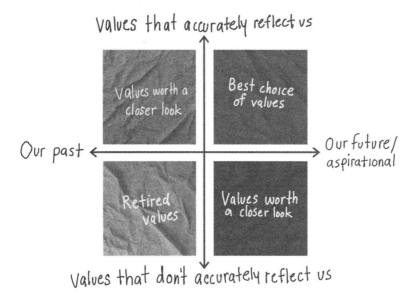

You may start to see clusters and trends emerge. If the chart is more of a dispersed scatterplot, maybe it's revealing that your culture doesn't yet have a clear, consistent voice.

As a group, gain consensus on the three to five values in the upper-right quadrant that keep coming up both in the survey and in the employee and customer stories that you share. They should feel distinct to your culture, actionable, and linked to the results you're trying to achieve. These may include new words that weren't initially identified in the pre-workshop survey yet capture a sentiment that keeps emerging in the stories you tell as a group.

Once your three to five values are selected, invite participants to reflect on the stories of how these values are lived in action at your organization. Find the emotions and business impact that connect to the values you've selected. Pressure-test the words. Is there another closely related word that captures the same idea but feels more representative of your company culture? Remember, your values should feel memorable and distinct to your organization.

After deciding on your refreshed values, begin to plan how to update the collateral that includes all references to your values. Craft a communications plan to cascade the new values and bring them to life for all of your employees.

## SCENE SEVEN SHOW NOTES

- **Use process to build a container for creativity**, but ensure creativity isn't engineered out.
- **Build a North Star that inspires creativity** and invites personal connection.
- Invest the time in **aligning with key stakeholders on shared values**, as well as what kind of culture you're aiming to create.
- **Mind the Messy Middle.**
- Consider the **communications** that will reinforce your purpose.

Your company's North Star sets the stage for your creativity culture, laying the important foundation for connection, innovation, and inclusion. In our next scene, you'll discover how to take your place as the conductor. This role extends beyond leadership and into the domain of a key influencer to culture transformation. I'll also reveal the Culture Strategy template tool, which you can use to approach culture like any other strategic lever of your business.

# BE THE CONDUCTOR: APPLYING THE CULTURE STRATEGY FRAMEWORK

*"Creativity isn't 'throw-it-at-the-wall and see what sticks'—
that's a misunderstanding. For creativity to thrive, you need
to have constraints and clarity, agreements and commitments."*

—John Foster, 4X Chief People Officer

I f you've taken the steps to get clear about your company purpose—your guiding North Star—the next step in building creativity culture involves crafting the strategy. Culture, if left unattended, usually regresses to dysfunction. In the early days of building a company, it's natural to feel a sense of (over) confidence about culture. You may think, *Culture will take care of itself if we simply hire the right people.* But as companies scale, there's typically an inflection point where the founders will no longer know every employee or feel aligned with each leader's style and values. The culture can begin to feel fragmented and siloed. That's where culture strategy comes in.

"You can't do it all, Anne," my then-CEO told me. I was near tears. "You don't have to be the expert in everything. Your job is to be the conductor."

Perhaps you can relate to the feeling of overwhelm when trying to spin all the plates and do everything well—simultaneously. Your capabilities may have been tested from the pressure to perform well in a college course, not getting the grade that used to come effortlessly. Or maybe missing a deadline to produce creative work left you questioning your talents, negatively impacting your confidence, causing you to wonder if you were in the right place. Maybe you picked up a new creative hobby that looked easy on its face but forced an awareness of how much practice would be required to gain competence, let alone mastery.

Years later, this offhanded comment about being the conductor stuck with me. It reminds me that the art of building a creativity culture includes giving yourself permission to let others shine. You can't do it all singlehandedly, regardless of how skilled a creative leader you are. To accomplish goals, it's more effective to build a vision and then empower others to also bring their creative best. They can then execute and co-create with you, as Seán Curran did with Build a Phrase. The same rules apply to the goal of creating a thriving organizational culture. It requires a capable conductor, well-tuned instruments, and artisans prepared to skillfully perform their craft.

That skill of influencing creativity culture is more than simply waving a baton, though. To expand on the metaphor of an orchestra, conducting involves intimately knowing the score, as if we had carefully written each note. In Act I, we started our journey together exploring the ingredients of individual creativity: creative confidence, strengthening our imaginations, gathering different perspectives and feedback. From Kris Bowers' ability to start his creative expression with an emotion to Shedrack Anderson III's instinct to focus on the lifestyle we want to create, these core creativity skills are shaped by the mindsets and behaviors we adopt.

In Act II, we layered in skills to lead creatively. We met creative leaders like Jen Brewer, Niki Armstrong, and Chelsea Grayson, and collaborative entrepreneurs and artists like Tommy Kail and Bob Reynolds, who shined a light on the techniques that inspire and nurture creativity in others. Here, our locus of control is expanded. We can set the tone with our teams, be mindful of the physical and psychological environment, and practice collaborative behaviors—knowing each person's Most Important Thing and bringing a combination of faculties and love to the jam session.

Now at the company level, we're widening the lens to spot behavior patterns and social norms that impact not only the individual and team, but the entire organization. We started by anchoring to the North Star, the inner purpose of the organization. Now we're ready to create the music. That's the conductor's job—to lead, inspire, and influence the entire orchestra to tell a story. The conductor sets the tone, tempo, and dynamics for each musician, but creates impact by knowing each crevasse, subtle (and grand) message, and the overall arc of the piece.

Back to that moment my heart first opened, I stood in the wings of a dimly lit backstage between thick black curtains hanging from the catwalk. Each musician expressed the instrument differently, much like you'll find among the players within your organization. That sacred hush was cued by the conductor, the singular person who signaled: *Okay, now we're ready. It's showtime.*

There will likely not be one arbiter of culture at your company, nor should there be. But stepping into the role of the conductor empowers you to signal that you're ready to begin. You begin by revealing the story, the culture journey, the strategy behind why, who, how, where, and when you'll come together to work. Conductors not only see and hear what's possible—they *feel* it.

## HOW SAFETY INFLUENCES CREATIVITY CULTURE

Building on the safety of trust falls we explored in Act II, much of the success of a company's creativity depends on the levels of safety employees feel—from psychological safety to job security to simply knowing what's expected of them. John Foster, former Chief People Officer and HR executive to companies like TrueCar, Hulu, Minted, and IDEO, thinks a lot about the underlying culture of the organization. He's witnessed how company and board leadership either enable a thriving people-first culture or contribute to one that's toxic and destructive.

**CREATIVITY BOOSTER:**

Take one of your meetings this week while walking outside in nature. Maybe you can walk with a colleague to discuss an upcoming project, or simply log into a team call and use your earbuds while walking. Notice how it impacts you. Do you find yourself able to feel more open to new ideas? Does it get your own creative juices flowing? Does it shift your mood by the end of the meeting?

John and I have taken to exchanging ideas while walking near the ocean on the Manhattan Beach Strand; generating that kinetic energy, surrounded by nature, facilitates our creative thinking. It allows for the expression of deeper perspectives. Recalling his experiences at IDEO, John has intimate knowledge of creative principles and practices from teamwork on fifteen-week client sprints. He described a surgical level of precision in these engagements—requiring not only exceptional creative leadership, but also collaboration, resources (think Post-it notes, Sharpies, and other colorful, idea-stimulating creative tools), processes (like the Design Thinking methodology IDEO shaped), and the understood team rules of engagement for creative output.

"Businesses have to get to results that matter," he reflected. "It needs commercial value. At the end of the day, someone is paying for the output. Creativity isn't this unmanageable, abstract, mysterious thing. People work together to come up with an innovative, inventive, never-seen-before idea. That's predictable."

John is quick to acknowledge that a creative process within the workplace is a delicate balance—too little process, and people feel unsafe. They don't know what's validated or whether they're on the right track. Too much process, and seasoned professionals can get annoyed—or worse, they completely check out. But in finding that sweet spot of process and pressure, creative cultures can provide the safe space for people to experiment, while also driving meaningful commercialized outcomes.

"Creativity requires humans to be in their most connected space," John reflected. "It doesn't happen when you tell them what to do. But connected space isn't a free-for-all. That's where people get caught up. They don't know what it looks like to manage creativity."

That push-pull dynamic within creativity cultures is essential. There must be enough safety for people to play and try new things, knowing that their jobs are stable and secure, but also the governing guardrails that yield business results. The skills we've covered in the first two acts—individual creative discipline and leadership techniques—permeate these workspaces. After all, this isn't creativity for creativity's sake; this is about propagating novel ideas across an organization that hold practical value. Safety in a creativity culture means trusting that you—and your creative colleagues—will find a way to yield the business results you're after.

## UNLOCKING CREATIVE VALUE WITH STRATEGIC PURPOSE

The governing guardrails to which I referred often show up as the rules of engagement across the employee experience. That's how value is unlocked across the employee journey—by knowing clearly what's expected of each person at each stage of the employee life cycle at the company. That's where the operating rhythms and cultural norms that you've established are codified. The moments are stitched together to become a culture strategy, something bigger than the sum of their individual parts.

This is more than just green lighting the Fun Club—building a culture strategy is about knowing your audience and personalizing an employee journey that's meaningful and enriching to every member. It's the ultimate empathetic process, a chance to consider different motivations, learning styles, and work preferences.

I once embarked on that empathetic process in a dusty conference room, my colleague and I huddled around a big whiteboard, ready to map the employee-experience life cycle. The process felt daunting. *How in the world are we going to capture all of the different moments of an employee's journey? Who are we to guess how employees perceive these different milestones along their path? And what if we get it wrong?*

If I'm being honest, the process of imagining the employee journey was more enlightening than the end product. We left that whiteboard covered with multicolored sticky notes and peaks and valleys of the employee experience, acknowledging people's discomfort of not always knowing where to get information, the overwhelm of lots of different communications platforms, the delight in human connection with colleagues or hitting a work milestone, and the confusion of not always having clarity on the team's priorities. These are likely common human experiences at any company, but certainly popped out as prevalent here.

We drilled down into the North Star (why people choose to work here), the people (who does what), the process (how and when they do it), the technology and systems (what platforms are used and how they interrelate), data (what information is stored and shared), and decisions (how insights influence next actions—or not!).

By the end of our exercise, a roadmap for what needed to change had emerged. We spotted patterns of communication breakdown, gaps in information sharing, and knowledge management opportunities. We noticed which pockets of the company serve as hubs for communication and how culture influencers could help drive more consistency in articulating why we exist. The communications channels that kept surfacing (e.g., the monthly company newsletter that everyone reads because of Ted's self-deprecating humor or the two-minute Friday afternoon videos with key client updates) felt like speedy information highways to reinforce the company North Star and bring values to life.

By focusing on how organizational purpose can show up across the employee life cycle, it starts to feel less like a nice-to-have company exercise; instead, the North Star becomes the lifeblood of the organization, the filter by which decisions are made, and the collection of guiding principles for the entire community. A clearer purpose creates momentum. It eliminates wasteful distractions. As you activate your North Star, priorities are illuminated and brought into sharper focus. It becomes a strategic imperative.

## INTRODUCING THE CULTURE STRATEGY FRAMEWORK

I first created the Culture Strategy tool as part of Andrew Bartlow's People Leader Accelerator Program, designed to help emerging Heads of People get a better strategic handle on their company's culture.

I must be a glutton for punishment in dealing with intangibles. When people ask what I do in my work, and I say I help leaders build strategy around their corporate culture to bring more creativity to the workplace, I'm usually met with a puzzled pause, head scratch, or blank look in response. *Huh?* When things feel ephemeral, it helps to put both structure and story around it. I once had an engineer plead with me in a learning experience, "Can we just remove all the feelings from this?" As our brains search for the comfort of categories, the Culture Strategy tool puts a process around how to get to a desired outcome—feelings optional.

You may be the Head of People, ready to use the Culture Strategy tool to engage with leaders across your enterprise. Perhaps you're a start-up founder who wants to be intentional about scaling your team's culture. Maybe you're earlier in your career, observing how certain teams seem to click, whereas others don't. The questions in this framework can help bring more clarity as to why certain teams don't gel—and what you might do about it. Regardless of your role within an organization, my hope is this tool will help lay the foundation for your creativity culture and drive a better employee experience for all.

In the Recommended Resources section at the end of the book, you can download the complete Culture Strategy tool. While you can address one section in isolation, you'll find they're also interdependent; it's the combination of the perspectives that captures a more complete picture of where your organizational culture is headed.

After diving into the questions in each section, the goal is to identify a few achievable initiatives to help strengthen the company culture you're aiming to create. For example, you may choose to address your onboarding process, so your culture is clearly defined for new employees. Maybe your feedback process could benefit from more plain-spoken descriptions of your core values in action. Or perhaps you'll notice you haven't yet identified organizational competencies, keeping colleagues from knowing what skills your company values most. Like any other part of your business, your culture will benefit from crafting a concrete vision, strategy, and operational plan to enable results.

Here's a peek at what the tool covers:

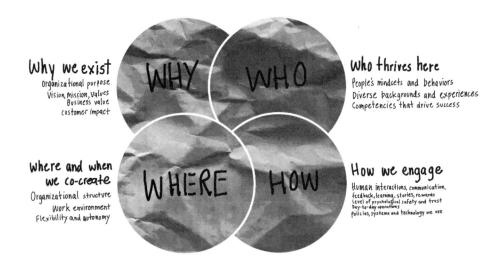

Why we exist
Organizational purpose
Vision, mission, values
Business value
customer impact

Who thrives here
People's mindsets and behaviors
Diverse backgrounds and experiences
Competencies that drive success

where and when
we co-create
Organizational structure
Work environment
Flexibility and autonomy

How we engage
Human interactions, communication,
feedback, learning, stories, rewards
Level of psychological safety and trust
Day-to-day operations
policies, systems and technology we use

## Culture Strategy 1: Why We Exist

The first stage in building a Creativity Culture strategy is to start with *Why*. (Props to Simon Sinek for popularizing this important technique.)[3] Why you do what you do, and feeling intimately connected to that driving motivation, helps draw focus to what's most important to your employees and customers.

The Big Why includes your organizational purpose or North Star, your Vision (the what), your Mission (the how), and Values (shared principles and behaviors), as well as your company value proposition. Consider: What problem is your business uniquely prepared to solve? When you deliver business value, what's the impact to your customers or clients? When you listen to their stories and learn how their lives are better off from your company's product or service, the Big Why becomes clear.

Have you ever considered why you work where you work? One fun and simple way to activate your North Star is by asking employees to submit short videos (a few seconds long) answering the question: "Why do you choose to work here?" You can then stitch together a few powerful *Why* testimonials and share them at the start of your all-hands meeting. Personalizing the Why helps harder-to-grasp concepts feel more tangible. Sharing them can drive stronger connection for those who might be struggling to put their personal Why into words.

One recent culture assessment revealed a powerful Why story that stopped me in my tracks. The founder shared a recorded customer testimonial, which he kept on his desktop for daily reference. In the video, his customer humbly admitted how the company not only *changed* his life for the better, but in a low moment of grief, it *saved* his life. While not all companies will have customer experiences as profound and intimate as this (after all, some companies simply need to manufacture soap), you can still anchor your company's North Star to the human impact you make. It might mean that brightening someone's day (I'll admit fragrant, eco-friendly soap has this effect on me!), simplifying someone's work experience, or offering life-saving support can stoke the embers of your creativity culture.

Here are a few key questions to help discover WHY your organization exists:

## Purpose, Vision, Mission

- Why does our company exist?
- How do we communicate that purpose?

## Core Values

- What three to five stories demonstrate the behaviors of living the values that each team member should know?
- What do we do when someone is *not* living our values?

### Value Proposition

- What are three to five customer impact stories that each member of our team should know?

These questions may prompt a deeper discussion among your leaders or team—a chance to find alignment and crystallize your shared approach. By starting the process of building a culture strategy, you begin to address the hard questions that may reveal gaps for improvement. Your operational plan to bridge those gaps will follow.

## Culture Strategy 2: Who Thrives Here

Once you have a handle on your organizational why, you need to know *who* thrives within your company. In this section, you may gain new insights about what behaviors are rewarded, reinforced, and promoted across the company. The "Who" might include people's mindsets and behaviors (for example, I'll soon share how Microsoft addressed this to promote a growth mindset), the diversity of people's backgrounds, identities, and experiences, as well as the shared competencies that drive success at your organization.

This is where you can start to look for pockets of creative thinking across your organization—not just in the typically creative functions like product design or marketing, but across the organization where you'd like to innovate, change, or make improvements. Take a closer look at your working teams. Do people have regular opportunities to learn from fresh perspectives or are they trapped in an echo chamber? Do you have a rotation program, so early-career teammates can learn different parts of the business and gain new experiences? The *Who* may also reveal opportunities to get creative with your talent acquisition and development plan. Notice where you have talent gaps. Could getting creative in how you source, mentor, and reskill make an impact?

Here are a few starter questions to prompt thinking around WHO thrives at your company:

## Demographics and DEIB (diversity, equity, inclusion, and belonging) strategy

- What strategies do we have in place to increase diversity and equity across the business?

## Competencies, behaviors, and learning

- What are our leadership principles and how are they consistently applied?
- What EQ/power skills do we want our people to develop and how do we support them?

## Culture fit and assessment

- Who are the change champions across our business and how do they embody our culture?
- How do we celebrate different identities, backgrounds, and lived experiences across our organization, through employee resource groups (ERGs) or other methods?

## Moments that matter, milestones, and social impact

- What social causes does our organization care about that are aligned to our values, and how do we support employee activism?

## Outgoing employees

- How do we gather feedback about the organizational culture from those who are leaving our company?

A deep dive into the *who* of your company may reveal blind spots. You can use this as an opportunity to build a baseline of DEIB metrics, but also shift to be more programmatic in your approach to support a thriving workforce.

## Culture Strategy 3: How We Engage

The How of your organization may feel like the biggest area for review, and potentially the ripest area for improvement. After all, how we engage and show up for each other is present in every micro and macro interaction at work.

To make this section feel more manageable, I often start with an audit of meetings. What is your meeting culture like? Who does the most talking? Do you typically have a clear agenda? Are you using technology to help synthesize information from meetings? What happens when there's disagreement (if that's even permitted)?

Since it's easy to resort to "Well, this is just the way we do things here . . . ," it can help to have newer employees involved in this audit process, particularly if they're joining from another organization with positive cultural attributes.

Get curious about the levels of psychological safety across your team. Are there standout leaders who consistently get rave reviews from their direct reports? What might they be doing that the other leaders aren't?

Finally, since you can't control how others behave each moment, consider the areas of the company where you have articulated guidelines of workplace standards. What do your policies or cultural artifacts communicate? What messages are you delivering at Town Halls or end-of-year celebrations? How do your systems and operational protocols influence or shape your culture?

Thinking back to the celebratory scavenger hunt around New York City, that team-building experience worked because of our mutual trust, safety, and appreciation of each team member. We had been in the trenches together, building, creating, stubbing our metaphorical toes, and picking each other back up—and learning and laughing while doing it. That's how social norms fuse together to create a culture. As Jess Yuen shared, creativity can start small, and then build as it's reinforced.

Here are additional questions to consider while analyzing HOW your team members engage:

## Listening and feedback

- What different methods do we have to listen and gather feedback on our culture from ALL stakeholders? (e.g., survey/platform, town halls, ask-me-anything email channels, small group listening circles, client and employee surveys, etc.)

- How do we model giving real-time feedback and ensure 1:1 manager–report meetings are happening?

## Business operations

- What constitutes an effective meeting and how do we measure success? (i.e., agenda, role to play for each participant, clear owners assigned to each next action, timeline, summary, *don't be boring,* etc.)

- How do people in different functions or regions collaborate on shared business challenges and opportunities?

## Goals

- How does goal achievement link to future growth opportunities (stretch assignments, promotions, etc.)?

## The learning process and career path

- How do leaders share their stumbles and what they've learned?

- How are we recognizing and rewarding outstanding performance, and do our total rewards reflect our values and culture?

## Team building and community

- How are we communicating our culture to our board and/or investor community?

- Do we have a culture dashboard, and if so, what are we measuring?

John Foster shared a powerful example of enabling the *how* as part of the customer experience. He and his daughter visited two coffee shops. The first was a high-end gluten-free bakery and coffee shop, filled with special culinary creations and sweet treats. After spending over $100 on buttery baked goods, John figured he'd grab a quick coffee refill before hitting the road. After handing his cup to the cashier who had rung him up only moments ago, he was charged another $4.95.

Contrast that experience with the second at another local coffee shop. There, after John enjoyed a last sip of java, the cashier took the initiative to ask if he wanted a fresh cup on his way out the door. No charge.

Neither of these workers did anything wrong, but *how* they delivered the customer experience was vastly different. At the second coffee shop, the cashier applied creativity. It's likely that somewhere within the training process, this worker was empowered to make a customer happy—they had been given discretion and authority to color outside the lines. In the first scenario, the training was likely different.

These two different approaches demonstrate what a creativity culture can enable. When team members across the organization are empowered to think on their own to solve problems, delight customers, and apply creativity to get their job done, the customer (and the employees) can have markedly different experiences.

In your work, think about *how* you engage with your colleagues. Do you inspire each other, looking for ways to improve your product or service for the customer experience? Or are you operating from a place of fear of violating the rules, where creativity may be discouraged?

## Culture Strategy 4: Where and When We Co-create

The last stage in the Culture Strategy template involves a closer look at where and when to co-create, including synchronous and asynchronous workflows, in-office, hybrid, and remote-first work arrangements, and the messaging around your company's philosophy about flexibility.

As we explored in Scene Five, where and when people work together has changed significantly following the pandemic, but also as technology has enabled new ways of collaborating.

Many of my clients struggle with getting their employees back in the office. One response has stuck with me—*Yeah, it's cool to have Lizzo perform at our company party, but unless she's now my manager, it won't change how I think about returning to the office.*

Here are a few questions to think about when reviewing WHEN and WHERE you co-create with colleagues at your company:

## Organizational structure and shared organizing principles

- When do we connect as a team to build relationships?
- When and where do we meet as a leadership team, either in person or virtually?

## Physical work environment

- What physical artifacts represent who we are as an organization?
- How do our virtual or in-office team-building experiences reflect our culture?

## Conflict and concerns

- Do team members know the code of conduct, policies, behavior guidelines, and what to do if something isn't right?

Creativity culture shows up in unexpected places. It might be demonstrated in the design of your new intern program or on full display with a new team's strategic planning offsite. You might find it when a mid-level manager notices things can be improved by trying something in a new way, developing the habit of experimenting to make things better.

Wherever you find creativity culture, be sure to stop and notice when you do. Celebrate it. Tell a story about it. Chances are, it's just a tiny fraction of the creativity and innovation that's possible across your organization. As you embrace your role as the conductor, your job is to help that creativity grow.

## THINK LIKE A MARKETER

If you engage with the Culture Strategy tool, chances are you'll unearth a slate of initiatives to bring culture to life across your organization. Prioritizing them is the first step. But you may also need to market them internally.

> *"Together, we prioritize purpose over profit and protect this*
> *wondrous planet, our only home."*
> **—Patagonia**[4]

> *"We exist to help more and more people experience financial well-being."*
> **—BlackRock**[5]

> *"We help customers realize their hopes and dreams by providing the*
> *best products and services to protect them from life's uncertainties*
> *and prepare them for the future."*
> **—Allstate**[6]

These gold standard purpose statements represent effective organizational cultures who have synthesized their North Star into high impact language. I'll admit that marketers (and sales professionals, for that matter) often get a bad rap. Even the thought of marketing can leave us with the squeamish, negative impression of meeting a snake oil salesman—that we're being sold a bill of goods.

Marketing—in whatever career you pursue—is a big part of the job. It's also an essential part of getting a creative idea to take flight, and fully embracing the role of the conductor. Delivering a message consistently, clearly, in a memorable way helps build a culture of creativity. Organizational leaders, as well as culture carriers at all levels, must first understand and connect to the message personally before they can transmit the message to others. It may feel exhaustingly redundant, but for your culture messages to fully land across your organization, you'll need consistency, repetition, and persistence.

When Satya Nadella joined Microsoft as CEO, the organization was struggling. Nadella introduced the growth mindset as the new defining characteristic of the culture. He underscored the importance of Carol Dweck's research, showcased in her book *Mindset* as the foundation for this belief. Instead of rewarding outcomes, they shifted to reinforcing learning. Rather than celebrate star performers, they acknowledged those who were committed to growth and making improvement. The Microsoft team infused this rallying cry message to prospective employees in the hiring process, modeled the behaviors of a growth mindset at the leadership level, and architected action-oriented growth mindset moments across the employee life cycle. It became the roadmap for culture change.[7]

Similarly, when Pure Storage committed to driving inclusive innovation across its organization and bringing its core value of creativity to life, they did so with a programmatic and coordinated approach. Rather than only focus on soliciting patentable inventions, they widened the gate to include all business innovations, propagating the mindset that everyone can create an idea with business value—regardless of who you are or where you sit in the company. They created a safe space and easy process to share new ideas and found playful, creative ways of recognizing the innovators.[8] This is how to artfully conduct a creativity culture.

When I partner with clients, we work to clearly define the North Star and strategize on how best to activate it. It's not enough for leaders to huddle in a room and get aligned with each other. These messages belong to everyone across the company. The language shows up in employee interviews and team chats. They play a role in all-hands meetings and team offsites. The North Star is present in performance conversations. When leaders evaluate who should be promoted or take on a new project, the North Star and values framework play a prominent part. Company values become the translucent gel screen for the spotlight we're shining on the team, coloring the unique work experience.

Effective marketing—as well as a distinctive workplace culture—is designed to feel fresh, not canned versions of things you've seen dozens of times before.

Many of my clients come to me, hat in hand, feeling sheepish about their organizational values. I view this as a massive opportunity for reinvention.

"We realized we needed values, so we just quickly picked the ones we liked from our previous company," one co-founder told me. Years later, they now recognize the distinct culture and heartbeat of their newly formed company. Not better, not worse, but a unique organism on its own. Its values should reflect that uniqueness. As you play the role of conductor, you cue the sacred hush, when to pause to discover that cultural alignment.

## SCENE DIALOGUE FOR BEING THE CONDUCTOR

**SETTING:**

(MICHELLE, Chief Innovation and Culture Officer, pours a packet of sweetener into her coffee and gives it a stir. She guards the luggage and waits for SAM, the Chief Executive Officer, to join her at the airport coffee shop table. SAM returns with a sandwich, coffee, and two bottles of water, one to share with MICHELLE.)

                  **SAM**

Still delayed?

                **MICHELLE**

Yep. Holding at thirty.

    (They both laugh and crack open their water bottles.)

                  **SAM**

Not sure about you, but I'm feeling good about the presentation today. Feels like the deal is likely.

                **MICHELLE**

You were great, Sam. Jessica did a great job hitting the points about the client value. Seth nailed the story about benefits—the way he tells that story about the impact we had—

                  **SAM**

I know. It gets me every time.

                    MICHELLE

And Pedro has such an art for storytelling with
data. I really think we won them over with those
stats.

                      SAM

I'm sensing hesitation in your voice, though.
What's up?

                    MICHELLE

Well, if they accept our offer to get acquired,
I get that you'll want to move forward. And the
board will probably advise that we do. But—

                      SAM

Let me guess. You're worried about their culture. What's the red flag?

                    MICHELLE

                (swigs her coffee)

I just got the sense that they're a really competitive group.

                      SAM

Isn't that a good thing? I mean, we want to win
too, right?

                    MICHELLE

It was in the *how*, Sam. I noticed a dynamic
between them—an edge. They were cutting each
other off, and at one point they totally under-
mined the Head of People, basically dismissing
her point, which I thought was a good one.

                      SAM

So... what do we do now?

                    MICHELLE

I feel like we need a third-party audit on this
one. Someone to objectively assess where they
are with their culture. I don't want to inherit
a group that doesn't know how to collaborate
and foster creative thinking—

                      SAM

I get it. Their problem becomes *our* problem—

**MICHELLE**

Yeah, but on a much bigger scale, right? For us
to fully realize the value of this deal, we need
people who know how to operate creatively as a
repeatable process—not cut each other down at
every turn. If they act that way with my team,
it'd be a disaster.

**SAM**

I hear you. Let's figure this out.

**(END OF SCENE)**

In this scene, Michelle is playing the conductor, seeing the bigger picture of how the orchestra will fit together in a newly merged company. While she has a strong point of view, she first dances with Sam in the conversation to explore where they sit on the issue, then calls out the culture concerns. A conductor doesn't need to be brazen with orders. It's about sensing the dynamics across the situation to move toward a creative solution.

## HOW A CREATIVITY CULTURE CAN REDISTRIBUTE POWER

John Foster has developed a counterperspective to companies that wield conventional forms of positional power at the top of the organization. For many companies, the traditional method of power distribution no longer serves its desired culture and business outcome. Instead, John has built a methodology called Start from Scratch, a nod to his daughter with celiac disease who experiences severe negative health effects from even a small bit of gluten. Instead, recipes need to *start from scratch*, engineering out the gluten, while not sacrificing nutrition or taste of the finished product. John's analogy crosses into our business world, where a tiny bit of dysfunction can poison the entire employee experience. Instead, we need a redesign.

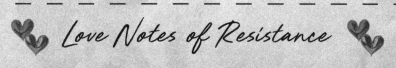

*Love Notes of Resistance*

You might sense the power dynamic across your leadership team is not healthy. Especially under high stress, leaders can exhibit power in dysfunctional ways, like building fiefdoms or making unreasonable team demands.

Consider how you might redistribute power. Engage team members to own initiatives. Find ways for earlier career professionals to also serve as mentors, offering their unique points of view.

Michael David Lewis has a similar perspective when it comes to traditional power structures within companies. Michael and I met in the early years of growing Axiom's Southern California presence. Hailing from the prestigious law firm Latham & Watkins and as a former business and legal executive at Warner Bros., Michael joined my team to apply his infectious relational and business skills to growing relationships in the entertainment sector. I quickly learned he's as generous as he is stylish: someone who can walk into a room dressed head-to-toe in a tailored fuchsia suit and then share half of his sweet potato fries over a client lunch.

With roots in the theatre and a shared love of narrative storytelling, Michael's life has been the slow unfolding of a creative act, from his philanthropic work as board member to HealthEd Connect, where he pioneered an initiative to invest in a Girls Achievement Program in Africa, to his pastoral work at the Brea Congregational United Church of Christ, creatively reaching the parishioners through story and music. Now SVP of Business Affairs and General Counsel to American Public Media Group (APMG), Michael thinks deeply about creativity culture in his daily leadership of the law department and as a core member of the executive team.

As the pandemic years found Michael bouncing between his home base in Los Angeles, California, and the APMG headquarters in St. Paul, Minnesota, he took the opportunity to live as a digital nomad, trading in a consistent home base for travel and adventure. Vowing not to die monolingual, Michael immersed himself in Spanish-speaking cultures for long stretches, from Medellín, Colombia, to Puerto Vallarta, Mexico. He visits restaurants touting sweeping panoramic ocean views as well as tiny, hidden local spots, rich with history. Taking a page from Anthony Bourdain's playbook, each escape is accompanied by a full order of the locals' favorite food and drink. He spends multiple-hour-long dining experiences as deep-dive lessons of the local culture—savoring the cuisine, communing with the natives—seizing the chance to understand others' walks of life. Each adventure invites a shift in perspective to find the universal human connection we all crave.

Despite limited physical time in the APMG office, Michael stays in tune with his leadership role to foster creativity culture. Rather than detract from that purpose, his travel fuels and reinforces it, exposing him to new ideas, discovering previously unseen possibilities, and flexing his creative muscles around curiosity and problem solving. Michael views travel as a chance to shake out creative energy, to mix things up and get outside of the traditional work environment. As a leader in a business whose purpose is to connect with listeners through human storytelling, it seems only natural to encourage this kind of creative thinking through a shift in the environment.

When Michael first assumed his role at APMG, he took great effort and care in meeting people. He wanted to know what their lives were like, to understand them as humans first, fellow colleagues second.

"I think a lot about unilateral power versus relational power," Michael explained. "Unilateral power is my ability to impact you without your consent. Relational power is an acknowledgment that power is co-created, and unless you and I agree that power is to be created, there is no power. Maybe we need to rethink how we define corporate leadership."

This redefinition of corporate leadership is what Michael has been doing ever since—from defining new rhythms and ways of working across his legal team to collaborating with different business stakeholders. One practice the executive team has adopted is a reflection meeting following each board meeting. By using that open space to look back on what went well and highlight what they'd like to repeat, to being open to evaluating what they might change going forward, core leaders can continuously improve and recommit to their shared working relationship.

As one of his company's conductors of creativity culture, Michael sees the value of a flattened organizational structure. Rather than rewarding people for seniority in years, his focus lies on the value that's being delivered to the collective ecosystem. That redesign to a more collaborative, less hierarchical construct enables creativity to flow up, down, and sideways. Rewards aren't handed out for sticking around longer, but for contributing in new ways, which sometimes means lateral moves through the organization.

"Being creative at work is a big risk," Michael reflected. "Senior leaders need to send a loud and clear message that it's a safe place to be creative, think outside of your job description, and take risks. Question other people about *why* they're doing what they're doing and be curious."

In the creativity culture that Michael describes, curiosity is rewarded before critical judgment. Team members are encouraged to think differently and be bold. At the pace at which we're seeing businesses transform, that creative thinking isn't a nice-to-have, it's an essential quality for survival and business evolution.

Most would agree that the power of an orchestra rests with the conductor. But it's also in the score. It's in each musician, working collaboratively, aligned to a common purpose. Power sits with the audience, receptive to that sacred hush. The baton is raised. It's the moment right before we begin.

## EXERCISE: IDENTIFYING YOUR CREATIVITY CULTURE PRIORITIES

By now, you may have noticed a pattern in how we address the culture influencers of Why, Who, How, and Where/When. You may have discovered questions that are challenging to answer, or ones that people across your company might answer differently depending on where they sit. This next exercise helps identify your company's priority culture initiatives so you can take further action.

Instructions: At your next leadership offsite, spend 90 minutes discussing the following questions to narrow in on your creativity culture priorities.

## People

- Who are the culture carriers across your organization? In other words, who best embodies the mindsets, behaviors, and shared principles that you'd like replicated across the company?
- How do you engage these culture carriers or share their stories with the rest of the company?
- What steps can you take in the next 90 days to engage these culture carriers even more?

## Processes and policies

- How do new employees learn about and connect with your culture and values?
- How do your managers model and reinforce desired mindsets and behaviors?
- What materials (if any) do you have in place to ensure all team members are aligned on what good looks like?
- In the next 90 days, how can you enhance the onboarding process to make values and culture a more meaningful experience?

## Technology and systems

- How do you gather feedback, input, and ideas about the employee experience?
- What platforms or systems do you use to solicit, gather, evaluate, and recognize creative ideas?
- What system can you evaluate (or try) in the next 90 days to encourage sharing business ideas and making suggestions for improvements?

Next, review the list of potential employee moments that matter that can serve as catalysts to strengthening your culture. As individuals, circle the top two that you believe need immediate attention. Finally, as a team, come to agreement on the top three areas you'll focus on and commit resources to in the next quarter.

- **Job-posting description**—providing differentiated details about your organizational culture

- **Interview process**—sharing culture stories directly from those at the company

- **Onboarding**—culture immersion and sharing companywide stories from colleagues and customers

- **First manager 1:1**—defining what success looks like here, along with cultural norms

- **Team meetings**—sharing commonly accepted behaviors and practices, including collaboration

- **All hands**—communicating company priorities and demonstrating inter-leadership communication

- **Sales kickoff (SKO)** or **quarterly business review (QBR)**—reinforcing key priorities and motivating team members to pursue clearly defined goals

- **Feedback**—receiving and delivering feedback among colleagues, direct reports, and/or more senior team members

- **Learning**—gaining perspective on what skills and experiences are valued

- **Goal-setting process**—gaining insight into company and team priority initiatives and outcomes

- **Employee Engagement Survey or listening forum**—inviting shared feedback on the employee experience, including the organizational culture

By the end of this leadership exercise, aim to walk away with at least three commitments for the quarter ahead, including an owner, timeline, budget (as applicable), and set of next steps.

## SCENE EIGHT SHOW NOTES

- You don't have to be an expert at everything to build a creativity culture; be the **conductor.**
- **Safety** in a creativity culture includes job security, clarity, and shared rules of engagement to deliver results.
- Workplace culture is influenced by **why you exist, who thrives there, how you engage,** and **when** and **where** you **co-create.**
- **Think like a marketer** to transmit your culture messages.
- Don't be afraid to **start from scratch** to redistribute power across your creativity culture.

Being the conductor is much more than simply standing on a podium. Embodying the mindset of a conductor within a creativity culture means deeply listening. It means applying a strategic outlook to shape the arc of the employee experience. In our final scene, we'll take the conductor's mindset and apply it to the practice of storytelling. Then you can activate your company's values through stories and cultural rituals.

# ACTIVATING VALUES WITH STORIES AND RITUALS

*"What we see in organizations that are creative and successful in their creative endeavors is that they view failures as learning opportunities. Okay, this was not successful, what did we learn? What can we do with this information? Can we do something with what we already have and learn for the future?"*

—Dr. Roni Reiter-Palmon, Distinguished Professor of Industrial-Organizational Psychologists and Director of Innovation at the Center for Collaboration Science at the University of Nebraska, Omaha

The two executives on my Zoom screen shook their heads, clearly agitated and desperate for help. After years of trying to get their company focused on values, their CEO finally agreed to a culture assessment. One of the executives, a newcomer who joined the company through an acquisition, felt the itch of discomfort from the new company environment. He longed for the formative days of building his company culture when values were top of mind.

"I think our CEO figured that if he bought my company, maybe he could simply adopt the values and culture that *my previous* company built," the leader admitted. "But it's not the same. *My old* company values aren't *our new* company

values. They need to be distinct. We need to figure out what this newly combined company stands for."

It's a common, thorny challenge. *How do we articulate what we value across
the organization? How do we quantify our workplace culture in a way that feels
uniquely ours? What stories shape what we believe, who we are, and where we're
going? And how does creativity become part of our company story as we continue to
innovate, disrupt, and build?*

In that kickoff call, my clients instinctually knew something needed to
change. They felt the pressure of leading a growing organization and needing
to recruit and retain top talent. They lived the urgency to tell a cohesive and
consistent story to employees with the absence of a North Star to fix their
gaze. They knew the magic of their culture was brewing right under the surface
but found themselves caught in the swirl of the day-to-day grind. Hustling to
tackle each new day's garden variety challenge, they were left craving a common language and purpose.

There's a childlike wonder to this problem. When we strip away the façade
of our grown-up titles and big work responsibilities, we're all trying to figure
out how to play well together in the sandbox. We long for clarity in the dream
we're pursuing. To fully realize a creativity culture, we each need to return to that
moment our heart first opened, tap into our passion, that sense of awe, and share
the rediscovered energy with our colleagues.

We each start our creative lives as children. We do hard things—learn, discover, imagine—and it's effortless. Like breathing. Yes, we fall. We fail to climb
up the stairs. We might struggle to learn how best to communicate or regulate
our emotions. We muddle through the creative process like my five-year-old
son, frustrated by seeing a clear image in his mind but not yet able to get it out
on paper the way he'd like.

So we iterate. We scrap the first paper and get a clean blank one. We create
again. And again. And again.

This is the creative process.

It becomes our story.

But soon, our creativity is also expressed within a community. Our story doesn't
just belong to us, it's woven through interactions with our team. We start to build

an identity within groups—whether it's at school or in our work lives. We look for spaces where we belong. The creativity we express (or that's suppressed!) in our workplaces knits together as the organizational culture story.

I'll admit the term *storytelling* is on the verge of being overworn. The art of creating a *story* can quickly turn dark—like spin or a false narrative. The kind of story I'm referring to, though, takes you on an emotional journey so you know what your company stands for. It might be the organization's origin story, the driving reason it exists to solve a problem. The story could be the company's North Star, its purpose and unique set of moments that shape the employee experience. These defining moments become the narrative of the company culture, the set of behaviors and social norms that motivate colleagues, light the fire, and fuel the creative journey.

In our final scene, I'll pull together the elements of your individual creative spark and creative leadership skills and examine how to influence your organization's story by activating your values. We'll take your company purpose and conductor's strategy and reveal rituals that can bring those company values to life. We'll address where and when to activate a creativity culture, depending on the size and scale of your organization. Finally, we'll learn how companies that are successful in manifesting creativity can operationalize this skill to breed a stronger creativity culture.

## THE LAST FIRST TOOTH

Whether we recognize them or not, rituals are all around us. They might show up as patterns of behavior as you start your day—a morning cup of coffee or quick stretch before checking your email. For many of us, we incorporate rituals in our lives to mark the passage of time or celebrate a milestone—an annual birthday celebration or graduation. But pausing to assess the quality and weight of these rituals is an important part of shaping a creativity culture.

On a flight back from Hawaii, our son lost his first tooth. As our youngest child, this was our family's last first tooth. My daughter, by then an experienced shedder of teeth, delighted in his rite of passage. Despite my wistful reflection of some glory days of work, I don't consider myself overly sentimental when it comes to my kids growing up. I'm happily done with diapers and onesies. There were no tears when the crib went away.

But for some reason, this tooth really got me.

It signaled a bittersweet passage of time. Alec Guettel, my mentor, once remarked how we tend to romanticize the hard early days of business building. The memories of getting things off the ground through repeated failures feel fonder from the rearview mirror.

As Axiom started to scale to new geographic regions, Alec and his family moved over to London to launch a new office. As co-founder, Alec knew every nook and cranny of the business. He could hire the right talent, win business with clients, and manage the P&L. But the most valuable asset Alec brought to the United Kingdom wasn't his knowledge of balance sheets or his skilled problem solving with legal execs; Alec carried the heart of the company culture. He brought organizational rituals. He transferred creative intuition and enthusiasm to invent the new while respecting what had come before.

Creativity culture, if done well, means shedding a lot of teeth, and getting comfortable with that process. It means welcoming in the new and discarding what no longer serves you. It's easy to cling to patterns and old ways of doing things. They feel comfortable and certain. We know what to expect. We rely on their familiarity to get through a hard day or long list of tasks. But a creativity culture requires challenging ourselves to periodically reflect and ask, "Does it make sense for us to continue doing things this way?"

Despite my championing of new ideas, innovation, and continuous improvement, I value pausing to reflect on why some things ought to stay the same. Those are the things that ground us, keep our feet firmly rooted on the ground as our head spins in multiple creative directions.

To help us stay rooted at work, the old guard (OG) has a powerful role to play. These culture carriers help model what's possible. They coach new hires to learn the ropes and avoid repeated pitfalls. In a healthy culture, early employees keep the business drumbeat as new joiners layer in new perspectives, riffs, and rhythmic syncopation of their own. Ideally, a fuller, more sustainable song emerges. Then, we can be willing to accept the last first tooth with an appreciation for what's ahead, without diminishing the loss of what's right in front of us.

## THE PERSONALIZATION OF RITUALS

I caught my first glimpse of the power of ritual back in my theatrical performing days. At ten, I played the little Dutch girl who sang with Sinterklaas (Santa) in the Pacific Conservatory of the Performing Arts production of *Here's Love.* On opening night (as I had learned was the ritual in the theatre), we shared gifts and messages to fellow cast members: a special ornament for a tree, a sparkly rock, a small token of love and appreciation.

That night, the seasoned thespian playing Kris Kringle left me an opening night gift at my dressing room spot. A gift from the oldest cast member to the youngest cast member. Inside a tiny cardboard box was a velvet bag filled with ten different silver coins from countries all around the world, including the Netherlands, my character's home. It was accompanied by a handwritten note in tidy cursive with a message far from the generic *break a leg!* Instead, the actor shared a thoughtful, personal note reflecting on his life in the theatre and the trips he had taken to these countries, presumably where he collected these coins. It felt like the passing of the torch, a heartfelt wish for my adventures ahead as a performer.

It was personal. Memorable. Ritualized.

Beyond the face value of these rituals, it's the sentiment behind them that really matters. The same goes for corporate life. Sure, receiving a monetary bonus is nice, but the ritualized moments and gestures of individual appreciation can mean much more. That might prompt you to borrow from Google's practice of picking a half day to pay respects to the failed ideas from the past quarter, or toasting employees leaving the organization with celebratory messages.[9] Rituals play powerful roles in shaping culture.

Personalized gestures inform employees about the company's unique way of doing things. Much like Bob Reynolds's recognition of the value of knowing everyone's Most Important Thing, these modes of operating (good or bad!) become the standard. And igniting those little sparks becomes contagious.

Building a creativity culture is the amassing of hundreds of these little sparks, nurturing the blaze to fuel the bonfire. Knowing how and when to put these creativity exercises into action is the final technique to apply. None of this is one-size-fits-all. The mere fact that culture is a creative process means it will adapt and change at different company maturity stages, sizes, industries, and environments. It needs context. Here's a starter guide to get you thinking about how to approach culture initiatives given the size and scale of your organization:

## TABLE 9.1: A QUICK REFERENCE GUIDE ON WHEN AND HOW TO APPLY CREATIVITY CULTURE INITIATIVES

| CREATIVITY CULTURE INITIATIVE | <100 EMPLOYEES | 101–1000 EMPLOYEES | >1000 EMPLOYEES |
|---|---|---|---|
| **WHY—Define your North Star (Purpose, Vision, Mission)** | Ensure execs are aligned quarterly; workshop annually | Ensure leaders are aligned semiannually; workshop annually | Annual review; integrate North Star across employee life cycle |
| **WHY—Core Values** | Revisit semiannually | Revisit annually w/ core values awards | Integrate across employee life cycle; core values awards |
| **WHY—Your Company Value Proposition** | Proof of concept/ revisit quarterly depending on growth | Revisit semiannually | Revisit annually |
| **WHO—Recruiting, interviewing, and hiring philosophy** | Build playbooks and define POV | Incremental improvements quarterly | Monthly tracking, depending on growth velocity |
| **WHO—Track employee demographics and set DEI strategy** | Ensure execs are aligned annually | Quarterly dashboards | Quarterly dashboard w/trending data and clear business goals |
| **WHO—Competencies, behaviors, leadership principles** | Ensure execs are aligned annually; set aside time to reflect | Develop leadership program | Scale leadership program to ICs to build future leaders |
| **WHO—Moments that matter, ERGs, and social impact** | Gather growth mindset stories and understand what matters to employees | Integrate stories across org and fund ERGs; analyze data around success stories and gaps | Build programming for community building and ERG governance |
| **WHO—Outgoing employees** | Gather exit interview data/reflect; celebrate outgoing employees | Address gaps in employee expectations and the company promise; engage with Glassdoor, Best Places to Work, etc. | Build and invest in alumni community |
| **HOW—Onboarding experience** | Create interactive new hire experience that integrates values and culture | Ensure a "buddy" system enables info transfer and belonging | Invest in immersive new hire cohorts; consider rotation programs |

| CREATIVITY CULTURE INITIATIVE | <100 EMPLOYEES | 101–1000 EMPLOYEES | >1000 EMPLOYEES |
|---|---|---|---|
| HOW—Listening, feedback, performance management | Ensure mix of OG of new hires to gather different perspectives | Employee engagement surveys (quarterly); ongoing feedback processes | Listening circles, anonymous culture channels, ask-me-anything email queues, idea boxes |
| HOW—Business operating rhythm (meeting hygiene) | Define a successful meeting; assign clear roles | Ensure cross-functional info sharing occurs (engage AI) | Experiment with asynchronous and synchronous collaboration tools |
| HOW—Goal setting | Ensure all employees know top three org and team priorities (quarterly) | Teams craft goals to pursue, measure, and celebrate (quarterly) | Integrate team goals (at scale) to be aligned to org's priorities (annual) |
| HOW—Learning and development strategy, process, career pathing, succession planning | Develop philosophy about sharing learning, conduct lunch and learns, share stories and insights | Map employee journey; develop and communicate paths | Launch succession planning and next-level-leader readiness |
| HOW—Team building, rituals, and community | Establish core team rituals organically | Evaluate what rituals serve the new scale (annually) | Refresh and evolve rituals; customize for microcultures |
| WHEN + WHERE—Org structure and organizing principles | Align on philosophy and priorities to support the business (annually) | Start future mapping the org (building for capacity) | Experiment with centers of excellence, scaling for efficiencies while preserving space for creativity |
| WHEN + WHERE—Physical work environment | Align on philosophy and priorities (annually) | Gather feedback on environment | Find and share best-in-class experiences and practices |
| WHEN + WHERE—Conflict and concerns | Align on philosophy and priorities (annually) | Integrate conflict resolution and elevating concerns into comms | Create transparency (whenever possible) on conflict resolution and decision processes |
| WHEN + WHERE—Company Offsites | Annual in-person gatherings, if possible | In-person gathering every 18 months, if possible | In-person sales kickoff (SKO) annually, if possible |
| WHEN + WHERE—Leadership Offsites | Weekly exec huddles; quarterly gatherings | Weekly exec huddles; develop team QBRs to scale up to execs; annual leadership retreats | Bi-weekly exec huddle; quarterly QBRs; annual leadership retreats |

As your company scales, be sure to:

- Ensure your onboarding process has an experiential way of activating company values.
- Take regular people-pulse surveys and examine key culture questions quarterly.
- Review meetings, town halls, and company communications to layer in North Star principles, semiannually.
- Reassess core values annually, ensuring they still feel relevant to your growing business.
- If there's growing tension between new joiners and the OG, create culture carrier opportunities, like Tiger Team working groups or rotation stretch opportunities, to strengthen bonds between the two groups.

Consider:

- What business rituals can we develop or continue?
- What leadership habits should we let go of and retire?
- What are the values and behaviors we'd like to carry forward in our next chapter, and how can we reward and celebrate them?
- How can we intentionally set up collaborative teams that honor our veteran team members yet welcome new perspectives?

Even after culture has been established within a more mature organization, there are still ongoing opportunities to influence and shape it. Many of my clients in later-stage organizations admit to a mild case of arrested development—they still operate like a start-up in many ways. As I gather info about their operating norms and processes during culture assessments, my clients often shrug and privately roll their eyes, as if to say *you'd think we'd have a better process for this by now . . .* Often they don't—or at least don't have one that's stuck! And you know what? That's okay. Behind the veneer of having things all figured out, many organizations are simply making things work as they go, quarter to quarter, scene to scene, and day by day.

# SCENE DIALOGUE FOR STORYTELLING WITH VALUES

**SETTING:**

(FATIMA sits at the head of the conference room table, waiting for colleagues to join. She nervously clicks her pen. BRYAN joins, sweaty from running from his last meeting. GRACE and JIM follow and shut the door behind them.)

### JIM

Fatima, thanks for setting up this meeting.

### FATIMA

Absolutely.

### BRYAN

(Wiping his brow)

Sorry to look like a drowned rat.

(GROUP laughs.)

### FATIMA

It's okay, Bryan. Thanks to all of you for making the effort to be here, especially last minute. As I said in my email, I wanted to talk about our values in action—

### GRACE

Is it true what you said in the email about—

### FATIMA

Yep, we'll get to that. But the reason I brought you all here is to talk about our values. You all model them daily. Grace, when it comes to *We're Customer Obsessed*, you live that! It shows up in how you structure meaningful conversations to deepen our customer relationships. You lead your team by empowering them to do right by our customers—

### BRYAN

Copy that!

### FATIMA

But we know that living our values isn't consistent right now across our leadership team. And we've got a big decision to make.

**JIM**

Can we address the elephant in the room? Harold is a bully. I see it not only in how he treats his Marketing team, but how he relates to us—

**GRACE**

I've seen it for a while, too. It really comes down to *We Empathize First*. Clearly he knows his stuff—but his approach is off. He's dismissive with his team and shuts down any ideas that aren't aligned to his.

**BRYAN**

Yeah, I don't disagree. I know we got him a coach. We've given him clear feedback. Does he know his job is at risk?

**FATIMA**

He does. And this last interaction with Skylar felt like a decision point to me. If we apply the filter of living our values like we said we would, having him stick around for another quarter doesn't make sense.

**JIM**

Man, it's going to be hard to find a replacement in this market—

**FATIMA**

But that's not the point. It's more harmful to our culture to keep him around. How many other team members will feel disempowered... or worse? So, is everyone with me?

**GRACE**

I am. But even with this tough decision to be made, would it be okay if I acknowledge a bright spot?

**BRYAN**

Yep, let's look for the good—

**GRACE**

I want to share a quick story about Heidi. She was up against some big obstacles last quarter. When our top customer canceled our contract, she switched to rebuild mode. But instead of reverting to what's been done in the past, she reinvented. She used it as a chance to experiment with the new tech and take some smart risks. It's completely shifted her team's working dynamic. And the new product is blowing customers away...

**JIM**

I've seen it, too. They've totally rebuilt the pipeline. It's inspiring. They're continuously trying new stuff—and Heidi's a talent magnet. How did she do it?

**FATIMA**

Heidi sees challenges as opportunities. She's really good at asking for feedback and empowers her team to go try stuff. She celebrates the process, even when the result isn't a slam dunk. She's got the clear vision and enables her team to co-create. How might we apply this strategy—which clearly shifted Heidi's team performance—to Harold's team?

**BRYAN**

Hmm.

(pauses)

This might be totally off base, but what if we had some of Harold's team do rotations into Heidi's group? They need to collaborate anyway, and that structural change might mix up the energy.

**GRACE**

I really like that. Start with Skylar—give her a chance to be the Subject Matter Expert and get exposure to all of Heidi's team rituals. I bet with some support she could step up as interim CMO if we part ways with Harold.

**FATIMA**

Great ideas, team. Jim, anything to add?

**JIM**

Nah, I love it. When can we realistically kick it off?

**(END OF SCENE)**

This scene demonstrates a story of someone on the team acting *outside* of the values, contrasted with a story of a cultural bright spot. Building culture with intention takes an awareness of the behaviors that either support or detract from the environment you're aiming to create. It takes a stomach for embracing change. It means calling attention to the stories of values in action that inform your people strategy and being ready to experiment when the situation calls for it.

## STORIES OF CREATIVITY ACROSS THE EMPLOYEE LIFE CYCLE

The rituals we create at work are great ways to scale creativity across your business. When I conduct culture assessments for companies, I'm often struck by the level of specificity people use to describe what they value most about their work. It often comes down to the relationships they've formed. They want to see people's cats, babies, puppies, and plants—little windows into people's lives. People crave connection.

> **CREATIVITY BOOSTER:**
>
> Dedicate time for pure social connection with your team. That might mean the first five to ten minutes of your weekly team meeting is spent on an around-the-room personal share. Some teams prefer to have dedicated 30-minute meetings each week sharing personal stories: updating the team on your home renovation project, private cooking class, or your kid's near win at the spelling bee.

Puppies and plants don't often grow the business, though. There's the pesky issue of bringing in revenue and delivering value to customers and clients. When a creativity culture is activated, a focus on the core business can feel just as fun and fresh. True culture building isn't something done off to the side of the business—it's the storytelling *within the business.* It shows up in:

- **Employee interviews**. Do you have a story prepared to share with your prospective employees that demonstrates your culture in action? What story might you talk about that authentically reveals how your organization values new ideas, experimentation, and learning from missteps?

- **All-hands meetings**. Are there opportunities to share stories of your customers and the impact you're having on their lives/business? Do you hold space to share stories of team wins and celebrate team contributions?

- **1:1 Catch-ups and feedback conversations**. Is part of your agenda dedicated to hearing stories of values lived in action? Can you challenge your team member to rethink how they handled something at work that could have been more in line with your organization's values?

- **Team celebrations**. How do you mark the occasion of hitting a goal? Can you make personalized quirky toasts that call out individuals' contributions to the team goal? Are there ways of creatively sharing experiences together, like a scavenger hunt, escape room, or cooking class?

- **Promotions, work anniversaries, and personal life milestones**. How does your company recognize moments in life that are most meaningful? Does the team sign a card? Does the company invest in a personalized gift? When the organization makes a gesture that demonstrates you matter not only for your work, but also for your personhood, the dynamic of the relationship shifts. These moments that matter form the employee experience in a personalized and memorable way.

The process of building a distinct organizational culture builds a story. You're co-creating the narrative—for your investors, board, customers and clients, community, and of course, each other. Think about a company that needs to make the gut-wrenching decision to conduct a reduction in force. How it's handled, from the people decisions, communications, timeline, severance package, and departure process, will become part of your company's story. When these difficult moments are handled with care, clarity, and kindness, they can be defining for those who leave, as well as those who stay.

Scaling in high-growth phases can also introduce storytelling moments that matter. You may find yourself growing so quickly that founders and leaders no longer know everyone personally within the organization or team. New energy can disrupt the team rhythm (even under the best of circumstances), so returning to the North Star helps anchor new team members to the stories that matter.

When storytelling is done well with specific examples, engaging delivery, clear tension, and meaningful resolution, tribal knowledge is transferred across the organization. It builds deeper grooves in the healthy patterns you're creating at work. Rituals might be a secret cookie monster who leaves a treat at someone's desk on a Friday afternoon, a tradition of Halloween Wig Day, or an annual social impact experience, like volunteering to write encouraging letters to kids who submit stories to story pirates. The real story is the way in which your team spends time connecting—either virtually or in person. Your creativity feeds the connection.

## TIME AND SPACE TO BE CREATIVE

Simply knowing that individual and shared creative experiences among your workforce will fuel your organizational culture isn't enough. There must be dedicated time for it.

Dr. Roni Reiter-Palmon has built her career on studying institutional creativity. Distinguished Professor of Industrial-Organizational Psychologists at the University of Nebraska, Roni studies how creativity shows up within teams and organizations, researching innovative teams and creativity skill development. Despite her life-long immersion in creativity culture, as a parent, she admits a distaste for what many may associate with creativity: all things glitter and glue. She doesn't classify herself as *artsy*. And yet, she recognizes that her creativity is expressed through problem solving, thinking through things in a new way, or creatively convincing her kids to do something hard, when many (perhaps less creative) parents would have quickly surrendered.

When it comes to organizational creativity, Roni revealed the 15 or so indicators of creativity at work. A big one, which we've addressed in Act II, is the tone at the top, the managers' ability to nurture creativity, model it, and give the time and space for it.

"Organizations come to me and say, '*Well, we want to be more creative,*'" she shared. "And I'll ask them, 'Do they have time to sit and think about how to solve problems in a creative way?' And they tell me, 'Oh, we can't do that! We have too much work to do!' They're not going to come up with creative solutions if they can't stop and breathe for a minute."

Another key creativity indicator across organizations is how information is shared. When teams are siloed without cross-functional approaches or integrated perspective taking, there's tunnel vision. Creativity suffers from information hoarding. On the flip side, creative cultures have mechanisms for sharing relevant information to reach a more novel and useful solution together. They plug in moments to share information and different perspectives into the operating rhythm, which can have a big influence on creative output.

"The diversity that matters is one where we look at the problem and think about it differently," Roni explained. "It gives you a much richer understanding of all of the perspectives of the problem. So not only are you coming up with more novel ideas, you're also likely coming up with a much more complete solution." As you think about the process of developing a more creative culture, these team structures play a big role. Are cross-functional team members naturally colliding in the flow of work, or are they more siloed, falling victim to the potential risk of tunnel vision? Do team members have opportunities to collaborate on projects with a shared investment in their success? By building operating rhythms and team structures that facilitate the time and space to be creative with the right amount of information sharing across functions, creativity can flourish.

Roni was quick to share how time pressure generally kills creativity. When the stakes are high, the instinct is often to rely on what's worked in the past. If there's a perception of risk, instead of finding new, potentially better solutions, organizations quickly revert to past successes.

## THE SWEET SPOT TO SUPPORT WELL-BEING

Roni Reiter-Palmon's comment about time pressure struck a chord. Many creative leaders refer to their complicated relationship with time. There appears to be an optimal level of pressure—either externally or internally—that helps facilitate a burst of creative output. Time pressure, other people's expectations, as well as high performance standards can accelerate the creative process. Instead of seeing it as a liability, I've seen many creative leaders embrace it as an asset. It's as if this pressure—internal or external—is a member of the creative team.

John Foster recalled his repeated work cycle of 15-week client engagements while at IDEO, which mirrored many a creative project I've experienced. The early weeks of the project contain relaxed organic ideation, brainstorming, and blue-sky envisioning of what's possible. It's that space to be creative that Dr. Roni Reiter-Palmon encourages. As the project progresses, the pace intensifies. Work accelerates. Toward the end of the sprint, expectations increase, workloads spike, and there's pressure to perform, deliver, and yield creative results. You likely experience similar rhythms with your work projects: the breezy phase one of discovery, the Messy Middle of phase two where you find your footing and slog through uncertainty, and phase three's potential mad dash to the finish line.

To recover from those later periods of intensity, creativity cultures acknowledge the need for team members to recharge. That might mean structuring breaks of a week or two (sometimes longer), depending on the situation. Those essential periods of downtime enable stasis and equilibrium, a chance to rebalance and recover from peak work. It makes space for creative well-being.

Today, prioritizing well-being and mental health is paramount to fostering a healthy organizational culture. For employees to feel cared for and protected from the high risk of burnout, well-being is ideally a shared cultural commitment. With the growing rate of employee burnout within high-pressure, innovative companies, leaders have a responsibility to stay attuned to the personalized needs of their employees.

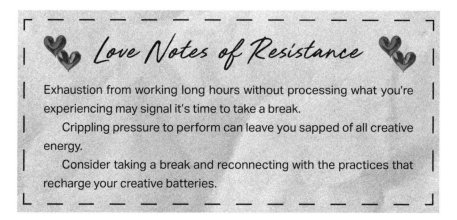

**Love Notes of Resistance**

Exhaustion from working long hours without processing what you're experiencing may signal it's time to take a break.

Crippling pressure to perform can leave you sapped of all creative energy.

Consider taking a break and reconnecting with the practices that recharge your creative batteries.

In the United States, there's a common glorification of overwork. It transcends industries and work environments. I experienced it as a performer, praised for doing double-duty while cast in two shows simultaneously that left little time for rest. And I felt it in my corporate life, being the first one in the office and last to leave, logging in late at night to respond to *just one more message* to reach my global colleagues. I'll confess I still get a dopamine hit by replying promptly to emails. But being busy doesn't equate to adding value. Creativity cultures support working smarter, not harder.

Most of us want to feel a sense of purpose in our work. We want our work to be appreciated and feel like it matters. When we experience belonging to a community and knowing that our work has meaning, that's where we find the sweet spot of pressure for a creativity culture. It's the zone where we feel our work is valued, yet we're not tossing and turning all night obsessing about it.

Finding this sweet spot requires modeling. When leaders value curiosity, exploration, and experimentation with an indefatigable commitment to continuous improvement, it must be combined with caring for the creative people across the organization. It calls for comfort with imperfection, asking for and providing continuous direct feedback, and managing conflict as it arises. When high performance standards are combined with an environment of creative well-being, this zone enables bursts of creative activity that lead to business results. It's where you're inspired by your colleagues who also bring their best ideas, while operating in an environment that supports and encourages well-being. This is where sustainable innovative results are possible.

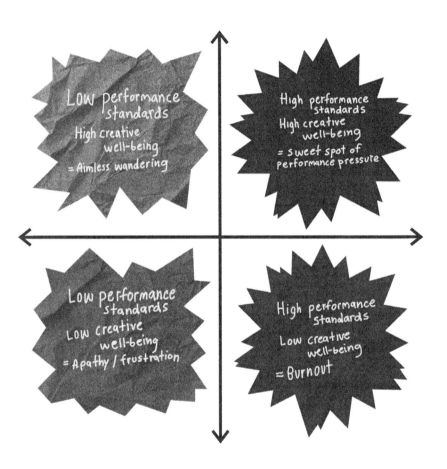

In your career, it's possible you experience either high performance standards or a high focus on well-being—one without the other. Maybe your charismatic boss is skilled at inspiring the team to innovate but never takes breaks, works through vacations, and sends frantic emails at all hours of the night. It could be your leader is gentle and affirming, encouraging you to be mindful of your health, but accepts mediocrity across the team, leaving you lacking inspiration, surrounded by apathetic peers with subpar performance. In a creativity culture, that sweet spot of performance pressure combines high standards of excellence with healthy work habits. Ambitious goals are hit, celebrated, and teams support mental and physical health along the way. It's an upward spiral of creativity.

## WHAT'S GRATITUDE GOT TO DO WITH IT?

As teams operate in this sweet spot, working collaboratively to find high value, creative solutions, there's an opportunity to pause and recognize what's working and what's not—the meaningful practice of reflection. Dr. Roni Reiter-Palmon revealed new research on the impact that these brief, introspective moments can have on the creative process.

"Reflection in teams has been found to be related to creativity and innovation," Roni shared. "Teams that naturally engage in this reflection process, meaning they've done something, learned some things from it, made changes based on what they've learned, changed the stuff that didn't work, and kept the stuff that did work—those teams tend to be more creative and innovative."

Roni's experiments show that even a 15- to 20-minute intervention to inspire reflection can impact levels of creativity. This debunks the myth that reflection will somehow interrupt the urgent call to transition quickly to the next project. Instead, a brief pause to share insights and lessons learned can influence a team's future creative output. It also creates space for gratitude and team appreciation, essential ingredients of creativity cultures.

Dr. Glenn Fox, Assistant Professor at the University of Southern California's Lloyd Greif Center for Entrepreneurial Studies in the Marshall School of Business, reminded me of the link between creativity and gratitude. While teaching at USC, he started the Found Well Initiative, a program tailored to budding entrepreneurs by strengthening sustainable life skills. As the name suggests, the emphasis isn't on toxic do-it-all cultures or pulling all-nighters to blow through revenue targets. Instead, its mission is to develop competencies that ensure founders can build businesses for years to come.

Founders, particularly highly creative ones, are susceptible to work-obsessed patterns of behavior that can lead to failed relationships, addiction, and worse. We spend a lot of time working on the business skills of getting a company off the ground, and far less on making it a fulfilling, healthy, and integrated human experience.

With an estimated 30 percent of entrepreneurs suffering from depression, compared to an average of 7 percent of the general population, it's clear that mental health concerns are negatively impacting today's innovative workplaces. A study from UC Berkeley found that a stunning 72 percent of entrepreneurs struggle with a mental health issue.[10] The well-being principles to which I refer aren't nice-to-have vitamins; it's time to shift mindsets and treat a disease that's plaguing our modern workforce. Conscious creativity cultures can help us manage this issue, offering a more humane, fulfilling way of working for all.

Although the pandemic threw accelerant on the root cause, this state of VUCA (volatile, uncertain, complex, ambiguous) or TUNA (tumultuous, uncertain, novel, ambiguous) in our workplaces has been brewing for years. Combined with rapid technology transformation and the deluge of information our brains are asked to process, it's no wonder we end our days (if we have an end to our day) feeling depleted, sapped of energy, and as Adam Grant famously called out, languishing.[11]

There is good news, though.

## CREATIVITY BOOSTER:

Try kicking off your team meetings by each sharing one thing for which you're grateful. Challenge each other by never repeating the same thing.

If you work in an office, start a gratitude board near your coffee machine where you can post pictures or write words that reflect your team's appreciation.

At your monthly team meeting, pick one (rotating) person to celebrate and recognize. Share specific stories about why you're grateful to have them on the team.

When we practice gratitude as one of the core rituals across our teams, we can reframe challenging moments as learning opportunities. We can feel gratitude for the Messy Middle and the Love Notes of Resistance. We can anchor to the North Star, our shared direction at work. We can thoughtfully reflect on our ikigai, feeling grateful for our reason for being.

Our workplace cultures will inevitably change shape. Company financial performance shows a snapshot in time—and then it changes. The client relationships we build and the stories we create are constantly in flux. To some, this is terrifying. But when faced with this impermanence, we're invited to value the present moment. We can choose to co-create with those on our team today, celebrating their unique strengths. We can fill our lives with meaning, gather new inputs and perspectives, share information, and reflect to make our next creative endeavor better than the last.

Practicing gratitude yields more gratitude. Practicing creativity yields more creativity.

As you take stock of your company's unique stories and values, chances are you were a big part in creating that journey—or you will be. By activating more creativity in our lives as individuals, leaders, and organizational culture conductors, we begin to play a more active role in the direction of our own lives.

Shawn Achor, happiness researcher and author of *Big Potential*, talks about gratitude as a method for creating a protective, insulating layer for organizations. It guards teams against the inevitable bruising that often occurs in business.[12] That active gratitude keeps us remembering the Why, our organizational purpose. Practicing gratitude allows us to celebrate each other and appreciate the collaborative work we do together.

Praise, personal acknowledgment, and gratitude can serve as meaningful company rituals. The recommended 6:1 praise-to-criticism ratio for high-performing teams reminds us that as much as we need to share constructive feedback to continuously improve, it's in celebrating what's going well that puts the wind in our sails.[13]

As a team leader, I schedule a recurring Friday afternoon calendar reminder called "Reflection and Gratitude." In the throes of winding down the week, that appointment reminds me to stop and take stock, prompting me to share gratitude with my team in a personal way. There are weeks when there have been bumps in the road, where things didn't go as smoothly as we would have liked. But there is always something for which to be grateful, be it a shared inside joke or moment of levity, or better-than-expected results from an employee survey. Sometimes it's the simple appreciation for the willingness to help on a project. This ritualized reflection and gratitude ran the risk of being corny, for sure. But each team member privately reached out to express how much it mattered to them.

People at work matter. The work you do matters. When we create habits of these micro-moments of appreciation, gratitude gets woven into our culture. It builds that protective barrier that we all covet.

## WHERE DO WE GO FROM HERE?

As I wound down my client's culture assessment, the two executives waited patiently as I pulled up the Insights Report on my laptop. Following dozens of employee interviews, focus groups, and the review of documents, artifacts, and surveys, my findings were complete. They delighted in having the good stuff reflected back, little hidden pockets of light. As for improvements, they valued having a clearer culture strategy roadmap, what practical changes to make, and where to focus.

As tempting as it is to offer one recipe for success, your organizational culture will ebb and flow—and it needs to be tailored. An initiative that's a soaring success for one company may crash and burn at another, so I will stop short of offering one step-by-step plan. The following guiding principles can help you shape your creativity culture:

- **Connection**. Consider how relationships are formed at your organization. Do people feel safe to try new things and possibly fail? Do people trust each other and have each other's backs? Are they given the time, space, and resources to feel emotionally invested in each other? Is there a magnetic pull to work with and help each other thrive? Are they connected to a shared company purpose, vision, mission, and values?

- **Innovation.** Think about how people across the company are invited to share their novel, useful ideas. Are they given clear guardrails, direction, and access to relevant, cross-functional information? Do they focus on the right things, have clarity on business priorities, and know what success looks like? Do they have the tools and resources to experiment and bring their useful ideas to life? Are their innovative ideas acknowledged or celebrated, even if they're not operationalized?

- **Inclusion.** Reflect on ways you integrate different relevant perspectives to address business challenges. Does the team have a strong sense of belonging? Are all voices heard and considered? Are they recognized and appropriately rewarded for their effort and hard work, brought in at the right time, and valued for their contributions? Is there a strong consensus around what leadership behaviors are sought after and rewarded?

These pillars shape creativity culture. As more of us crave a work experience that inspires us to bring our best creative ideas, enables us to lead others creatively, and be part of a workplace culture of creativity, we can finally get all fired up about our work. That's the energy that moves us. You now have the tools to put it into action. You, too, can co-create the story of your own creative career—in whatever professional path you choose. That's how a spark creates a bonfire.

## For Your Tool Kit: Activating Your Company Values

Our final exercise of Act III builds on the important work you've done to first develop your Creativity Culture Strategy. By now, you've identified gaps that are keeping you from fully experiencing the benefits of a Creativity Culture and prioritized where your organization is willing to invest in changes. This exercise is about the operational plan to get there.

Participants: Functional leaders plus two or three culture carriers across the business who may not be at the leadership level. Your target working group is approximately 8–12 people.

Instructions: Dedicate a block of 90–120 minutes for interaction and discussion about your culture. Write your values so all can see for reference. Under each of the values, write the following stages of your employee life cycle, which you can tailor to reflect your specific organization:

INTERVIEW/RECRUITMENT PROCESS
HIRING AND ONBOARDING PROCESS
1:1 MANAGER–TEAM MEMBER CHECK-INS
DAILY STANDUPS OR TEAM MEETINGS
ALL-HANDS MEETINGS
QUARTERLY BUSINESS REVIEWS
PROJECT KICKOFF IN WORKING TEAMS
PROJECT COMPLETION/MILESTONE
PERFORMANCE FEEDBACK CONVERSATIONS
CUSTOMER OR CLIENT INTERACTION
WORK ANNIVERSARIES, PROMOTIONS, OR EXPANDED ROLES
PERFORMANCE IMPROVEMENT PLANS
LEARNING EXPERIENCES
SOCIAL TEAM-BUILDING EXPERIENCES
LIFE EVENT MILESTONES
EXITING EMPLOYEE
ALUMNI COMMUNITY

Next, invite leaders to privately write down stories on sticky notes that demonstrate values being lived in one of the stages. After 10 minutes of silent writing, invite participants to place their sticky notes next to the categories that are connected to the relevant value.

Allow participants to narrate the stories to each other. Look for common stories, or examples that overlap. Notice if there are parts of the employee life cycle where values aren't being recognized. Consider why that might be.

As a group, commit to the top three to five stories that best reflect your organization's story and experience. Each participant should commit to bringing this story to life in their respective team. They may also conduct a similar exercise with their direct reports to unearth new values stories.

Finally, to operationalize these stories, map out where they might live as a reference guide—in your onboarding materials, handbooks, feedback guides, or short videos on your intranet. If possible, share the responsibility to operationalize them across functions. When leadership commits to bringing values to life through stories, it humanizes and personalizes what your company deems important. It's the necessary imprinting of a thriving creativity culture.

### SCENE NINE SHOW NOTES

- Be mindful of the **practices that no longer serve your organization** or team.
- Reflect on the meaningful **rituals that you want to preserve** as you grow.
- Consider the **different maturity stage and size** of your organization when operationalizing initiatives and building creativity culture.
- Scale creativity by **sharing and operationalizing memorable stories.**
- Aim to operate in the **sweet spot of performance pressure**: high expectations and a culture of well-being.
- **Integrate gratitude** into the fabric of your organizational culture.

CURTAIN FALLS

# DIRECTOR'S NOTES: AFTER THE FINAL CURTAIN CALL

O n a spring Saturday morning, with my husband and kids still asleep, it's not uncommon for me to sneak into the other room to crack open my laptop before our flurry of weekend activities. My brain's processing from the prior night's sleep leaves me bubbling with ideas. Then I get a familiar sensation. *You're almost done* (whisper my Love Notes of Resistance), *but aren't you forgetting something? Isn't there a message that you haven't yet landed?*

I stare at the screen, rereading what's been created.

I sketch out ideas and concepts by hand—the points that might be missing.

But as every creator knows, the work is never truly done.

## CREATIVE LABORS OF LOVE

Writing this book has been one of the hardest personal and professional endeavors I've attempted. Perhaps it's because it feels so personal—it's nearly impossible for me to separate my life experiences from my thoughts and ideas about creativity. Maybe it's the concentrated chaos of this stage of my life—juggling client demands while racing to get my kids to dance and swimming, then scrambling to make dinner before my *evening shift* when I might capture a few more minutes (hours?) to work or catch up on emails.

I've done my best to apply creative discipline to this process. Those years at

LACHSA have been put to good use—time blocking, building creative contain-
ers to move the process forward, breaking things down to Build a Phrase—never
relying on intermittent and fickle flashes of creative inspiration, but instead,
methodically chipping away at it, slowly carving the block of wood to reveal
something recognizable.

I've whittled away a lot of junk to create this story. Translating dozens of creative
anecdotes into bite-sized repeatable processes—those learnable bits of wisdom—
has at times felt like an insurmountable task, an ambitious beast of a project. But
mostly, it's been a giant, humbling honor of a lifetime.

I've come to discover that the technique of applying creativity is a little like
stepping into your first day of rehearsal. You accept the invitation to join an
unknown cast and new creative process, unfamiliar with what the journey ahead
might be. You're vulnerable, accepting the challenge to learn in the sweet spot of
performance pressure. What lies on the other side are all things wonderful and
invigorating, but also terrifying. After all, you can't go back. Once you're all fired
up, playing an active, creative role in your life's work, it's difficult to retreat to
what was before.

When you embrace your creative confidence to come up with a bunch of
bad ideas, something within you shifts. You may even start attracting others like
you, those who value experimenting with gusto to discover something novel and
useful. Soon, checking for blind spots and taking the note becomes almost second nature. You adopt the habits as faithful friends, behaviors woven into your
mode of operating.

The more I've become aware of my creative patterns of behavior, the more
I consciously choose to *activate my creativity*—especially when facing big obstacles. I remind myself I don't need to do what's on Day 8 when I'm still on Day 3.
I embrace the Messy Middle for what it is, trusting that soon I'll feel the surge of
energy that carries me to the finish line, ready to take a break and recharge. And
I recognize how failing can be my biggest teacher, a moment to reflect, gain new
insights, and refine my approach.

This book has been my creative labor of love. It's what brought me back
to the moment my heart first opened, that cacophonous orchestral tuning and
shared vibration before the sacred hush. Creativity is what fueled me to move

from my small-town roots in tiny rehearsal rooms to boardrooms with executive leaders and stages with audiences in the hundreds (sometimes thousands) in some of the biggest cities in the world. It's enabled me to do things I never thought possible, *be* things I only dreamed of, and help others who long for their own creative visions to become a reality.

Right now, you might be nurturing your own creative labor of love—a career-making work initiative or a side hustle that fills your soul but not your bank account (yet). That spark lights you up. It reminds you of your purpose, your ikigai. Now that you hear more clearly the creative potential that's calling you, it's time to answer it.

## CREATIVE BEGINNINGS

Creative potential, if developed, can lead us to unexpected places. A Northwestern University classmate of mine, Carrington Vilmont, was cast in *Phantom of the Opera* on Broadway shortly after graduating in 2000. Other than a few brief leaves of absence to take on other creative projects, Carrington stayed in the production until its close in April 2023, performing in a total of 6,066 performances in the Broadway company and playing roughly 15 different tracks, ranging from every member of the male ensemble to two principal roles.

While each audience provided some variation on the experience, Carrington admitted it soon felt more akin to working in a factory, rather than producing a creative art form. He learned to rely on the feedback notes process—from stage management, the music department, or the production supervisor—as his primary source of creative inspiration, a reminder to keep learning. It was in the rehearsal room where creativity reappeared.

"When you've been doing a show for a long period of time, it's easy to feel like you know what you're doing, and to push back against any notes," Carrington confessed. "But at some point, I realized, oh, that's actually a great opportunity to imbue it with something fresh. Keep it alive."

In your day-to-day, you may face similar periods where you start to slip into automatic routine, or where work is on life support. You may find yourself multitasking on team Zoom calls or going through the motions in yet another performance-review cycle. Applying creativity in our work—or in our personal lives—is a lifelong effort. We may need to seek out the feedback notes process to discover ways to improve, look at things in a fresh light, and embrace our beginner's mind. No matter how skilled and experienced we are, there's always more to learn. We come to trust that even after producing great creative works, there's a nascent opportunity waiting in the wings, prompting us to begin again.

At the start of each new project or experience, we can look for the tiny sparks that will light us up. Sometimes those sparks are already within us—we may delight in the chance to collaborate with new people or tackle a fresh challenge—and sometimes, during moments where we feel blocked or stuck, we may rely on those around us to ignite the fire.

Part of the joy I experience in working with a variety of workplace cultures and teams is the renewed energy I get each time I launch a new work engagement. I get to learn about my clients' Most Important Thing and listen to what motivates them. These beginnings get me supercharged—I try to synthesize all of the good stuff I see and reflect it back to them, so they, too, can feed on the energy.

Imagine for a minute that whatever role you're in right now or project you're wrestling to the ground, you're coming in new to the process. How might you describe the project to your (new) self? What feedback notes would you offer? What patterns of behavior might you shed, and what rituals can you dial up and celebrate even more? These are the practices of creativity.

In our process of demystifying creativity, I hope you've found it's not an intangible, mythical creature. You might now notice how creativity shows up (or not) in your team meetings, processes, and leadership behaviors. With your beginner's mind, perhaps you're ready to try the Culture Strategy tool or identify one or two initiatives to bring your North Star to life. Being the conductor, you can now zoom out to see the bigger picture, the way creativity is expressed across different teams and working groups. As you notice the tides of each project's beginning-middle-end life cycle, you can listen for the whisper, *What will you create next?*

## KEEP CONNECTING IN THE FACE OF CHANGE

When we apply creativity in our workspaces—taking part in those irresistible whiteboard sessions where ideas are flying, and the team pizza is left half-eaten because everyone's too excited about what new insights are emerging—these are social experiences. Effective collaboration demands connection within a community; that jam session doesn't happen with one single instrument or if the love isn't there.

Instead, we empathize and care—*really care*—for those on our team. We care enough to learn about each person's Most Important Thing. We care enough to empower someone to embrace the nonlinear workday (after all, racing to get to your daughter's dance class on time or pick up your aunt from chemo doesn't make you any less committed to your work). It's in those moments that we're reminded how we're all part of a networked community. For creativity to flourish, we need to show up as wholly and imperfectly human within a system of fellow co-creators.

Carrington referred to how his fellow *Phantom* cast members became less like coworkers, and more like a family unit. There were moments of sibling conflict, and long-running inside jokes, all rolling up to the shared cultural experience of the production. And now, after the final curtain call, the family is disbanded. He faces an entirely new—and unwritten—professional chapter. It's time to embrace change.

Whether we welcome it or not, change within our workplaces will only accelerate over the next decade. A recent survey of 2000 CEOs found that 40 percent believe their "company as it exists today will not be in business 10 years from now."[1] Another revealed a group of 1500 CEOs who identified creativity as *the top* sought-after leadership skill.[2] These stunning statistics are the rallying cry for more creativity in our workplaces to drive business transformation, imagine future possibilities, and put them on their feet to make these changes a reality.

Cultivating creativity as a core skill and cultural characteristic has never been more urgent. As more technology enters our workspaces, we'll soon be called to apply our human creativity in novel forms. We'll need to inspire and engage our workforce in new ways, redesign processes and workflows, and experiment with different tools. Operating in environments where you feel safe (safe to be yourself, secure in your position at the company, or about the future health of the organization) will all impact your ability to fully apply this necessary skill of creativity. Take note of that. If you find yourself feeling creatively stifled in your work, consider your environment.

## YOU NOW HAVE TOOLS TO INNOVATE

If your workplace is conducive to applying your creativity, think about the tools you now have that can be put into action. From applying your personal creative mindset, to experimenting with team exercises, Creativity Boosters, and a tool to shape your culture strategy, you're equipped to drive business value.

Beyond helping the bottom line, applying creativity *just feels good*. It's personally fulfilling—it gets us all fired up! Creativity Boosters are designed to lift your mood, as well as team morale. Imagine how offering your encouraging feedback on a colleague's new idea might be the one thing that makes their day—or month! Dialoguing about your company's North Star could uncover a deeper shared organizational purpose and bring your core values to life, keeping people from disengaging, hunting for another job, or worse, like contributing to workplace toxicity. When we're open to the possibilities and primed to activate our imaginations, we're ready to play. It sets the tone for taking a risk to try something new—an essential ingredient for innovation.

Thankfully, innovation belongs to everyone. You could be the person who helps the Pittsburgh office manager realize that she, too, has an idea that holds business value—it might just need a little refinement. You might motivate her to share and run with this idea, serving in the "yes, and" position to make it even better. Who knows, maybe you've got the positional power to green-light it, full stop. Whatever your role, your comfort with creativity will influence not only your own new ideas, but also the ideas of those with whom you work. Think about it: if we all encouraged and nurtured even 1 percent more innovative ideas, what might that look like in the aggregate across our businesses and communities?

Innovative cultures are built from the ground up. They're formed when people set the expectation to challenge the status quo because it's the cultural norm. They take shape when people prioritize building trust, creating a safe space to share fresh ideas, like putting a QR code on packaging that links to a license agreement. Innovative cultures can make room for diverse colleagues to inspire each other through storytelling, collaboration—or even scavenger hunts through Central Park. It's easy to put innovation in a box. It's common to expect that some other function will come up with the shiny ideas, like Design or Engineering. But the responsibility (and privilege) of innovation belongs to all of us.

## YOU BELONG. YOU ARE BORN TO CREATE.

This precious, deeply human need to belong is pervasive. It shows up when you start a new corporate job or law firm. Belonging might comfort you in your school alumni group, yoga class, poker club, or PTA meeting. Maybe the feeling of belonging is most prominent in your family (or your chosen family group of friends). For creativity to thrive—in your life and work—belonging is what will help you take the plunge and express your creativity. As you seek out different perspectives in your creative process, the stories you uncover can strengthen that sense of belonging and enable everyone to see themselves as a meaningful player in them.

I hope you've seen yourself in this story, as you're very much a part of it. Maybe you've found yourself wrestling with an idea, unable to find a solid block of time to dedicate to it. Perhaps you're stepping up to lead a new team and want to foster fresh ideas. Or maybe you're charged with transforming your team or company culture, looking for practical steps to define why you exist and chart the course ahead. In each of these scenarios, your story will be largely influenced by your creative approach to the experience. The blaze you build by cultivating creativity—in yourself and with others—will fuel the courage that's needed.

You're now officially invited to the party to get all fired up about work. And if your work doesn't currently light you up, it could be time to focus on something else that does. Life is short. With an estimated one-third of our lives spent at work, I believe more creativity can help it become something that fuels you.

## YOUR CREATIVE SELF-PORTRAIT

One of my favorite stories is about an elementary school open house. Parents walk through two first grade classrooms, both displaying the six-year-olds' self-portraits on the walls. The first classroom art looks typical—what you might expect to find. Paint-blob faces and stick-figure bodies are posted around the room. The other classroom, in stark contrast, is filled with masterpieces. Each painting is striking in its composition and color choices. Parents marvel at the young artists' work and eagerly approach the teacher to learn the secret to her instruction.

"How did you do it?" the parents ask. "What's different in your approach?"

"It's easy," replies the teacher. "I know when to take their paintbrushes away."

So now, I put down my paintbrush. Not because I feel like I'm done, but to step back and reflect on what's been created. To sit with it for a moment. I'm ready to generously share what I've learned so that you can build on the ideas that resonate with you—and discard those that don't.

Now it's your turn. The fire is burning brightly. Everything you could ever need to create is already within you—your personal spark is lit, you're ready to cultivate creativity in others and foster a creativity culture across your organization. Yes, you'll encounter Creativity Killers and Blockers, those who don't yet value what your creativity can offer. You may have Jesus-on-the-donkey moments where your creative work gets dismissed, without the loving guidance of a collaborator. You may face storms in your life that will threaten to put out the fire you've toiled away to build. (Maybe you're in one of those storms right now.) But there's still energy burning underneath. You can rebuild the bonfire. I can't wait to see what you create.

# ACKNOWLEDGMENTS

There are countless people to thank for either direct support or indirect inspiration in my years-long process of writing this book.

Caroline and Parker, you are my biggest teachers. You were my heart even before you came into existence. To my husband, Chris Fria, I'm grateful you love me as you do—even if I do load the dishwasher like a raccoon on meth.

To my community of readers of the Creativity at Work newsletters, who take the time to reach out with a supportive word, you are the Creativity Boosters I often need. To my Spring Street Solutions clients, thank you for trusting me with your most precious challenges, opportunities, and workplace culture initiatives.

Blair Thornburgh and Megan Stevenson, thank you. Anne Sanow and the Greenleaf team, your encouragement was just what I needed. Moira Conlon and the Financial Profiles team, your generosity and belief in me is appreciated beyond measure.

My fellow creators from LACHSA and the LACHSA Foundation, Northwestern University, the Chicago theatre community, NYU Stern School of Business, Axiom, RGP, the NeuroLeadership Institute, and the PeopleTech Partners Advisor community, you have nurtured my creative spark. I'm grateful.

Finally, huge thanks to all of the incredible humans who opened up to me about their experiences with creativity or took time to offer guidance, especially Alec Guettel, Mark Harris, Mehul Patel, Henry Jones, Kristin Hoebermann, Gina G., Lew, Amy L. Cooper, Susan Vigon, Suzy Nece, Tommy Kail, Glenn Fox, Nicole Marra, Kris Bowers, Kim Rohrer, Jess Yuen, Chelsea Grayson, Rod Lathim, Pat Bass, Michael Lewis, Nora Brickman, Bob Reynolds, Roni Reiter-Palmon, Liz Dick, Lisa Cornell, Meredyth Jensen, Sasha Strauss, Kate Duchene, Kate Kibler,

Carrington Vilmont, Aaron Mitchell, Jonathan Mueller, Niki Armstrong, Jen Brewer, Benjamin "Jamie" Salka, Shedrack Anderson III, Michael-Bryant Hicks, Ward Hendon, Frances Winkler, Joe Kucera, John Foster, Andrew Bartlow, Claudia Fulga, Kevin Kinkor, Genein Letford, Karen Mozes, and Laura Boysen-Aragon.

Finally, to my ever-supportive family, I won the lottery of life with you. I couldn't have done this without my sister, Kristen Jacoby, my dad, Paul Jacoby, and my mom, Gerry Jacoby. I love you.

# RECOMMENDED RESOURCES

Throughout this book I've referred to nuggets of inspiration that have helped shape my point of view on individual creativity, ways to creatively lead, and organizations that operate with a creativity culture. Below are a few of my recommended resources to feed your curiosity and continue your exploration.

- *The Confidence Code: The Science and Art of Self-Assurance—What Women Should Know*, by Claire Shipman and Katty Kay (New York: Harper Business, 2014).

- BetterUp Labs: https://www.betterup.com/research

- NeuroLeadership Institute™ SCARF® Assessment: https://neuroleadership.com/research/tools/nli-scarf-assessment/

- *Mindset: The New Psychology of Success—How We Can Learn to Fulfill Our Potential*, by Carol S. Dweck, PhD (New York: Penguin, 2006).

- *The Fearless Organization: Creating Psychological Safety in the Workplace for Learning, Innovation, and Growth*, by Amy C. Edmondson (Hoboken, NJ: Wiley, 2019).

- *Creative Change . . . Why We Resist It . . . How We Can Embrace It*, by Jennifer Mueller, PhD (New York: Houghton Mifflin Harcourt, 2017).

- *Start With Why: How Great Leaders Inspire Everyone to Take Action*, by Simon Sinek (New York: Penguin Group, 2009).

- *Big Potential: How Transforming the Pursuit of Success Raises Our Achievement, Happiness, and Well-Being,* by Shawn Achor (New York: Penguin, 2018).

- *What Do You Do With an Idea?* by Kobi Yamada and illustrated by Mae Besom (Seattle, WA: Compendium, 2014).

- *The Creative Act: A Way of Being,* by Rick Rubin (New York: Penguin, 2023).

- *Dare to Lead: Brave Work. Tough Conversations. Whole Hearts,* by Brené Brown (New York: Random House, 2018).

- *Drive: The Surprising Truth about What Motivates Us*, by Daniel H. Pink (New York: Riverhead Books, 2009).

- *Tomorrowmind: Thriving at Work with Resilience, Creativity, and Connection—Now and in an Uncertain Future,* by Gabriella Rosen Kellerman and Martin Seligman (New York: Simon & Schuster, 2023).

- As mentioned in some scenes, many of my Spring Street Solutions clients engage my tools and templates to bring these creativity culture concepts to life. You can access the "Digital Creativity Log" (Scene Two), "Perspective-Taking Exercise" (Scene Six), and "Culture Strategy Tool" (Scene Eight) by visiting my website, springstreetco.com/resources, and using the code BornToCreate to get your free downloads.

If your team or organization could benefit from a culture assessment or strategic culture consultation, leadership or learning workshop, or coaching support, I hope you'll be in touch. To join your community of fellow creative leaders, you can find or follow me at:

www.linkedin.com/in/annejacoby
springstreetco.com/press-connect
Instagram.com/annejacoby.author

# NOTES

## PREVIEW: CREATIVITY IS NOT ROCKET SCIENCE

1. Scott Barry Kaufman, "The Neuroscience of Creativity: A Q&A with Anna Abraham," *Beautiful Minds* (blog), *Scientific American*, January 4, 2019, https://blogs.scientificamerican.com/beautiful-minds/the-neuroscience-of-creativity-a-q-a-with-anna-abraham/.

2. Kaufman, "The Neuroscience of Creativity."

3. Forrester Consulting, *The Creative Dividend: How Creativity Impacts Business Results* (Adobe, 2015), https://landing.adobe.com/dam/downloads/whitepapers/55563 .en.creative-dividends.pdf.

4. Uplift Conference, March 2020, Berkeley, California.

5. Claire Cain Miller, "Do Chance Meetings at the Office Boost Innovation? There's No Evidence of It," The Upshot, *New York Times*, June 23, 2021, https://www.nytimes.com /2021/06/23/upshot/remote-work-innovation-office.html.

## ACT I. THE SPARK: IGNITING YOUR CREATIVE MINDSET

1. Katty Kay and Claire Shipman, *The Confidence Code* (New York: Harper Business, 2014).

2. Upwork, "Freelancers Predicted to Become the U.S. Workforce Majority within a Decade, with Nearly 50% of Millennial Workers Already Freelancing, Annual 'Freelancing in America' Study Finds" (press release), October 17, 2017, https://www.upwork.com/press /releases/freelancing-in-america-2017.

3. *Alone*, produced by Ryan Pender, David George, Dan Bree, and Grant Kahler.

4. Roger E. Beaty, Yoed N. Kenett, Alexander P. Christensen, and Paul J. Sylvia, "Robust Prediction of Individual Creative Ability from Brain Functional Connectivity," *PNAS*, 115, no. 5 (January 2018): 1087–1092, https://www.pnas.org/doi/10.1073/pnas.1713532115; Roger E. Beatty, "The Creative Brain," *Cerebrum* (January 2020), https://cpb-us-e1 .wpmucdn.com/sites/psu.edu/dist/c/122043/files/2020/08/2020_Beaty_Cerebrum.pdf.

5. NeuroLeadership Institute, "The SCARF° Assessment," https://neuroleadership.com /research/tools/nli-scarf-assessment/.

6. NeuroLeadership Institute, "The SCARF° Assessment."

7. Aaron Mitchell and Shannon Alwyn, "Banking on Us: Fulfilling Our Pledge to the Black Community," Netflix, December 1, 2021, https://about.netflix.com/en/news /banking-on-us-fulfilling-our-pledge-to-the-black-community.

## ACT II. THE BLAZE: CULTIVATING CREATIVITY IN OTHERS TO INNOVATE

1. Charles Duhigg, "What Google Learned from Its Quest to Build the Perfect Team," *The New York Times Magazine*, February 25, 2016, https://www.nytimes.com /2016/02/28/magazine/what-google-learned-from-its-quest-to-build-the-perfect-team .html?smid=pl-share.

2. Amy Edmondson, *The Fearless Organization: Creating Psychological Safety in the Workplace for Learning, Innovation, and Growth* (Hoboken, NJ: Wiley, 2019).

3. Miller, "Do Chance Meetings at the Office Boost Innovation?"

4. Jennifer Mueller, PhD, *Creative Change: Why We Resist It . . . How We Can Embrace It* (New York: Houghton Mifflin Harcourt, 2017).

5. Jaimar Tuarez, "What Part of the Brain Controls Imagination?," Neurotray, February 22, 2021, https://neurotray.com/what-part-of-the-brain-controls-imagination/.

## ACT III. THE BONFIRE: FOSTERING CREATIVITY CULTURE ACROSS YOUR ORGANIZATION

1. Donald Sull, Stefano Turconi, and Charles Sull, "When It Comes to Culture, Does Your Company Walk the Talk?," MIT Sloan Management Review, July 21, 2020, https:// sloanreview.mit.edu/article/when-it-comes-to-culture-does-your-company-walk-the-talk/.

2. *Stutz*, directed by Jonah Hill (Netflix Originals, 2022), https://www.netflix.com /title/81387962.

3. Simon Sinek, *Start with Why: How Great Leaders Inspire Everyone to Take Action* (New York: Penguin Group, 2009).

4. Patagonia, "Our Core Values," 2023, https://www.patagonia.com/core-values/.

5. BlackRock, "Principles," 2023, https://www.blackrock.com/corporate/about-us /mission-and-principles.

6. https://www.allstatecorporation.com/about/our-shared-purpose.

7. The Case Solutions, "Satya Nadella at Microsoft: Instilling a Growth Mindset Case Harvard Case Solution & Analysis," https://www.thecasesolutions.com /satya-nadella-at-microsoft-instilling-a-growth-mindset-case-174161.

8. Frances Winkler, "From Gatekeeper to Gateway: Pure Storage Patent Team Continues to Redefine Inclusive Innovation," IAM, April 21, 2023, https://www.iam-media.com/article /gatekeeper-gateway-pure-storage-patent-team-continues-redefine-inclusive-innovation.

9. Jessica Leber, "How Google's Moonshot X Division Helps Its Employees Embrace Failure," Fast Company, April 14, 2016, https://www.fastcompany.com/3058866 /how-googles-moonshot-x-division-helps-its-employees-embrace-failure.

10. Michael A. Freeman, Sheri L. Johnson, Paige J. Staudenmaier, and Mackenzie R. Zisser, "Are Entrepreneurs 'Touched with Fire'?," April 17, 2015 (Pre-publication manuscript), https://michaelafreemanmd.com/Research_files/Are%20Entrepreneurs%20Touched%20 with%20Fire-summary.pdf.

11. Adam Grant, "There's a Name for the Blah You're Feeling: It's Called Languishing," *The New York Times*, April 19, 2021, https://www.nytimes.com/2021/04/19/well/mind/covid-mental-health-languishing.html.

12. Shawn Achor, *Big Potential: How Transforming the Pursuit of Success Raises Our Achievement, Happiness, and Well-Being* (New York: Penguin, 2018).

13. Jack Zenger and Joseph Folkman, "The Ideal Praise-to-Criticism Ratio," *Harvard Business Review*, March 15, 2013, https://hbr.org/2013/03/the-ideal-praise-to-criticism.

## DIRECTOR'S NOTES

1. PWC, "Winning Today's Race While Running Tomorrow's," January 16, 2023, https://www.pwc.com/ceosurvey#whats-the-half-life-of-your-business.

2. IBM Global Business Services, *Capitalizing on Complexity: Insights from the Global Chief Executive Officer Study*, 2010, https://www.ibm.com/downloads/cas/XAO0ANPL.

# INDEX

# ABOUT
# THE AUTHOR

**ANNE JACOBY** is founder and CEO of Spring Street Solutions, a consultancy dedicated to sparking creativity at work. Through culture assessments, workplace strategy, leadership programs, and coaching engagements, Anne partners with corporate leaders who crave more connection, innovation, and inclusion across their teams. Prior to launching her own company, she helped create a new category of disruptive professional services firms where she hired, developed, and led teams to establish a best-in-class engagement management program, helping to scale the firm to hundreds of new clients and thousands of employees in three countries.

With an MBA from NYU's Stern School of Business, Anne has been instrumental in delivering innovative solutions to the world's most dynamic companies. She has launched offices in Chicago and Southern California markets, helped rebuild and lead a companywide learning and development function, hosted a popular internal podcast series, activated a new global brand, and facilitated transformational change initiatives. She has served hundreds of clients, including F100 investment banks, F500 pharmaceutical companies, international entertainment and media firms, and emerging tech start-ups, and has led workshops in dozens of locations around the world. Her leadership roles have spanned from General Manager and VP of Sales Strategy and Operations in a high-growth private company to the head of Learning, Development + Culture at a multinational public company of 4000+ employees.

Before her transition to the corporate world, Anne spent 15 years as a professional singer, actor, dancer and voice-over artist in Los Angeles, Chicago,
and New York City. She has performed from coast to coast, appearing on stages
from Radio City Music Hall to the Paramount Pictures studio lot. Her healthy
obsession with storytelling began in her youth, and she attributes her creativity,
curiosity, and grit to her climb from waitress to business leader and entrepreneur.
Anne is an advocate for arts education for young people and proudly served on
the foundation board of her alma mater, the Los Angeles County High School
for the Arts. She is based in Redondo Beach, California, where she lives with her
husband and two creative kids.